QUEER FAMILY ~~VALUES~~

Debunking the Myth
of the Nuclear Family

In the series

Queer Politics, Queer Theories

edited by Shane Phelan

QUEER FAMILY VALUES

Debunking the Myth of the Nuclear Family

Valerie Lehr

Temple University Press   **PHILADELPHIA**

Temple University Press, Philadelphia 19122
Copyright © 1999 by Temple University
All rights reserved
Published 1999
Printed in the United States of America

Library of Congress Cataloging-in-Publication Data

Lehr. Valerie. 1961–
    Queer family values : debunking the myth of the nuclear family / Valerie Lehr.
      p.   cm. — (Queer politics, queer theories)
    Includes bibliographical references and index.
    ISBN 1-56639-683-2 (cloth : alk. paper). — ISBN 1-56639-684-0 (paper : alk. paper)
    1. Gay parents—United States.   2. Family—United States.   3. Gay rights—
United States.   I. Title.   II. Series.
HQ76.3.U5L44   1999
306.85′0973—dc21   98-45411
                                            CIP

To everyone

whose love,

support,

and care have

nurtured me

Contents

Acknowledgments

When I first began to think about issues of family as a graduate student, I had only a vague idea that this interest could be connected to what seemed like a different and less feasible area of study within the discipline of Political Science: lesbian and gay politics. My ability to develop this connection has come from the growing literature in this area, but even more, it has come from the opportunities that I have gotten from the Lesbian, Gay, and Bisexual Political Science Caucus to present my work, receive feedback about it, and hear the work of others. Thus, I want to acknowledge the important work that the caucus founders and organizers do in encouraging and promoting the work of political scientists who are committed to exploring gay/lesbian/bisexual/queer issues and ideas.

I have also benefited from being in a community of scholars dedicated to exploring questions of identity, culture, and feminism in a variety of faculty reading groups at St. Lawrence. I want to thank my colleagues and fellow participants for keeping such engaging and thought-provoking conversations alive in my daily life on campus.

There are also individuals who have provided me with the professional and personal nurturance necessary to develop the ideas in this book. I want to thank Joe Kling for the encouragement and assistance that he has given me over the past ten years. His support has helped me to develop as a scholar and as a teacher. Martha Ackelsberg and Dorothy Miller read and commented on this manuscript with great thoughtfulness and care. The comments of each have prompted me to make beneficial revisions. Shane Phelan and Doris Braendel have been wonderful editors; their responses have often been challenging, yet their challenges were always mixed with enthusiastic encouragement. Finally, I want to acknowledge my deep gratitude to Marta Albert not only for reading and commenting on multiple drafts of the manuscript, but also for numerous hours of conversation about issues raised in this book. My thinking has benefited greatly from her insights.

QUEER FAMILY VALUES

Debunking the Myth
of the Nuclear Family

Introduction

On a daily basis, stories about families and family matters enter each of our lives. In beginning to explore the complexity of family, I offer the following small sample of stories. With each, I discuss questions and issues that frame the understanding of family and private life that I will put forth in the book.

- As a member of the Faculty Council at the university where I work, I was able to vote on a proposal to extend domestic partner benefits to employees. The proposal on which we voted was similar to many others passed by either municipalities or businesses: it stipulated that the university would extend the same benefits to domestic partners as were already available to spouses.[1] The conversation about this policy began with a libertarian member of council observing that he did not understand why we were considering it. "Wouldn't it make more sense," he asked, "for the university to give each faculty or staff member an equal share of the total pool of money spent on benefits with which he or she could do whatever s/he wished?" "Why," he continued, "do we give money to people for benefits for children, but not for parents or siblings?" One way to answer these questions is to explore the historical development of the family wage in order to understand why only particular dependents receive benefits. But historical exploration does not fully answer the question, which I believe merits serious consideration. My own needs and experiences in part account for why I consider this an important question. The ability to cover my parents under my health insurance policy would be more beneficial to me than being able to cover my partner, who already has health care benefits. In fact, I could think of few couples on campus who would benefit substantially in material ways from this policy change.

The provisions of the policy itself are worth considering in greater detail. Again, like most such policies, it contained provisions that are much like those embedded in marriage: couples need to live together or be financially interdependent and be in an exclusive relationship.[2] These are, as I will discuss later, provisions that I believe gays and lesbians should find difficult to accept as normative standards, or as criteria for determining whether an individual should have access to so basic a need as health care. Despite these reservations, the passage of this policy would bring material benefits to a few and would also bring significant symbolic benefits, particularly since, at least according to campus conversation, the Board of Trustees had rejected a similar proposal the previous year, not because of cost but because they did not want to appear too gay-friendly to the external world. Faculty Council passed the proposal and, with the support of the president, the Board of Trustees approved it. Yet for me questions linger. Although the policy seems to increase "fairness," the question of what was "fair" could only begin from the presumption that marriage was the norm that lesbians and gays, as well as nonmarried heterosexual couples, should emulate if we want economic benefits. The possibility that people other than partners/lovers and children may be dependent on or partially dependent on adult employees remains absent from discussion. The availability of benefits for partners also expands the number of people in society who receive necessary resources only because of their relationship to someone else.

- A heterosexual couple has been foster-parenting a now seven-year-old boy for the past few years. They have worked hard to help him catch up in school, continue to develop, and maintain contact with his mother and siblings. At times over the past few years, social services has followed its mandate to keep children with their biological parents if at all possible by encouraging the biological mother of the child to take steps to reclaim custody. Recently, the child's biological mother began to do this, with the understanding that the boy may soon be able to move in with her again. The state takes these steps in the "best interests of the child" because dominant family ideology asserts that residing with a biological parent is always best, regardless of the relationships that the child has built with others. The threat that these foster parents now face is, of course, a threat faced by all foster parents. The extent to which the state makes this threat real depends upon how family values rhetoric is operating at any particular moment to create ideological understandings of "the best interests of the child." Of course for gay and lesbian foster parents, one significant factor is how strongly homophobia is part of family values rhetoric at any given moment. This incident raises a number of questions: What are the costs to children of a rhetoric of family that understands biological parents as inherently superior? How do such presumptions influence adults who are considering becoming foster parents? Why is it necessary to see either the biological parent *or* the foster parent as central to the child? That is, why does social services not try to create a more complex system of nurturing, one that honors the multiple relationships a child has already formed? Whose needs are served by a construction that denies such complex "family" configurations? How does this affect second-parent adoptions by lesbian, gay, or heterosexual nonmarried couples? Shouldn't ramifications of political ideology such as this be explicitly part of political discourse?

• Recently I taught Adrienne Rich's classic text *Of Woman Born* (1976) in a feminist theory class. I had considered not including this book in the course in favor of more recent theoretical writing. Yet I discovered that it made a deep impression on a number of my female students, who had previously understood mothering as a central and inherently positive aspect of their female identity that they would enact when conditions were right. The book made an impression on them because they felt that it was the first time in their lives they had heard or read that mothers (perhaps most importantly biological mothers) can and do feel intensely ambivalent about their children. Their reactions to the book should not have surprised me, given that popular culture constantly puts forth the ideological assertion that women are appropriately mothers through images of joyous, nonambivalent, and natural mothering.[3] It is, therefore, no wonder that lesbians, like other women, continue to see those women who choose not to have children as "unwomanly" and selfish; the power of maternal ideology remains strong. In a sense, the increased ability to choose when to

have children has made this ideology even stronger, while also reinforcing a discourse of blame that controls those who become pregnant without "choosing" to do so. Again this raises questions: How
do we, as a society, create conditions that would lessen the pressures
on mothers? How can the "choices" that women, including lesbians,
have in relation to reproduction be made more meaningful? Further, we also might ask how men understand parenting and paternal
ideology.

- Over the past ten years, I have seen my three grandmothers each
  struggle with the question of how they can maintain independent
  lives in their mid to late eighties. The options available have varied.
  Most significantly, the variance has had nothing to do with how hard
  they worked either in the paid workforce or in the home. Rather, it is
  has had to do with the benefits available to their husbands, the investment decisions that their husbands made (if they had the resources to make such decisions), luck in relation to how long their
  husbands lived, and the resources of their adult children. As a lesbian
  who does not expect to have children, I find this reality frightening.[4]
  Tamsin Wilton notes, "We have no means of knowing how many
  elderly people are lesbians, but it is likely that many elderly lesbians
  are living in hardship and loneliness and, given the refusal of the lesbian and gay community to consider the needs of its elders, this is a
  group likely to remain invisible for a long time" (1995, 200–201).
  Further, Janet Kornblum reports that twice as many gays and lesbians
  over the age of sixty-five live alone than heterosexual people over
  sixty-five (1997, 46). This reality, combined with my grandmothers'
  opportunities and choices, encourages me to consider both my own
  future and the futures of lesbians and gays whose sacrifices, including
  economic, have enabled many like me to be open about our sexual
  identities and to have greater flexibility in how we live our gender.[5]

Three other stories have helped me to form the questions that I want
to ask throughout this book, though in these cases my exposure has
been less direct—that is, through reading.

- Currently, judges can deny relationships that are emotionally powerful and therefore render them legally nonexistent. One much pub-
  licized example is the denial of custody to Sharon Bottoms of her

young son Tyler. A Virginia judge granted custody to Bottoms's mother, who had "challenged the custody rights of her daughter on the grounds that exposure to Sharon's sexual orientation would damage the child's psychological development." In particular, she argued that he would "grow up confused about his gender identity if allowed to remain with [Bottoms and her partner, April Wade] (Bull 1993, 24). The ruling that granted custody to Bottoms's mother, although not formally based on the fact that Bottoms lives with her female lover, seems to reflect the judge's view of lesbian parenting. Tzivia Gover, writing for *The Advocate* about custody decisions that involve lesbians and gays, explains that although many states, including Virginia where Bottoms's case was heard, technically hold that sexual orientation alone cannot be the basis for denying custody, bias still exists: "'[Judges] now try to say their decision is based on some other behavior,' says Abby R. Rubenfeld, a Tennessee lawyer who has won many custody cases in favor of gay and lesbian parents.' This was the situation in the Bottoms ruling, where everything from the fact that Bottoms did not complete high school to the fact that she accepted a deal with ABC to make a movie about her life was cited in the judge's decision against her" (1996a, 22).[6]

Another consequence of awarding custody based on heterosexual norms is that when lesbian and gay relationships end, a biological parent can deny visitation and custody rights to an ex-partner who had played, and would like to continue to play, critical roles in a child's life. In relation to a case in which a biological partner denied her ex-partner custody rights, Gover writes, "Denied access to her son by her ex-partner, Fowler took her case to court. But while she was prepared to fight in the legal arena, she was taken aback by the reaction she got from other lesbians. 'What really surprised and disappointed me is that people said, "maybe you're not his mother,"'' Fowler said. Others simply preferred not to talk about the subject. And although she has found support from some lesbian rights groups, others were less forthcoming. 'I think they saw it as infighting,' she says" (1996b, 31).[7]

These two situations only begin to illustrate the complex and contentious ways in which discussions of gay and lesbian families set forth standards by which we believe judgments should be made about the relationship between adults and children. When we also consider the possible use and regulation of reproductive technologies, including artificial insemination and surrogate or contract birth, the issues and sources of controversy become even more complex. The fact that these technologies can be, and sometimes are, justified in ways that potentially harm others suggests that lesbians and gays as a community need to ask serious questions of ourselves and each other about the circumstances under which we will advocate their use.

- Second-parent adoptions are, at least in some states, one quasi legal means of guaranteeing that a child's nonbiological parent has legal standing. Second-parent adoptions, when they are possible, are predicated on a positive appraisal of parental fitness by social services. Phyllis Burke's discussion of this process reveals the difficulties that such investigations pose. She suggests that one impact of her experience with second-parent adoption was the threat to her relationship with her partner, since she withdrew out of fear of not being granted parental status. Her description of the scheduling of the visit by a social worker makes clear the tension: "Only Jesse [her son] and I were to be there, so [the social worker] could observe us interact. I had been waiting for so long that I had forgotten that the process was real. The anxiety that I had been masking with activism intensified, and I was almost overcome with dread. I couldn't eat and it was difficult to sleep" (1993, 204–205). Given, as the social worker reminds Burke, that the process of partner adoptions is not "quite legal," this anxiety is necessary. The process that Burke describes raises complex questions about the relationship between nurturing roles negotiated by adults and the intervention of a social service system that defines only one form of parental relationship—a monogamous heterosexual relationship—as normal. Further, it makes clear the extent to which the state can and will intervene to reframe relationships.

- Finally, any vision of family that is able to address gay and lesbian issues effectively needs to recognize and be able to address the reality that for the most part heterosexual parents raise gay and lesbian youth. This poses difficulties unlike those faced by ethnic and racial minorities since the nurturance of nonheterosexual children takes place not only in a hostile society, but often in either hostile families or in families where homosexuality is ignored rather than demonized. Linnea Due's interviews with gay and lesbian youth reveal the consequences of increased gay visibility combined with few positive interactions between gay and lesbian adults and youths. One young lesbian states: "I don't think there is anyone more isolated than queer kids. You don't see yourself anywhere. At least racial minorities have their families. With queers, oftentimes our families are who we're the *most* alienated from. So what do we have? Maybe a room. A room and nothing" (1995, 118). Of course, many gay kids often do not even have a room, and there are few social services provided by either gay communities or social services for these young adults. Older gays and lesbians may often fail to ask about gay/lesbian/transsexual youths, perhaps because in order to ask about the circumstances of their lives we need to revisit the difficulties that we encountered ourselves, and because we think that greater acceptability of gay adults will have a trickle-down effect. Due makes it clear that this is more fantasy than reality: trickle-down self-esteem is no more effective than trickle-down economics.

Although the question of how we create better lives for gay and lesbian youth is generally not very prominent in writing about gay families, Kath Weston's description of her motivation for dedicating *Families We Choose* to Julie Cordell is a deeply moving and disturbing account of why a family politics that fails to address this issues is inadequate. Julie Cordell, she tells us, was a young lesbian with few economic resources from a working class, Fundamentalist family. The gay community in early-1980s San Francisco could not provide her with the resources that she needed. Weston reports that shortly before committing suicide, Julie felt she had no option but to return to her hometown: "Although Julie had turned to friends in the past for help during emergencies, she did not feel she could rely upon them for basic necessities of life. Instead, she turned to the only people she could name as family: relatives by blood and adoption" (1996, 280). Weston believes that had lesbians and gays been creating families of choice at this time, Julie would have had an alternative to her "family." Although it is possible given Julie's age that this would have happened, the young adults to whom Due speaks do not provide much encouragement. Rather, their voices suggest that youth need to have greater freedom and more resources to enable them to use that freedom.[8] How, I want to ask, can we best enable gay kids, as well as other young adults who are questioning sexual or gender identity and those perceived as gay because of gender nonconformity, to experience less violence, less depression, and fewer suicide attempts and suicides?

Focusing on gay and lesbian youth does not fully address the issues that gays and lesbians might wish to consider in relation to youth, however. I want to extend the focus on youth by arguing that unless we are able to help to build a political movement that takes a greater interest in all youth, we are likely to continue living in a world where antigay/lesbian violence, along with racist and sexist violence, is prevalent. Due notes that "in a study of college freshman, thirty-seven percent of men reported verbally harassing gay men, while nine percent of women had harassed lesbians. Fully nine percent of the male students had hit, kicked or beat gay men." She goes on to observe, "Violence rates are rising—supposedly from panic over AIDS coupled with increased visibility. I'll buy panic as the culprit, but I believe the scum at the bottom of this well of hate has more to do with fears over sexuality and gender than disease" (1995, xxxi). The power of fears over sexuality and gender is obvious to those of us who work with eighteen- to twenty-two-year-old college students on a daily basis.

The challenges and insecurity that many youth face in the 1990s are also visible in my life because of my partner's work with a school dropout prevention program in a poor, rural community. This area is unique in some ways, yet it is not at all unusual in that young men are most likely to obtain services and support from outside of the family only if they break the law and young women only if they become pregnant. Not only do peers encourage conformity with gender norms, but one must enact "gendered" transgressions in order to get help from social services or the wider society. Of course even this "help" is generally punitive. The consequences of this system of non-intervention until a gendered crisis has struck are enormous for heterosexual youth. For gay youth, as suicide rates indicate, they are highly destructive. Although a particular focus on gay and lesbian youth is important, unless we are able to understand better the insecurity that all youth face, and that neither parents nor schools help them to confront, the lives of gay youth and adults are likely to remain threatened.

Each of these stories reflects something important about how we understand family in American culture. Each also raises to awareness the extent to which our family lives are structured by and occur within in-stitutional structures, whether the workplace, child protective services, the media, the press, law enforcement, social services, or the political arena. In developing a gay and lesbian analysis of family, we need to consider the issues raised by each.

Over the same period of time that I have been trying to make con-nections between these stories and gay and lesbian visions of family, the possibility of Hawaiian courts ruling that the denial of marriage rights to same-sex couples is illegal had, until the recent referendum made this impossible, become very real, raising the hopes and expectations of many gays and lesbians, including many political activists and theorists who have argued that marriage rights should be central to gay and les-bian agendas. Those who have made this argument in recently pub-lished books include Urvashi Vaid, Andrew Sullivan, William Eskridge, and Torie Osborn. It is apparent if one compares the perspectives of these authors that this is one of the only points on which they agree; even so, they do not agree about the consequences of legal gay and lesbian marriage. For example, Sullivan believes that marriage rights would further an agenda that would allow at least some gay males to grow up free to be their true selves, that is, "virtually normal." Describ-ing his own evolution as he accepted his natural homosexuality, Sullivan writes, "Once I found the strength to be myself, I had no need to act myself. And it came as no surprise that once I had become more open about my homosexuality, these mannerisms declined. So my clothes be-came progressively more regular and slovenly; I lost my interest in drama; my writing moved from fiction to journalism; my speech actu-ally became less affected" (1996, 199). Thus in part marriage rights, and in general social acceptance, are valuable to Sullivan because they would enable him and other middle-class white men to become less queer and more stereotypically masculine.

Vaid (1996), on the other hand, argues that the gay liberation agenda, with marriage rights as a component, can and should encourage the breakdown of hegemonic cultural norms, including gender norms, some of which Sullivan identifies as part of his "natural" self. Eskridge agrees with Vaid, suggesting that the extension of marriage rights to gays and lesbians is an important step for breaking down gender roles, as well as extending important social benefits, since "the state's prohibition of same-sex marriage reflects two related caste systems: an apartheid of the kitchen harmful to women and an apartheid of the closet harmful to gay people" (1996, 161). In the book as a whole, however, Eskridge does not focus on connecting his argument about gay marriage to feminist literature. Rather, he focuses on how we might build a more civil society, in part by better civilizing gay men.

In this book, I will argue that in order to address the situations and conflicts present in the stories discussed earlier, the more radical goals asserted by Vaid, or to a lesser extent by Eskridge, need to be central to our agenda. Achieving marriage rights is unlikely to accomplish these goals fully. The "family" problems that gays and lesbians face in the United States and other post-industrial nations are much more extensive than what marriage rights can address. Further, without an alternative to liberal, rights-based political frameworks—one that can provide a more radical discourse of family—it will be difficult for gays and lesbians to work with others to develop and advocate social policies that could address these other needs and help resolve some of the conflicts presented in the preceding scenarios. Fostering an alternative discourse that takes seriously all of the family needs of gay people, including gay youth, has the potential to create a stronger movement—one in which the more radical component of the movement might make the demands of liberals appear more reasonable, while also building a discourse with the power to keep alive a movement that addresses family and private life even if liberal demands begin to be met—but not, I would expect, to solve all of the problems that many liberals believe the reforms that they advocate will solve. In this context, Kath Weston's *Families We Choose* (1991) is an instructive book. Weston tells us that gays and lesbians are creating multiple forms of families. Yet few of these families of choice receive support from the larger society, and many would not receive support even if liberal reforms such as marriage rights were granted to gays and lesbians.

In order to suggest how these questions and issues can be significant parts of lesbian and gay politics, I will examine not only the values embedded in current definitions of family and social regulations that construct the problems that I have identified, but also the theory and values that inform gay/lesbian/queer politics. The argument that I will develop in this book focuses on family issues, but it is equally importantly an argument about politics and democracy. In fact, one argument that I will make is that we need to understand gay and lesbian family agendas less as agendas for legal reform and more as political agendas, political agendas that can be part of a vision of politics and democracy explicitly intended to counter the Rightist vision that has dominated American politics since at least the 1980s. Articulating such a vision requires that we examine how sexuality, gender, race, and class oppression and privilege come together in the dominant vision of family in our society.

The assertion that gender, race, and class need to be examined along with sexuality in order to develop an understanding of family—and, therefore, an understanding of the negative consequences of focusing gay politics on marriage and legal reform—raises a critical question for both my analysis in this book, and for gay and lesbian political organizing: Given that gay politics have been dominated by white men with the financial resources to gain political access (see Vaid 1996), is it at all possible for an analysis that critiques the power and privilege of these men to become central, or even influential, within gay and lesbian politics? Both Vaid and Osborn wish to see lesbians and gays advocate an agenda that moves beyond questions of gay rights, connecting the ability to enhance freedom to wider political and social change. "The honest, relevant discussion," Osborn writes, "would be driven by real moral values, beginning by acknowledging that the true enemy of family is not the queer, the single teenage mom, or the welfare recipient. The enemy of family love is violence" (1996, 91).[9] Vaid argues that gay and lesbian political success requires a return to a focus on liberation, a focus that acknowledges the importance of social change and transformation. Such goals and analysis are generally absent in Eskridge's analysis and present in Sullivan's only when he rejects them for violating the principles of liberalism. Feminist critique of the family as an institution continues to be more influential in the work of lesbians. At the same time, family plays multiple roles in the lives of gays and lesbians, roles conditioned by race/ethnicity, class, and gender. Whether splits along the lines of race/ethnicity, class, and gender can be overcome is a difficult question to answer, though I believe that to concede the more narrow, rights-focused goals in advance of discussion and debate is a mistake.[10] That is, regardless of the outcome, discussing and debating why a wider family agenda might be desirable is a necessity. Indeed, it may be important for encouraging the development of the kind of "bottom up" movement that Vaid envisions as a corrective to current elite-dominated gay politics.

In chapter 1, I explore the limits of a family politics that draws largely from liberal perspectives to seek inclusion into current institutional structures, most importantly marriage. The liberal perspectives of theorists such as Sullivan and Eskridge, although drawing from dominant political discourse in the United States, fail to understand the extent to which the family is a socially defined institution, one that has been central for defining status for people as men and women within society and that works to maintain inequalities among people. A rights-based approach cannot challenge power as much as it can simply let a few privileged lesbians and gays gain further entry to power.

It is possible to expand on and further develop the central arguments of the first chapter by examining how family norms have been a divisive force in gay politics for the past twenty-five years. This examination, which will be central to chapter 2, indicates that understanding and critiquing the role of family within society and politics is important because the formation of a more unified gay movement is contingent upon our ability to understand the ways by which hegemonic family constructions have worked to reinforce multiple conflicts within gay and lesbian communities. The liberal, rights-based approach is an unsatisfactory approach to family issues because it cannot build bridges between those who wish to be conventional and those who desire greater freedom. It is, however, possible to conceive of an alternative way of framing family issues that has the potential to allow ties to be built by different groups within gay and lesbian life.

Assuming that the importance of framing an alternative to liberal politics for gay and lesbian family politics is clear, questions remain concerning the form that such a political movement might take. I will discuss this question in chapter 3. Thus far, the primary alternative to liberal politics in gay communities has been identity politics, but this is also not an approach to political organizing that will be effective for reframing family politics. Understanding identity politics can, however, be a step in theorizing a new possibility: radical democratic politics. This perspective would challenge gays and lesbians to understand identity as less fixed and, therefore, a function of history and public discourse. This more complex understanding of identity is necessary in order to engage in both structural critique and cultural critique, each of which is important for constructing an alternative understanding of family and private life.

Although chapter 3 relies primarily on theoretical writing to argue that radical democratic theory can be an important resource for those within gay and lesbian communities concerned with questions of family and private life, in chapter 4 I will argue that this is a theoretical framework that can, in very practical ways, help us to think through the difficulties that lesbians and gays have had in building alliances with other social groups harmed by dominant constructions of family and by the public policy that has resulted from these ideological assertions. One of the critical issues that we must face is how gays and lesbians define the children and youth about whom we are concerned. In chapter 5, I will ask what social policies gay and lesbian adults need to advocate if we wish to help lesbian and gay youth, or other youth questioning either their sexual identity or gender identity. The difficulties that gay youth face force us to recognize gay concerns as spanning people's lives, and thus an alliance politics focused on redefining social needs and status—rather than solely on the concerns of middle-aged adults—is critical. Finally, in chapter 6 I will briefly explore some of the demands on government that those interested in building greater choice in private life might consider. These demands would be intended not to bring the state into people's lives, but to use state power to enable citizens to have the resources that they need to make real choices.

1

Rights, Freedom, and the Limits of Inclusion

Two strands of political theorizing have been common elements in gay theory and politics. One is identity-based, liberationist politics. The other—gay rights in relation to family—is the focus of this chapter. Gay and lesbian rights organizations such as the Human Rights Campaign (HRC) and the National Gay and Lesbian Task Force (NGLTF) privilege fighting for rights over working for a more general transformation of both discourse and institutional structures.[1] The liberal democratic discourse dominant in U.S. politics heavily influences these organizations. This political theory also informs their discussion of marriage rights. Within political theory, however, there are significant critiques of liberalism, in particular critiques arguing that liberal solutions are inadequate for addressing the complex problems that the United States and other post-industrial democracies face as nations. Central to my critique is the argument that the extension of rights depoliticizes issues that need to be subject to public debate and discussion. To foreclose such controversies through the extension of rights is not to resolve them; it is to deny the full significance of such questions for society by containing debate. The extension of marriage and family rights to gays and lesbians would serve to foreclose serious questioning of the values embedded within current understandings of marriage and family.

14

Such foreclosure would mean that the extension of rights will have taken away the possibility of enhancing freedom.

The relationship between rights and freedom, assumed so often within American political discourse, keeps us from asking what "freedom" means. We assume that it means individuals have rights in order to allow them to act on their own desires free from outside interference.[2] As feminist political theorist Wendy Brown (1995) discusses, this formulation of freedom is not the only one that has been present in American politics, but it has gained a significant renaissance since the mid 1970s. It is this understanding of freedom and the role of rights that the Right embraced. As a result, a political discourse that defines freedom as free enterprise and that understands individuals as rightly having the power to make decisions for themselves, without the interference of a state mandating social goods such as equality or ending oppression, now dominates. Brown suggests that although this liberal understanding of freedom assumes that we are free when we do not feel power operating, we need to understand that power is always operating. Total freedom is not a feasible goal, but as citizens we can engage in struggles with the potential to decrease domination and increase freedom.

The Right is not the only segment of society to believe that decreased social regulation is equivalent to increased freedom. Many lesbian and gay leaders and civil rights organizations suggest that the ideal rhetorical justification for extending marriage rights is one that makes clear the denial of individual choice currently existing for lesbians and gays. The Human Rights Campaign makes this connection explicit in a publication that advocates marriage rights. In the organization's "marriage organizing booklet," produced to help lesbian and gay activists counter antimarriage rights arguments, the organization suggests that those who argue for marriage should construct their argument using the following key terms: "basic human right," "personal decision," and "individuals, not government, should decide" (Birch 1997). Together these three terms indicate that the Human Rights Campaign believes people can be persuaded that marriage rights should be extended to gays and lesbians because these are a basic human right, and that without this right individuals cannot exercise choice because the government has infringed upon their realm of personal decision making.

When proponents of gay marriage argue that marriage is a basic human right, the denial of which means that an individual cannot really be free, they are drawing on an understanding of marriage common in our society. William Eskridge argues that the marital family is critical for civilizing humans—a task, he states, that would be more successful with the extension of marriage rights to gays and lesbians. Gays and lesbians would be civilized because we would build more stable (monogamous) partnerships with legal recognition. At the same time, the institution of marriage would be civilized because gays and lesbians would create more egalitarian relationships, thus providing models for heterosexuals (1996, 118). Eskridge builds his understanding of marriage as a civilizing institution on the assumption that marriage is so intrinsic to human desire that it is a basic human right. In making this argument, Eskridge draws on the dominant understanding of marriage within American society and the law. He approvingly quotes Justice Douglas's opinion in *Griswold v. Connecticut:*[3]

> We deal with a right of privacy older than the Bill of Rights—older than our political parties, older than our school system. Marriage is a coming together, for better or worse, hopefully enduring, and intimate to the degree of being sacred. It is an association that promotes a way of life, not causes; a harmony in living, not political faiths; a bilateral loyalty, not commercial or social projects. Yet it is an association for as noble a purpose as any involved in our prior decisions. (1996, 126)

Marriage, according to Douglas and Eskridge, is such a basic component of human relationships that to deny someone the ability to marry is to deny their freedom. Chief Justice Earl Warren's majority opinion in *Loving v. Virginia* expressed this connection between choice and freedom in relation to marriage:[4]

> Marriage is one of the "basic civil rights of man," fundamental to our very existence and survival. . . . To deny this fundamental freedom on so insupportable a basis as the racial classifications embodied in these statutes, classifications so directly subversive of the principle of equality at the heart of the Fourteenth Amendment, is surely to deprive all the State's citizens of liberty without due process of law. (qtd. in Rubenstein 1993, 396)

Andrew Sullivan, in staking out what he identifies as a liberal/conservative position on gay equality, asserts that rights such as marriage—that is, rights that he believes do not assert causes, political faiths, or social projects—are all that liberal democratic society can legitimately grant. When we demand more, such as antidiscrimination policies or right-to-rent legislation, we have crossed the boundary between public life and civil society that defines liberal democracies. To Sullivan, cross-ing this boundary limits the ability that people have to choose. The position that Sullivan sets forth draws on and attempts to reinforce a traditional liberal political perspective, one that understands civil soci-ety (which includes the economic realm) as the domain of freedom be-cause it is a domain in which individuals are not interfered with by the state. "There is a line," he tells us, "over which liberal citizens will not cross; he or she refuses to see the state as a way to inculcate virtue or to promote one way of living over another; the state has no role in promoting understanding, or compassion, or tolerance, as opposed to toleration, or indeed to celebrate one set of 'values' over another; and where the state and the individual conflict, the liberal will almost always side with the individual" (1996, 139). The idea that individuals should be privileged when their choices conflict with the values of others is also present in HRC's language. HRC found in focus group research that this language is most likely to appeal to average Americans. It should not be surprising that this formulation is most likely to persuade the American public; it is very much the language of liberalism. Yet putting the advocacy of marriage into this language—a language used to argue for many things, including some of the Right's primary polit-ical goals [5]—should serve as a warning that perhaps we need to examine in greater depth the issues involved. The following questions can guide our exploration of these issues: Is marriage really such a basic human right that entering into the institution of marriage enhances human freedom? What does "choice" mean in liberal democracy if we can choose to marry but possible employers can limit our choice in employ-ment by legal discrimination? How is choice related to freedom?

Liberalism and Individual Freedom

Liberals assert that individuals are most appropriately able to define for themselves the meaning of the "good," and that government works best when it removes obstacles from the path of those who wish to further their own interests, as long as they do not violate the basic rights of others. The distinction between the state and civil society (the realm in which people define and act on their own definitions of the good) is basic to liberalism. Within this framework, as both Andrew Sullivan and William Eskridge argue, it may well be difficult to defend a position that denies gays and lesbians marriage rights. As adults, if we wish to define our "good" in terms of sexual relationships with people of the same sex, there either must be a compelling argument about how this choice harms others, or we should have the right to marry. Yet large numbers of U.S. citizens continue to believe that extending marriage rights to gays and lesbians is wrong. This either means that the clear and rational connection between gay marriage and individual freedom has not penetrated the consciousness of average citizens, or it means that the role that family plays in society is more complex than proponents of liberal ideology care to admit. If, as some critics of liberalism assert, liberalism requires interference based on some notion of the good, then perhaps we can understand this hostility as a product of politics and culture. If this is the case, rational argument about human rights is unlikely to convince citizens that granting gays and lesbians the right to marry enhances freedom. Further, if marriage is not really a road to freedom, even if gays achieve the right to marry, we might have gained something that is less desirable than we believe.

The understanding of both civil society and the individual within it that Sullivan relates has been present in liberalism since its formulation in the political theory of John Locke. It is also an understanding of civil society and the individual within it that has been seen as faulty by a number of modern political theorists. They argue that the "state of nature" construction that liberal theorists from the seventeenth century to the present have used to develop their arguments about the appropriate role of government masks the extent to which liberal individuals are the product of assumptions asserted as natural or obvious by the theorists. For example, Locke portrays individuals in the state of nature, at least if they own property, as rational and industrious men whose primary aim is to increase their wealth through their labor (see Macpherson 1962). They are also married, having naturally recognized that a male-dominated family is the best way to maximize reason and industry. From these initial, highly questionable assumptions, Locke is able to derive the need for government to uphold the rights of the rational from the interference of the irrational, that is, those who do not own property. In significant ways, the Lockean individual did not define the good at all; Locke assumed that a significant part of the good, including the private relationships that the individual forms and the way that he will interact with his children, was found by the individual through reason.[6]

Feminist critics such as Susan Moller Okin (1989) and Carole Pateman (1988) develop the critique of liberalism in ways that are important for lesbian and gay politics and theory. They begin by noting that the liberal individual is inherently male with his basic necessities met within a male-dominated family. The ability to be a rights-bearing individual rests on a division between public life and private life (a division specifically invoked by Sullivan to support his argument for marriage rights) that continues to disadvantage women to the present. Joan Tronto (1993) extends this analysis by noticing that the disadvantage is present in the lives of all of those who have primary responsibility for providing care. This critique of liberalism is important for a gay and lesbian analysis because it begins to make clear the extent to which the citizen who is granted rights, including marriage rights, is assumed to have a particular set of values and responsibilities, ones that may not be compatible with forming the families that we choose.

To display the falsity of the "natural" nuclear family, Michelle Barrett explored the many different forms that family takes in human societies by examining anthropological and historical works. "At an ideological level," she wrote, "the bourgeoisie has certainly secured a hegemonic definition of family life: as 'naturally' based on close kinship, as properly organized through a male breadwinner with financially dependent wife and children, and as a haven of privacy beyond the realm of commerce and industry" (1980, 204). If we reject the ideological assertion that the state is merely protecting natural relationships, then we need to ask whose interests the family-household system embedded in twentieth-century American liberalism serves.[7] Collier, Rosaldo, and Yanagisako argue that the creation and maintenance of privatized family units is connected to the role that the ideology of the family plays in capitalism: "We discover that what gives shape to much of our conception of The Family is its symbolic opposition to work and business, in other words to capitalism. For it is in the market, where we sell our labor and negotiate contract relations of business, that we associate with competitive, temporary, contingent relations that must be buttressed by law and legal sanctions" (1982, 34). The family, according to the dominant ideology, is a realm in which we build permanent and caring relations, rather than fleeting and competitive relations. These relations will sustain those who labor in the harsh public world of the market. Because these private relations are nurturing, it is necessary to keep the impersonal force of the state out of family relations (1982, 35). Yet the state—which has the power to set the terms for marriage contracts, for child custody, and for privacy—is never outside of the family.

The ability to create a privatized household depends on financial resources that are unavailable to many, particularly families that do not have a white, male wage-earner. Thus, one initial observation might be that the privatized units created by marriage best fulfill the needs and desires of a particular group of people. Those who cannot satisfy the material prerequisites of family life do not create the same kind of privatized units as those of the more economically privileged. Patricia Hill Collins notes, "Privatization is less likely when survival depends on rapid circulation of limited resources. African-American families exhibit these fluid public/private boundaries because racial oppression has impoverished disproportionate numbers of Black families" (1990, 47). Ellen Lewin (1993) points out that for single mothers, both lesbian and heterosexual, having support networks of both one's biological family and other women and their children to provide loans, babysitting, and emotional support significantly reduces the strain that they inevitably face. The development and perpetuation of wider connections can also leave people vulnerable since, as Eli Zaretsky points out, state policies attempt to maintain families as separate, independent units, not as extended systems: "My argument is that the family has been preserved [by the welfare state] as an economically private unit and that most of the normative aspects of state policy are based on that" (1982, 195). Carol Stack (1974) demonstrates that many poor families only survive with such sharing, even though an individual who shares her/his state benefits risks losing them, as well as being prosecuted for fraud. Further, the assumption that one only requires benefits for those in their nuclear family also causes problems for people attempting to climb the class ladder, a problem that Wilkerson (1995) argues has had a particularly strong impact on black middle-class people, since extended families continue to rely on their economic resources.

Different theorists have posited a number of explanations for why law and social policy privilege private heterosexual economic units supported (at least primarily) by a male wage/salary. One theory put forth by feminists is that a capitalist form of patriarchy developed to maintain male power and privilege after the decline of the formally patriarchal order.[8] Even if individual men lacked power in the capitalist, public world, they would still have power in the private world of the family.

Other explanations for this particular form of family include the need to ensure paternity (at least for property owners) so that inheritance follows paternal lines; the capitalist need for consumer units, units that are important for capitalism because they create markets for the goods produced (Barrett 1980); the importance of dependent wives and children on male workers for minimizing the resistance of labor;[9] the importance of nuclear family dynamics for creating the psychological predispositions necessary for capitalism and liberalism;[10] the support that the family-household ideology provides for an understanding of masculinity that is critical for producing male laborers and male citizens; and the creation of a reserve labor pool of women workers through the formation of a dual labor market. In each of these arguments, the family-household system exists and works to reinforce a sex/gender system embedded in the family and the economic realm. Yet the social functions served by the family-household system are denied through the ideological assertion that this way of life is natural.

Some critics of liberalism, such as Michael Sandel (1982) and Charles Taylor (1985), argue that the abstract individualism of liberalism masks the extent to which human beings define their goals in interaction with and as a result of social norms. In the process, liberalism denies to people the ability to construct themselves as actors. That is, if we define the good and our sense of self in relation to whatever desires we happen to have, we do not have the ability to step back and ask if we are the kind of person we would like to be. To ask this question requires that we understand ourselves as embedded within the communities of which we are a part, or that we understand our identity as "defined to some extent by the communities of which we are a part" (Sandel 1982, 150). How we understand ourselves, including our desires and how we define the good, is a complex interplay of community and self, with the state, the economic system, and resistance movements each playing an important role in conditioning how we understand ourselves and our desires. If we accept social structures, such as monogamous marriage, as simply natural, we lose the opportunity to engage in the processes of self-reflection and self-construction. That is, we lose the possibility of enhancing our freedom.

Michel Foucault's work helps us to understand further the extent to which the concept of "normalcy" constructs our self-definition. The extension of liberal freedom, he argues, occurred with the rise of disciplinary power, by which he means the ability, largely but not exclusively, of bureaucratized institutions to define and control in order to construct the normal. To Foucault, even if overt domination and physical coercion have decreased in comparison to pre-liberal society, we do not have greater freedom:

> Historically the process by which the bourgeoisie became in the course of the eighteenth century the politically dominant class was masked by the establishment of an explicit and formally egalitarian juridical framework, made possible by the organization of a parliamentary, representative regime. But the development and generalization of disciplinary mechanisms constituted the other, dark side of these processes. The general juridical form that guaranteed a system of rights that were egalitarian in principle was supported by these tiny, everyday, physical mechanisms, by all those systems of micropower that are essentially non-egalitarian and asymmetrical that we call the disciplines. (1995, 222)

The power to define normality and to control people is exerted in multiple ways and within multiple institutional structures, including those that encourage people to enter into a specific form of family by constructing other alternatives as abnormal or deviant. What is most critical about this power is that people rarely feel it as the exercise of power. Often, the exertion of power takes place through professionals, that is through the power of "experts" who define and enforce that which is natural and normal. From this, we can conclude that in order to understand "family" in the United States, we not only need to examine universal rights and the law, but also the disciplinary practices that are the necessary other side of a legal system that promises individual choice and equality.

Liberalism's formal guarantee of equality rests on a system of classification that defines and maintains status. People feel that liberal freedom and equality are positive and progressive because we contrast current society with the fixed status relationships of feudal society. One important component of disciplinary practices is that they work not only to produce people who are "normal," but also people who will fill particular roles within society. That is, even if we are no longer born to a particular and fixed place within the social system, disciplinary practices can still work to produce individuals formed through status differentials. "The disciplines," Foucault notes, "should be regarded as a sort of counter-law. They have the precise role of introducing insuperable asymmetries and excluding reciprocities" (1995, 222). It is individuals with differing power who negotiate contracts. Further, Foucault tells us, the ability to negotiate contracts rests on preconstituted inequalities (1995 : 169, 223). If freedom means only that we can choose to engage in contracts, we are free only to a very limited extent.

In this context, we can explore the role of marriage and family. Although the contractually agreed-to marriages of today may seem like a significant advance over the pre-arranged, clearly economic arrangements made for many men and women in the past, this understanding presupposes that monogamous, dyadic sexual relationships should have higher status and receive greater benefits than other forms of relationships. This superiority is asserted often through a variety of disciplinary mechanisms, including mental health experts, the media, schools, religious institutions, and the law. In this sense, marriage itself can—and should—be seen as a disciplinary system, one that promotes social goals, such as creating households of consumers and promoting a dual-wage structure, rather than as a natural institution that enhances individual freedom.

Marriage and the State

Liberalism, as I have noted, developed in response to patriarchal society, where fixed social relations existed within status relationships and one's place in the community was central to identity. John Gillis's discussion of the change in marriage from "ritual to romance," a change that took place in the nineteenth century, is suggestive of the transformation that took place for persons. Marriage, he writes, changed from a ritual designed to secure a place for the married couple within the community to a private, contractual agreement: "The public rites of the old betrothal were replaced by the private engagement, witnessed only by the family. The ring lost its magical properties and became a mere symbol; the binding power now invested in law of church and state, witnessed to by contracts drawn up in the lawyer's office" (1988, 103). The full import of this change is apparent when we observe that ritual can be an important mechanism for managing emotion; in the case of marriage, Gillis specifically mentions the importance of playing particular roles for managing the envy of others attracted to either the bride or the groom. The decreased meaning of the ritual and increased meaning of the marriage contract indicate the loss of concern with managing emotions in order to preserve a sense of community; instead, respect for private, contractual relationships became central. Yet, as Pateman argues, these contractual relationships are dependent upon trust and commitment, values that are expected to develop and be sustained in the private sphere. "Ethical life," she writes, "depends upon marriage because marriage is the origin of the family. In the family, children learn, and adults are continually reminded of, what it means to be member of a small association and so are prepared—or, rather, men are prepared—for the universal public sphere of civil society and the state" (1988, 176). The ability of private life to perform this task requires that people enter into marriage not as individuals, but as men and women, each of whom will play a particular role in constituting the emotional world that makes public contracts possible.

In the fictional state of nature used by liberal theorists to articulate the basis of human rights and freedom, the concern with managing emotion as one enters a community disappeared because emotion in general is missing from their discussions. In justifying the move away from patriarchal power, these theorists portrayed even family relationships as the outcome of rational calculation and choice. Locke tells us that it is not a natural relationship that binds the son to the father. Instead, reasoned choice makes him committed to his father: the son knows that his father can choose whether or not to leave him an inheritance (1963 [1698], secs. 72–73). Similarly, the husband and wife choose to form a marital relationship because reason suggests that this is the best way to satisfy desire and raise children. Ideologically, the language of freedom and individual choice replaced that of duty and status. At the same time, even within the rhetoric of liberal political thought, choices about family relationships are not free of material considerations, even if a language of freedom justifies these material decisions.[11] Pateman helps us to consider the limits of the marriage contract and, in particular, warns that although we should be skeptical of the extent to which liberalism increased the freedom of most people, we should be particularly skeptical in relation to women. We can best understand the need for such skepticism by examining how sexual status is maintained in the marriage contract.

Pateman's analysis, like Foucault's, indicates that we should reconsider the ideological assertion of freedom and choice in relation to marriage (as well as other facets of life). She reads some of the grounding texts of liberalism in new ways which indicate that the "individual" of liberal society is a person who is male and generally not free, other than in his relations with women. Within this social organization, women remain subordinate and defined primarily in terms of a status relationship. The ability to freely enter into contracts, Pateman explains, is not as positive even for free, individual men as the ideology asserts; the concept of the contract hides the continued power, inequality, and lack of freedom present in society. "If contract is not to be a vain endeavor, the means must be available to ensure that the service contracted for is faithfully performed. The party who demands the service (the employer, the husband, the client) must have the right to command that a body is put to use, or access to the body is made available, in the requisite manner. Contracts about property in the person must always create obedience and constitute a man as a civil master" (1988, 231). Thus, when men contract the use of their services, they are contracting power over their bodies to people with the means to ensure that their bodies are used as the contractor demands. Because disciplinary practices so effectively construct workers, power remains invisible most of the time. It is, as a result, generally unnecessary to employ the coercive power that underlies labor contract. But, coercive power does come to the surface when organized workers challenge the power of their employers.

For women, however, contracting has even more negative consequences. As contracts replaced status, women were only able to enter into the marriage contract—a contract that contained, and continues to contain, some rather odd provisions compared to other contracts. Its content is codified into law, rather than negotiated by its individual contractors. It is a contract that mandates sexual intercourse in that it can be invalidated if a marriage is not consummated, a provision that under any other circumstances in the United States would be defined as a contract for prostitution [12] and that contributes to the presumption of marital rape as a definitional impossibility. Further, the marriage contract specifies the sexes of the two parties who will enter into the agreement, thus clearly indicating that it is a contract not between individuals, but between a man and a woman. It is, Pateman argues, not a contract at all, but a means of defining status for people as men and women.

One might assume that the extension to gays and lesbians of the right to form marriage contracts would be positive in that it would help to remove the last vestiges of status by expanding the understanding of individual to include women and by making marriage less of a status relationship and more of a contractual relationship. Individuals then would be able to exercise freedom as they controlled the conditions under which they entered the private realm. This is, after all, what

Eskridge (1996), Stoddard (1989), and gay civil rights organizations hope to see happen. Pateman, however, provides an argument that rejects the hopes held out by these theorists and organizations. What these theorists ignore, she argues, is that "the 'individual' is a patriarchal category. Contract may be the enemy of status, but it is also the mainstay of patriarchy" (1988, 168) because the differential abilities that people have to negotiate contracts are central to the hidden patriarchal power of modern industrial capitalism. Marriage, stripped of all of its legal requirements, becomes nothing more than a prearranged divorce, or a negotiated deal in which he or she with the greatest bargaining power will get the best deal. In this sense, just as a worker is unlikely to get a beneficial contract from an employer unless there are social regulations influencing the bargaining process, the person with less power is unlikely to get a good marriage/divorce contract. In heterosexual relationships, the power to bargain would help men to maintain patriarchal power unless significant social and cultural change came with the new understanding of marriage. Similarly, the power to bargain does not in itself give working-class men significant bargaining power. Although the visible presence of couples without such gendered power differentials working to negotiate more equitable relationships could help to promote social and cultural change, such change likely depends on challenging inequality first.

Wendy Brown helps us to understand that gendered power can be sustained within society even without all men and all women participating in the institution of marriage. She points out that "to the extent that many elements of women's subordination are tied to a division of labor that does not require all biological women to occupy the position assigned their gender, the emancipation of particular women can be 'purchased' through the subordination of substitutes" (1995, 164). In her discussion of what we might learn from President Clinton's withdrawal of his nomination of Zoe Baird to be the Attorney General, a withdrawal that occurred because Baird had employed undocumented immigrants and failed to pay social security taxes for them, Grace Chang points out that Baird's story, when combined with many others, "suggests [that] the advances of many middle-class white women in the workforce have been largely predicated on the exploitation of poor immigrant women. While middle- and upper-class women entrust their children and homes to undocumented immigrant women, the immigrant women must often leave their own children in order to work"

(1994, 153; see also Amott 1993). Thus status, and in particular gender status, may be foundational in the marriage contract, but removing the gender requirements within marriage by itself will not change the overall dynamic of the sexual division of labor.[13] Eskridge's own discussion of same-sex marriage in other cultures displays very effectively the reality that it can be quite compatible with and reinforcing of a gendered division of labor.[14] Thus, in many of the cultures that he discusses, marriage was contingent upon one partner adopting the social role of the other sex. As a result, the institution of marriage with a gendered division of labor was not only not threatened by homosexual relationships, it was reinforced.

We can also explore some of the implications of Pateman and Brown's arguments by considering the connection between the marital relationship and the legitimate birth and nurturance of children. Martha Fineman and Gillian Dunne each note that the marital relationship is particularly important because the family-household system dominant in industrial capitalism is one that understands the sexual relationship between adults as central to the definition of a real family. Fineman connects the valorization of marital sexuality to the construction of nonmarried mothers as deviant. "The very label 'single mother,'" she writes, "separates some practices of mothering from the institution of 'Mother' by reference to the mother's marital situation" (1995, 148). Similarly, Dunne observes that privileging marital relationships works both to institutionalize heterosexuality and to devalue primary nonsexual relationships, whether same-sex or "opposite"-sex (1997, 13–14). Why, we might ask, is sexuality so important to marriage? We should further ask, how is "appropriate" sexuality guaranteed within cultural ideology and the legal regulation of marital relationships? How our understanding of marriage and sexuality might change with the legalization of gay and lesbian marriage is worth speculation because such speculation reveals both the limits of inclusion within the institution of marriage and the potential consequences of extending contract further into private life.

The Regulation of Sex in Marriage

Fineman argues that there is some, but not much, flexibility built into what courts will recognize as "the sexual family": "To a large extent, the new visions of the family merely reformulate basic assumptions about the nature of intimacy. They reflect the dyadic nature of the old (sexual) family story, retaining the centrality of sexuality to the organization and understanding of intimacy." Later she adds: "The dominance of the idealized sexual family in social and legal thought has restricted real reform and doomed us to recreate patriarchy" (1995, 147). Ruthann Robson makes a similar point in arguing that understanding the contradictory nature of legal decisions involving lesbians, gays, and questions of family requires that we see how the state recognizes only those relationships that do not challenge dominant understandings of property. She writes:

> Braschi's emphasis on the "exclusivity and longevity of relationships," Kowalski's attention to the issue of monogamy, and the domestic partnerships affidavits mandating affirmation that the other is one's "sole domestic partner" all demonstrate the property model of relationship by valorizing exclusivity in sexual relationships. . . . The not-so-implicit message is that lesbian/gay relationships will be accorded the status of family only to the extent that they replicate the traditional husband/wife couple, a tradition based on property relationships. (1994, 987)

Through regulation of the private—re-creating a family system that has historically guaranteed the provision of the labor of care in a private setting—it is possible to create and regulate gay and lesbian households, while also protecting a moral order that plays an important role in supporting capitalism. Because the law understood wives and children as little more than a husband's property, it was able to create a justification for the power of the male head of household—power used to extract the labor of care from his wife and to control children.

We can consider further the importance of sexual exclusivity within marriage and the impact of inclusion into the marriage contract by exploring the regulation of marriage through the requirement of consummation, which guarantees that the family is a sexual family. Richard Collier (1995) provides a detailed analysis of the construction of appropriate sexuality and masculine identity in British law through legal cases contesting the consummation of particular marriages. In these cases, the courts decide what counts as meaningful enough sexual interaction within a marriage so that the marriage should continue. This obviously raises an important question: What is the state's goal in recognizing marriage and requiring consummation? After a judge determines this, s/he must decide whether the sexual acts in which the couple has engaged (if any) are adequate for accomplishing the goal. Courts have tended to identify two aims: to prevent licentiousness and to encourage procreation. These two assumptions about the role of marriage have led judges to mandate a particular form of heterosexual sex: vaginal penetration by the penis. Collier, who argues that preventing licentiousness is now the primary goal, notes that "a husband may have to submit to the misfortune of a barren wife, but as long as he can still experience pleasure, he will not be tempted elsewhere" (1995, 160). The courts, we might say, agree with Eskridge that an important function of marriage is to civilize people (mainly men), while going further to suggest that such civilizing is only likely to happen if a particular form of sexual activity takes place within the marriage. Given the important social function of minimizing nonmarital sex, the courts can void those contracts where they—generally in conversation with "experts" such as medical professionals—determine that appropriate sexuality has not taken place.

This raises the intriguing and frightening question of how courts would define consummation in relation to lesbian and gay couples. Given the focus on penile penetration and male pleasure, it is difficult to conceive of what courts would say in relation to lesbian sexuality, particularly since it is already at least arguable that much of lesbian sexuality does not fit neatly into social understandings of "having sex." As Marilyn Frye (1990) notes,[15] we can either assume that studies of sexual activity are accurate and that lesbians simply have less sex than either heterosexuals or gay men, or we might see these research results as an indication that lesbian sexuality in particular and women's sexuality in general are definitionally either unlikely or impossible in a society focused on male orgasm. If this is the case, courts forced to determine whether lesbians have "had sex" will either be challenged to view sexuality more broadly, or can more easily nullify lesbian marriages due to lack of consummation. Nullification could become a powerful weapon in custody cases that biological mothers could use to deny rights to partners, since courts often understand biological parents as having primary rights. If courts begin to understand sex more broadly, they will also understand adultery more broadly, something that again might not be desirable.

This discussion may seem somewhat bizarre and far removed from the realities that most lesbians and gays will face with the extension of marriage rights. But, courts *will* make rulings in relation to questions such as these. Additionally, such discussion and debate is not unknown among legal theorists and practitioners even now. For example, in exploring the impact of insemination with donor sperm (AID) on family and marriage law, William O'Donnell and David A. Jones discuss whether AID can "count" toward consummation—an issue on which there have in fact been court rulings. They note that conservative lawmakers might be reluctant to allow AID to stand in for consummation because "the inability to consummate an intimate relationship is frequently cited as a major ground for denying certain marriages, particularly same-sex unions. Under the latter expansion, however, lesbian couples could consummate just as easily as heterosexuals, simply by arranging AID for one of the parties" (1982, 223). This point is one that lends significant weight to Pateman's fears concerning the gendered nature of marriage and the way gender differences can influence marriage even if the institution is not explicitly heterosexual: what O'Donnell and Jones suggest as a possible definition of consummation would make pregnancy a definitional part of lesbian marriage. Thus, if one of the state's goals is to promote childbearing by some segments of society, courts could regulate lesbian marriage in ways quite compatible with this goal. At the same time, the focus within the law on penile penetration would make gay marriages consummatable without childbearing. Gender differences, in this scenario, would be just as important as they are currently; they would exist within marriage as an institution, not as an individual relationship. It may be that thought concerning consummation, how the definition of consummation works to construct the definition of marriage, and how the requirement that marriages be consummated regulates people are not as rare as might be believed. Given the definition of expertise that is accepted by judges, they will be making these decisions in consultation with psychologists, physicians, and other medical professionals, not intentionally with gay, lesbian, or feminist activists. Further, the rulings set down will construct the definition of family and sexual normalcy more widely, particularly in divorce proceeding and custody hearings.

The Limits of Lesbian and Gay Marriage

Political theory can provide powerful arguments against seeking inclusion into the institution of marriage, but these arguments may have little persuasive power for lesbian and gay couples trying to confront challenges such as the denial of health care benefits to partners or the denial of hospital visitation rights to partners. For these couples, marriage may appear to be the only means of addressing financial and legal challenges. How, we might ask, do the theoretical concerns that I have discussed thus far fit with the concrete benefits that marriage rights provide? In other words, while one function of marriage is to consolidate the status of people as men or women, marital status is nonetheless an important consideration in our society. Therefore, we need to understand what the status "married" brings to couples. To explore the limits of marriage in meeting needs, we must consider to what extent marriage enhances freedom by providing options for meeting human needs. Are there ways by which marriage as an institution limits the ability of human beings to explore and define their needs? If there are, we need to consider how we can weigh the costs and benefits. Following Brown's analysis, we can ask whether entrance into marriage would decrease domination, with domination understood as a situation in which state and economic policies are not meeting human needs, but rather restricting them. How would the extension of marriage rights work in relation to concrete problems, such as those outlined in the introduction?

An important place to begin is the financial consequences of marriage law. How does legal constitution as a family help households to be financially solvent? Certainly domestic partner benefits and the benefits that married couples receive automatically have a significant impact on the financial health of many couples. It is apparent in the interviews that Suzanne Sherman (1992) conducted with lesbian and gay couples that economic benefits are the primary reason many of these couples care about legalized marriage.[16] Yet by supporting marriage in order to get material benefits, we fail to ask whether basing benefits on marital status and whether the class bias involved in the current distribution of benefits are fair. As noted earlier in this chapter, lesbian and gay couples not covered by domestic partnership benefits face a constant economic question: How can they provide for themselves, each other, and, if they have them, their children? If they were heterosexual, either partner could extend her/his benefits to include the family as a whole. Since marriage is not possible, couples cannot automatically provide for either one another or for children. It is undeniable that this situation creates hardships for many couples. It is also true that many of these couples would benefit from marriage. There are, however, a number of important limitations, limitations that are indicative of the limits of marriage to enhance human freedom. First, and most obviously, a couple can enjoy economic benefits only in cases where at least one partner has a job that provides benefits. Given recent changes in the economy, and the widening gap between rich and poor, significant segments of the gay and lesbian population, like the heterosexual population, would fail to make significant economic gains even with legalized marriage. Thus it is important to be aware of the extent to which one's economic class has an impact on the benefits that will accrue from marriage (see Ettelbrick 1989).

The extension of marriage rights would also extend an already existing status differential, one that is essentially representative of class status. It is true, as Eskridge suggests, that in essence gay people subsidize the marriages of our heterosexual married fellow citizens. Yet this is only part of the story. There are three other points that deserve attention if our goal is to decrease domination for all gays and lesbians. First, since gender has a large influence on where men and women fit into the labor force, lesbians will be less likely than gay men to benefit positively from entrance into the institution of marriage.[17] Second, it is important to remember that all nonmarried people (or more accurately all people without domestic partnership or marriage benefits) subsidize the relationships of married people, or those who receive domestic partnership benefits. Thus, those who might choose to remain single or to have multiple partners would still pay economic penalties. The families that Weston discusses, though sometimes organized around current sexual relationships, often are not. Finally, since family benefits are benefits provided largely by private business and the state, they are highly regressive benefits. That is, they are most available to those with either unionized jobs or professional jobs, but all consumers pay for these benefits because pricing and taxation reflect their cost. Those who can least afford benefits, therefore, pay for the benefits of others each day when they make purchases and pay taxes. Thus, if the goal in advocating marriage is to help some gay and lesbian people to become economically better off, marriage will succeed; if the goal is to increase freedom and decrease domination, this is a policy that will fail.

One of the clearest cases in which marriage rights would bring immediate benefits is where one partner in a relationship is hospitalized or dies. Without marriage rights, hospitals often do not permit the other partner to make medical decisions, nor is that partner guaranteed the role of executor of the estate. As Eskridge points out, the AIDS pandemic has made it very clear how vulnerable gays and lesbians are in such situations. In the case of medical decision-making, the extension of marriage rights does provide a means of lessening vulnerability, but it does not do it very well. For those gays and lesbians who choose to marry, there would be clear guidelines regulating visitation. But, as Ettelbrick notes, marriage rights will not "address the pain and anguish of an unmarried lesbian who receives word of her partner's accident, rushes to the hospital, and is prohibited from entering the intensive ward or receiving information about her condition solely because she is not a spouse or family member" (1989). Additionally, for those who choose to not be monogamous or who organize their private relationships around a network of friends rather than or in addition to a lover or partner, the problem remains. Further, the possibility that a hospitalized or deceased person could have assured a different outcome by marrying can keep us from asking what is an important question: How do we allow adults to indicate their preferences for caretakers and executors regardless of formal family connections without also requiring that they incur legal expenses? Marriage rights may secure protection for some, but at the cost of ignoring more comprehensive social changes that might provide real options and real freedom. Again, Ettelbrick's analysis remains compelling: "Only when we de-institutionalize marriage and bridge the economic privilege gap between married and unmarried will each of us have a true choice. Otherwise, our choice not to marry will lack legal protection" (1989). That is, the extension of marriage might well make it harder for us to form the "families" that we choose by extending the reach of family as defined and regulated currently.

As we further consider the role that the family plays in recreating both patriarchy and property relations, it is important to remember that the ideal family begun with entrance into marriage is more than a contract between two adults. Within dominant social ideology and legal reasoning, the marriage contract is the first step in the parenting of children. Chief Judge Swanson, of the Washington State Court of Appeals, expressed well the ideological centrality of children to the marital relationship in his majority opinion in *Singer v. Hara:* "The fact remains that marriage exists as a protected institution primarily because of societal values associated with the propagation of the human race" (qtd. in Rubenstein 1993, 415). He, like others, goes on to argue that since same-sex couples cannot procreate, denying recognition to gay and lesbian relationships is not discriminatory on the basis of sex. Our examination of the family-household system, then, needs to pay careful attention to the regulation of men and women as parents. For gays and lesbians to demand entrance into the system of marriage is also to demand entrance into a system of parental regulation, one that in the complete absence of such regulation may appear attractive but that, in fact, may contain values that are constraining.

Another significant issue that lesbians and gays face concerns our ability to form significant relationships with children. For many lesbians, there is a fairly simple way to build such connections: we can bear children. Yet the relationships that many of us might form are likely to be with children who are not biologically our own. Thus far, lesbians and gays, along with many heterosexuals, have done this in various ways: co-parenting a partner's child; surrogacy arrangements; acting as a co-parent to a child being raised by a group of friends; adoption or foster parenting; and, in the words of Patricia Hill Collins (1990), "othermothering" or caring for a child who happens to need care at a particular moment. In many of these instances, gay and lesbian nurturers (like heterosexuals in similar situations) are in legally vulnerable situations. Marriage rights might be useful in cases where two adults in a sexual relationship decide that they would like to parent together, but in situations where the adults who wish to parent reject the definition of a "good" family as composed of children and two sexually monogamous parents, marriage would not be helpful.[18]

There are multiple issues embedded in the question of how adults gain and maintain rights and responsibilities in relation to children that marriage rights cannot address. The most obvious instance is maintaining the rights of multiple parents who may have no sexual relationship with one another. This is a question, in part, of the ethics that we bring to the formation of private relationships. Since there is evidence that lesbians have been willing to violate such agreements in order to deny custody to former partners, it is tempting to suggest that the state is an important alternative. Yet accepting state regulation in this instance works to reassert the two-parent family norm that harms lesbians and gays, as well as others, who choose to form families that deviate from this norm. The alternative is to contest the norm and, therefore, for lesbians and gays to develop a political position that encourages a cultural transformation in how our society thinks about relationships between adults and children. In this new form of relationship, there might be less focus on legal rights, particularly those that one has simply because of biology, and more focus on the care that adults provide in their relationships to children. Eskridge recognizes the challenge that gay and lesbian "families we choose" can pose to the law as it exists: "Because procreation will necessarily involve a third party, children will introduce differences. For instance, third-party sperm donors and surrogate mothers (and perhaps their partners)[19] are more likely to be part of the lesbian or gay family than is the case with heterosexual families. Lesbian and gay 'families we choose' would, in the short term at least, be more extended than heterosexual families" (1996, 117). What Eskridge does not ask is what impact marriage rights might have on the ability to form and protect the interests of those in these more extended families. That is, would the extension of marriage rights help to reinforce an understanding of family that is antithetical to building such extended units for the nurturance of children? If so, how might we frame an alternative vision of parenting?

Finally, as we attempt to understand the limits of entering into the institution of marriage, we should remember that central to marriage and marriage law is divorce and divorce law. Given that gay and lesbian relationships are unlikely to last longer than the relationships of heterosexuals, we also need to ask how single parents can support themselves and their children financially while receiving the emotional support that they need to raise their children. The emphasis on marriage rights sometimes accepts and reinforces the superiority of two-parent households in a way that draws from and reinforces current discourses of family and parenting. For example, Eskridge raises the superiority-of-two-parents argument as he discusses why denying marriage rights harms children: "A few studies," he reports, "have found that children raised in a two-parent lesbian household are better adjusted than children raised in a single-parent household, whether the single parent is straight or lesbian" (1996, 113). This sentence clearly sets up a ranking between different forms of family, one that provides no support for single parents—whether lesbian, gay, or heterosexual—and ignores evidence suggesting that single-parent families are quite capable of providing the nurturance that children need, if they have adequate resources (Stacey 1996).[20]

Freedom and the Family

One likely response by marriage proponents to the limitations on choice and freedom that I have delineated might be to agree that once one enters into the institution of marriage, there are significant regulations. That is true of any social institution, they might say, but it is not relevant to the discussion of marriage because the point is that if one has rights, s/he can choose whether or not s/he wants to exercise those rights. If a particular individual understands marriage as an oppressive institution, s/he should not choose to marry; s/he does not need to limit the choices of others, and certainly the society in which we live should not limit choice based on private sexual desires and behavior. Yet because we live together in a society, the choices that we make do in fact limit the ability of others to choose.

An analogy is helpful for making this point. It is possible to argue that marriage in this context is not much different from buying and driving a car: I am free to drive or not to drive, but if I drive, I need to follow the rules of the road that have been established because they best allow for our common life. Yet it is clear that many people, particularly those of us who live in rural areas, have little choice but to buy cars because other modes of transportation are not available. In this sense our choice is a nonchoice, one that became a nonchoice in large part because someone, in this case automobile manufacturers, benefit from the fact that cars have become a virtual necessity. Marriage is the same kind of nonchoice: Given that it can bring clear economic benefits, it is difficult for those who have the right to marry to resist doing so, even if they do not believe in the institution of marriage. One of the women (Patt) interviewed by Suzanne Sherman makes this especially clear. First, Patt discusses the problems that she sees with marriage: "People are attempting to squeeze themselves into what I consider an abhorrent ritual, where one person is basically made the property of the other. As much as you try to pull the ritual apart and make it work, it really doesn't seem equal" (1992, 31). Yet the fact that Patt and her partner could benefit from marriage leads her to conclude, "If there were clear benefits to legalized marriage, I'd certainly sign the papers, but I can't imagine that we'd walk up the aisle together. I think these ceremonies are going to be our downfall" (1993, 34). Regardless of individual intent, however, each time people "choose" to marry, they strengthen the institution, at least in part, because they have less of an incentive to oppose the benefits they receive as married people. Just as a new car owner has a powerful incentive to support road construction and not public transportation, a newly married couple has an incentive to support continued benefits for married people. In either the case of private automobiles or of marriages, a public good is privatized in such a way that many have little incentive to question the values and social consequences built into our very limited choices.

Yet even this does not fully answer the objections to my argument that a proponent of focusing gay and lesbian family politics on same-sex marriage is likely to raise. As we have seen, proponents of same-sex marriage also argue that it will challenge larger systems of domination within society by working to deconstruct gender norms. In this way, even if it reinforces class domination, it might challenge gender domination. One comparison made with some frequency by proponents of gay marriage is to miscegenation laws. *Loving v. Virginia*, the case in which the United States Supreme Court overturned miscegenation laws, is often cited by proponents as precedent for overturning the ban on gay marriages. It is not at all clear, however, that *Loving* played a significant role in furthering either a decline in racial discrimination or an increase in interracial interaction, since systems of domination are maintained in part by private relationships, but even more by structural constraints. Perhaps the question that best allows us to compare the impact of miscegenation laws to the potential impact of gay marriage is, How has *Loving v. Virginia* affected the socialization of children? That is, are parents, even those who do not consider themselves racist, more likely to encourage their children to see interracial marriage as a positive option? Are they happy when their children choose interracial relationships? Have positive cultural portrayals of interracial couples increased?

In a discussion of homophobia in black communities, bell hooks suggests that for some black families, interracial relationships may be less accepted than lesbian relationships: "Often black families who can accept and acknowledge gayness find inter-racial coupling harder to accept. Certainly among black lesbians, the issue of black women preferring solely white lovers is discussed but usually in private conversation. These relationships, like all cross-racial intimate relationships, are informed by the dynamics of racism and white supremacy" (1989, 124). The continued power of these dynamics, as hooks recognizes, makes these relationships more difficult to sustain. This is not unique to gay and lesbian relationships. Writing recently in *The New York Times Magazine*, Michael Lind noted that although racial intermarriage rates in general have increased significantly, black-white intermarriage rates remain dramatically lower than intermarriage rates between white and other racial groups. "What seems to be emerging," he notes, "is a new dichotomy between blacks and non-blacks. Increasingly, whites, Asians, and Hispanics are creating a broad community from which African-Americans are excluded" (1998, 38). In trying to explain this dynamic, he notes: "The major cause of low black out-marriage rates may well be anti-black prejudice—the most enduring feature of the American caste system. Furthermore, anti-black prejudice is often picked up by immigrants, even when it is not brought from their countries of origin" (1998, 39). He concludes the essay by suggesting that "intermarriage is the result, not the cause of racial integration" (1998, 39). Similarly, gay and lesbian marriage will be the result of a society that does not privilege heterosexuality; it will not lead to the existence of such a society.

The legalization of gay marriage is likely to be most positive in a cultural context where there is some openness to nontraditional values. Martin Dupuis (1995) argues that the possible legalization of gay marriage in Hawaii is not an accident; Hawaii is more accepting of nontraditional relationships than other states. In fact, even though in the November 1998 election voters expressed their desire to prohibit gay and lesbian marriage, the state now has one of the broadest domestic partnership laws in the country. Dupuis's analysis also suggests that a national climate of progressiveness, particularly in relation to sexuality, was a significant factor in the passage of marriage legislation in Denmark. If this is so, it is important to recognize and challenge the cultural norms that construct family in a particular and narrow way before, or at least along with, fighting for legal change. The argument that change is most likely to be effective when it occurs as a result of cultural norms implies another point: that it should ideally come through political and cultural struggle, not the legal process. Dupuis makes this argument specifically in relation to gay and lesbian marriage. Glendon (1987) makes a similar argument in her comparative work on abortion law and policy. The degree of conflict around the issue of abortion is much more pronounced in the United States than in a number of European countries that attained abortion rights not through constitutional law, but through political debate. Rights that came through legislative action may have been somewhat more restrictive, at least initially, but they are not under constant attack. Cultural norms are more powerful than a rights-based approach can enable us to confront, unless we understand rights more broadly than they have been understood within the liberal tradition and within a gay politics that seeks marriage rights as a discrete good that courts can provide.

Brown again can help us to understand why conducting such fights politically can be beneficial. She argues compellingly that a primary effect of extending rights is to remove from political discussion inequalities that continue to operate. In essence, once the state grants rights, it no longer has to confront the issue. Yet within civil society the conditions that create the discrimination are likely to continue operating. As a result, the extension of rights enhances neither freedom nor democracy, and we should therefore expect the degree of freedom within the culture prior to the extension of rights to be pretty similar to the degree of freedom after the extension of rights. In fact, Brown suggests that Marx was largely correct about seeking rights from the state: they are most useful for demonstrating to us that they can never really grant the freedom that we seek. To gain such freedom requires much more extensive social critique and political activism.

There are significant consequences in relation to gay and lesbian marriage that we can draw from this critique of liberal, rights-based approaches to social change. The primary consequence is that if gays and lesbians are to gain freedom in our personal lives, we need to understand those cultural norms and values that are most inimical to this change. Challenging these norms should be central to our political agenda. The primary obstacle clearly remains the continued sexual conservatism in the United States. The idea that sexual norms need to be challenged is not new to gay politics, yet it is also an idea that has not yet informed political activism in a way that can lead to building the alliances that are necessary for affecting widespread cultural or political change.

Politics Beyond Rights

Following the work of political theorists Iris Marion Young and Wendy Brown, we can see that meaningful citizenship requires an understanding of politics and citizenship that moves outside of the liberal framework of rights. In *Justice and the Politics of Difference* (1990), Young maintains that a critical problem with focusing on liberal rights is that this focus tends to translate all political questions into questions of distribution. In this sense, it is not surprising that the primary argument for the importance of marriage rights is economic. Eskridge, as we have seen, points out that because gays and lesbians do not receive the same benefits as heterosexual couples, homosexual people in essence subsidize heterosexuality through our employment contracts. At the same time, he believes that we could make a more compelling case for marriage if it were clear that the extension of rights would not cost very much and in some cases might actually save the state money.[21] In either case, a question that was once about rights is now a question of distribution. As a result of this transformation, Young tells us, what we lose in the discussion is what we have lost in our national political life: the ability to play a significant role in determining the conditions under which we live through meaningful participation and debate in the political world. Economic calculation replaces political debate as consumers replace citizens.

Instead of playing a role in determining the possible conditions under which we can live, lesbians and gays have been encouraged to accept two choices: either we remain invisible within political and legal institutions, thus giving us slightly more safety, or we choose inclusion within existing institutional structures, gained through the extension of rights. Brown critiques the latter alternative, arguing that the fight for rights is a fight for protection from the state and that the price of protection is high. "While minimal levels of protection may be an essential prerequisite to freedom, freedom in the barest sense of participation in the conditions and choices shaping a life, let alone in the richer sense of shaping a common world with others, is also in profound tension with externally provided protection. Whether one is dealing with the state, the Mafia, parents, pimps, police, or husbands, the heavy price of institutionalized protection is always a measure of dependence and agreement to abide by the protector's rules" (1995, 169). Although marriage rights may protect relationships, they also demand agreement with the state's rules of marriage. Brown argues that the masculinist character of the state means that these rules carry with them gender divisions and domination. She also reminds us that examining and critiquing the state's role in furthering domination requires attention to the domination of capital. For these reasons, Brown argues that the boundary between state and civil society that Sullivan and his liberal predecessors and contemporaries see as inviolable is exactly what those who wish to decrease domination need to call into question. Otherwise, the state acts to protect the power differentials that exist in civil society. Even when the state makes small or moderate reductions in distributional inequalities, it does this in a way that does not reduce domination.[22] Political activism that takes these issues seriously would engage in a process of redefining human needs, while working to create the social, economic, and political conditions that people would require to meet these newly understood needs.

In relation to the family, the possibility of constructing such alternative discourses may seem slight. Yet there is reason to believe otherwise. Changes in production and reproduction mean that we have more options for meeting these needs than we had in the past. Alberto Melucci, for example, argues that human beings are at an important crossroads: we can either create new ways of living or allow bureaucratic regulation to constrain our choices to an extent unimagined in the past. To do the former requires that we participate in the development of moral and ethical systems, "capable of directing human action when it is no longer dominated by natural fate and is therefore exposed to a more radical destiny: the destiny of choice and responsibility" (1989, 152). In particular, we must build a sense of individual identity that allows us to commit ourselves to relationships without the coercive power of either tradition or biology: family has become a choice, largely because sexuality and reproduction are now separable.

Melucci sees one possible result of the separation of sexuality from reproduction as a new foundation for parent-child relationships:

> When biological parentage is exposed to choice and contingency and escapes the compulsions of nature, the parent-child relationship may also be founded solely on reciprocity and choice. This implies a profound change in the parent-child relationship. The child is no longer only someone to be brought up, a vessel in which to pour the values and standards of society. He or she becomes an individual endowed with personal autonomy and a partner in a love relationship—a partner from whom the adult can learn to play and wonder (1989, 159).

The obstacles to this view of child-adult relationships are strong, yet the possibility does exist that gays and lesbians, because of our exclusion from the family as it has been understood within industrial, liberal democratic societies, might in fact have much to contribute to the development of an alternative understanding of family and moral understanding. As we work to develop such a discourse, we might begin by recognizing—as Hester Eisenstein sees feminism as having done—that the family "is a site in which certain needs are met: for intimacy, for nurturance, and for reproduction. This suggests that debates about family ought perhaps focus less on form than on substance" (1991, 94). An important component of focusing on substance is entering into debate and discussion about how reproductive technologies might best be used in our society. Unless we see policies connected to these technologies as a critical part of gay and lesbian political agendas, the technologies could become not a means to freedom, but a further means of oppression. This is exactly what Pateman sees occurring as contract is extended to surrogate motherhood. Thus, part of the rethinking of needs must include a recognition that contract is inappropriate as a basis for marriage and family. "When the repressed story of political genesis is brought to the surface," Pateman argues, "the political landscape can never look the same again. Nature, sex, masculinity and femininity, the private, marriage and prostitution become political problems; so, therefore, does the familiar patriarchal understanding of work and citizenship. New antipatriarchal roads must be mapped out to lead to democracy, socialism, and freedom" (1988, 233). Many gays and lesbians might respond to Pateman by agreeing that although it may be important for sex, masculinity, femininity, the private, marriage and prostitution to become political issues subject to debate and redefinition within a genuinely democratic political world, it is too much to ask lesbians and gays to play a significant role in leading the struggle to make these debates reality. However, these debates have significantly informed conflicts within gay and lesbian life for at least the past twenty-five years. Rather than seeing the magnitude of these issues as too much to take on for people already harmed by norms of gender, family, and private life, I suggest that gays and lesbians take these issues on every day, though often in covert ways that do little to further discussion. By recognizing how much family issues have informed many conflicts, gays and lesbians might be more inclined to ask not how we can gain entrance into these institutional structures, but whether there are other, less divisive ways to think about family and private life. Engaging in this rethinking would put us in a better position to build a community and to create a political discourse capable of building ties with other communities.

2

Are We Family?

G ays and lesbians have often used the term "family" to describe others who have claimed a gay or lesbian identity. This use of "family" indicates that despite whatever differences might separate those who are gay and lesbian, there is a common identity uniting them. Writing in 1991, Weston suggests that this had been the meaning of "family" within gay life, but that changing social conditions were making the term less commonly used: "While the use of kinship terminology has fallen into disfavor as the politics of identity has given way to a politics of difference, people still employed it from time to time as a way of hinting at sexual identity" (p. 127). One of the forces that plays an important role in dividing the gay and lesbian "family" is the ideology of family dominant within the larger society. Within gay and lesbian politics, there are a number of issues that have proven to be consistently divisive. These include whether homosexuality is a natural, essential part of individuals; whether those within gay and lesbian life who refuse to accept broader social norms are immature compared to those who settle into a "virtually normal" life; and what, if anything, gays and lesbians have in common that can lead to the formation of a unified movement. Exploring history and current discourses of appropriate family can help us to understand why these particular issues have been such a recurring problem. Additionally, this exploration can help us to understand that these divisions are embedded within ideological constructions of family and adulthood. Recognizing the extent to which dominant discourses of family help to foster these internal conflicts is critical for understanding what is at stake as gays and lesbians debate family issues.

It is tempting for oppressed groups to argue for their rights by portraying themselves as so similar to those who are dominant that the social denial of rights is irrational and counterproductive, creating a category of outsiders who could, if they were allowed inside, contribute much to the dominant society. The cost of the strategy of seeking inclusion, however, can be high. Within gay and lesbian politics, norms that are embedded in family ideology have been continually present as a divisive force. Only by understanding how conflicts—such as whether homosexuality is a natural, essential part of the self; how gender and sexuality are connected; and whether monogamy and maturity are linked—are connected to dominant constructions of appropriate family can we begin to move beyond them, offering instead a different vision of self, relationships, and politics centered on creating neither a unified gay family nor private families. The voices of the gays and lesbians interviewed by Sherman (1992) sometimes indicate a desire for marriage rights and acceptance as "normal," yet more often they indicate a desire for the freedom to build relationships that are neither just like those of heterosexual people (at least as these are portrayed in hegemonic constructions) nor constantly threatened by a society that refuses to help individuals or couples to have the resources necessary to be able to exercise choice and agency in their relationships.

In these voices there is simultaneously an understanding of the importance of social support and an understanding of the importance of privacy within relationships, privacy that allows individuals to work together to build a relationship based on their needs. For example, Sherman quotes Kathie Cinnater: "What I like about domestic-partnership legislation is that it includes people who live in households and do not necessarily have a traditional, sexual relationship. I like to think that there are a great variety of ways to live with people and relationships you can call families or partnerships" (1992, 34). In order to develop state policies that allow individuals this space, while also working to foster social goals, we need to understand better the current difficulties resulting from social policies that work to further goals based on economic rationality and the needs of the capitalist economy, rather than goals based on the needs of human beings who desire increased freedom.

As we try to build an alternative conception of family and freedom, it is useful to understand that the current narrative of family contains values and assumptions that are historically rooted in the development and consolidation of liberal industrial capitalism in the early 1900s. Because these values emerged in a particular historical moment, one very unlike that in which we now live, it is worth questioning whether the values that guided family understanding are now appropriate as a model of family life. In relation to gays and lesbians, they are values that constrain our freedom by limiting our ability to form relationships in an intentional way. It is not coincidental that a critique of this understanding of family, and an attempt at formulating an alternative vision, was present in the Gay Liberation Movement, which had strong theoretical ties to other social movements of the 1960s that centered on civil rights, women's liberation, and antiwar sentiment. These movements helped gay liberationists to connect their analysis of sexuality and family to the needs of a racist, sexist, capitalist economy (Jay and Young 1972).

The alternatives to the nuclear family put forth by Carl Wittman in *The Gay Manifesto* indicate that this radical analysis led some to a complete rethinking of family life: "We have to define a new pluralistic, role free social structure for ourselves. It must contain both the freedom and physical space for people to live alone, live together for awhile, live together for a long time, either as couples or in larger numbers; and the ability to flow easily from one of these states to another as our needs change" (1972, 334). The values harmful to gay and lesbian lives were then and remain now harmful to other social groups as well, because these family values are embedded in maintaining a social organization that privileges a few. As a result, the possibility of building political connections around "family values" exists, though conflicts and divisions within gay and lesbian communities make building such a political movement a challenging task.

The development of alternative ways of organizing private life is desirable not simply because it would allow many gays and lesbians to live as they desire, but also because those who are choosing to form private lives and families based on values inimical to those of the dominant culture are providing models of private life based on developing and exercising agency in a new and ethically justifiable way. Additionally, the ethical framework embedded in these alternative ways of life is one that can allow for traditional choices, whereas the ethical framework of gay liberals who seek to gain marriage and family rights is inevitably a moral system that will exclude many who understand themselves as gay, lesbian, or queer.

Make Room for Daddy!

The conservative nature of the values embedded in discourses of inclusion in family institutions is best understood by examining parallels in the value system and political agenda of gay theorists committed to the inclusion of gays in institutions such as marriage, and the values set forth by those who argue that social problems are related to the decline of traditional nuclear families. One such proponent of the idea that many current social problems are caused by changes in the family is David Blankenhorn, author of *Fatherless America* (1995). If his analysis is correct, or if it can maintain ideological primacy, state policy would focus on embedding social benefits in family status.

In *Fatherless America*, Blankenhorn argues explicitly that America will not be able to solve problems such as violence unless fathers are a strong presence within families. "Fatherlessness," he writes, "is the most harmful demographic trend of this generation. It is the leading cause of declining child well-being in our society. It is also the engine driving our most urgent social problems from crime to adolescent pregnancy, to domestic violence against women" (1995, 1).[1] Therefore, he concludes, it is critical to form a grassroots movement dedicated to the construction of a new cultural narrative of the "Good Family Man." Central to this narrative would be the understanding that to be a good father is to be a provider, an educator, and a nurturer, with each understood to complement, but be different from, the parallel role of the mother. Blankenhorn argues that the state should reinforce this narrative with social policies ranging from giving married couples priority in public housing to mandating that all policy be evaluated for its impact on married couples, to regulating sperm banks. Blankenhorn's work is interesting because he positions himself not with the political right, but as an advocate of civic virtue and populist democracy. In this sense, he is writing in, though rarely explicitly drawing from, a tradition that includes the work of Christopher Lasch and Jean Bethke Elshtain, each of whom feminists criticize for reinforcing patriarchal constructions of family and society.

Blankenhorn's arguments are being taken seriously. *Fatherless America* has been reviewed by journals from *The Economist* ("Feminist-Reversing

Fatherless" 1995) to *The Futurist* ("Fatherless America (Book Review)" 1995) to *Family Relations* (Hansen 1996). Although the reviews suggest that at times Blankenhorn may be pedantic or not as fair as possible, they also suggest that the book is well-argued and should be read and taught. Further, the ideas that Blankenhorn sets forth are similar to ones currently guiding the formation of policy. The *New York Times* reported recently on a project designed to bring fathers back into housing projects by creating jobs that pay them enough to be able to provide for families (Rabinowitz 1996). Although this policy does not require that the fathers live with the mothers, that is clearly a goal.[2] Another *New York Times* article, one in which Blankenhorn is quoted, is about the desirability of ending no-fault divorce in order to keep more marriages from ending (Johnson 1996). The impact of this drive to reinsert fathers into families is clear in welfare reform legislation, as the *Washington Post* notes: "Since its emergence nearly a century ago, public assistance has focused almost entirely on the plight of unwed or abandoned women with children.[3] But the federal welfare overhaul signed into law last August gradually upends the notion of cash benefits for single mothers and mandates that states promote stable, two-parent households that can make it on their own" (Jeter 1997). President Clinton's agreement to these changes should not be a surprise. Although Hillary Clinton's *It Takes a Village* does argue that we need to respect families that are not the two-parent sexual family, she indicates clearly that two-parent families are the better alternative. Referring to Daniel Patrick Moynihan's argument from "more than thirty years ago,"[4] she suggests that "the absence of fathers—in the lives of children, especially boys—leads to increased rates of violence and aggressiveness, as well as a general loss of the civilizing influence marriage and responsible parenthood historically provide any society" (1996, 40). Thus, Blankenhorn's is not an isolated voice; it is one of many currently working to create, or reinforce, a conservative narrative of fathering, a narrative supported by public policy.

When Blankenhorn argues that fatherlessness is our most pressing demographic problem, it is critical to understand the full import of his words: to be fatherless is to not live with one's *biological* father.[5] There are two distinct reasons why Blankenhorn finds this so important. First, men who do not father are a threat to society because they have nothing to temper their aggression. "Fatherhood, more than any other male activity, helps men to become good men: more likely to obey the law, to be good citizens, and to think about the needs of others. Put more abstractly, fatherhood bends maleness—in particular male aggression—toward prosocial purposes" (1995, 25). It does so by directing men's aggressiveness into providing for and protecting their families. If we fail to create a cultural ideal of fathering that has the power to encourage men to play this role, we are in danger of reverting to a Hobbesian State of Nature, for as Blankenhorn notes, both Hobbes and Locke believed that the founding of civilization occurred with the founding of fatherhood.[6] Although Blankenhorn admits that males sometimes direct aggressiveness toward the family, he see this as somewhat rare, particularly if the children being parented are a man's biological offspring.[7]

In addition to the problems that can be avoided by taming men, Blankenhorn identifies four benefits for children who live with their fathers: (1) the provision of physical protection; (2) the availability of greater financial resources; (3) access to "a father's distinctive capacity to contribute to identity, character, and competence"; and (4) the provision of day-to-day nurturing (1995, 25). Although these may seem to be fairly straightforward functions that any parent provides for a child, Blankenhorn sees them as gendered: "For in contrast to the more continuous and symbiotic mother-child bond, this daily mixture of closeness and distance, expressiveness and instrumentality, constitutes a typically distinctive feature of the father-child bond, both contributing to the child's development and informing the infant's attachment to the father's bigness and otherness" (1995, 55). The distinction between what mothers provide to children and what fathers provide is based on a belief in essential and socially productive sex differences.

Although it is possible to accept significant portions of rhetoric such as Blankenhorn's while arguing that gays and lesbians could contribute to social stability by forming our own families, constructing an answer to conservatives on the basis of this argument is counterproductive because it reinforces values that demand not the active definition of social and individual goods by individuals (leading to the formation of new and ever subject to change social roles), but rather conformity to predefined social roles. The values advocated by Blankenhorn are values that have come down to us from another era, one in which changes in production and public life created social instability that was, in part, responded to through the creation of a new understanding of family life that continues to inform our thought today. There are three values central to this understanding and to Blankenhorn's argument: the value of monogamy, the value of secure gender roles, and the desirability of the privatized family. These values are shared by pro-marriage gay theorists such as Sullivan and Eskridge. They are also, however, values that underlie a number of controversies and divisions within gay and lesbian life. As will be evident by tracing the historical development of these values and discussing how they operate within gay life today, accepting the narrative of the dominant culture poses great challenges to the values of many lesbians and gays. Therefore, political strategies based on these values should be rejected in favor of goals and strategies that allow those who want to form monogamous relationships to do so, while not creating hegemonic norms and public policies that limit the freedom of others.

Essential Gayness

One way of arguing for the inclusion of gays and lesbians within the institution of marriage and family is to point out that conservatives who oppose gay rights are setting forth a counterproductive argument. Since gays and lesbians cannot help but be homosexual, this counterargument goes, to prevent gay people from marriage and from entrance into social institutions guarantees that family institutions and family values will further erode. It is nonsensical to define the family as a central agent of social stability and socialization while simultaneously denying a significant portion of the population entrance into this institution. Additionally, given the social approval that comes with marriage, many homosexuals will enter into heterosexual marriage simply because it is the only way to gain social approval, harming themselves, their spouses, and their children. "It is quite common," Sullivan writes, "that homosexual fathers and mothers who are encouraged into heterosexual marriages subsequently find the charade too much to bear: spouses are betrayed, children are abandoned, families are broken, and lives are ruined" (1996, 104).[8] In the end, these homosexual people will be poor spouses and poor parents, ones likely to harm their families and further erode the family values of our society. Given that homosexual people have no choice about their sexuality, it would better to recognize that gay people will exist and welcome them into the stabilizing institution of marriage.

The understanding of gay identity contained in this argument is controversial within gay and lesbian communities and within queer politics because it understands homosexuality as an essential, unchangeable part of the self. Such an understanding fails to account for the lives and experiences of both bisexuals or homosexuals who feel that they have actively chosen their sexuality. As many bisexuals argue, an essentialist understanding of homosexuality makes it impossible to account for bisexuality as anything other than indecision, an attempt to take advantage of heterosexual privilege, or a perversion. This division within queer life—that is, the division between those who understand sexuality as dichotomous and essential and those who understand sexual identities as less fixed and less stable—has a history that is as long as gay and lesbian politics itself. Despite the work of historians and other social theorists who have explicated in detail the extent to which "homosexual" and "heterosexual" are social—rather than natural— categories, arguments which assume that homosexuality is a natural condition, and can therefore be an essential part of the self, persist.

The threat that bisexuality poses to both many heterosexuals and many homosexuals has been much discussed and is stated well in an essay by Sara Ford, a high school teacher. She describes an interaction with a student: "Last year one of the girls told me that she has no problem with homosexuality because, 'after all, a gay person can't help it.' Bisexuality is wrong, though, because bisexuals are choosing to have sex with someone of the same sex when they don't have to" (1994, 121). If one has a choice, as many would argue in agreement with this student, those who choose to be other than heterosexual do not deserve rights; unlike women or people of color who are discriminated against based on roles they do not choose, homosexuals are discriminated against based on roles they choose. Ford remarks, "I listen to the assumption underlying her 'tolerance': there is something inherently ugly in the act, but it can be forgiven as long as you have this biological excuse" (1994, 121). Embracing the biological excuse, as Gary Lehring observes, has become almost a necessity for gay politics in a conservative climate. Yet, he notes, failing to challenge the essential understanding of gayness is to dismiss, often without serious consideration, much of gay liberation theory, and to create a situation in which gays and lesbians will at best be inferior people who are tolerated (1997, 193).

Starting from the position that lesbians and gays deserve rights because sexual orientation is not chosen will make it impossible to build a movement able to build bridges between those who feel that they have always been gay and those who understand their sexuality as more flexible. Further, it will not enable gay and lesbian politics to confront internal divisions connected to differing conceptions of what appropriate gay and/or lesbian identities are. Because gay men are more likely than lesbians to understand their sexual identity as a natural and fixed part of the self, conflict over what sexual identity is reinforces gender divisions within gay communities. At the same time, the very possibility of changing lesbian sexuality has caused divisions within lesbian feminist theory and activism. Without a clearer understanding of the political and economic significance of the ways by which gender interacts with sexual identify, gay and lesbian people may well spend more time arguing with one another over the meaning of sexual identity than fighting external institutions that reinforce gay/lesbian inferiority.

Laura Brown notes that fixed understandings of sexual identity make sense for gay men in a way that they do not for lesbians: "Arguably such a model [of a fixed, nonchanging sexual self] may be important in understanding gay men who subjectively report a more unchanging experience of sexual identity; but lesbian sexuality, like other aspects of female sexuality, does not appear to be well-described by any model assuming fixed sexual orientation" (1995, 12). Perhaps it is for this reason that many lesbians' understanding of their identity has divided them from other lesbians, as well as from bisexual women. Central to this conflict is the identification of lesbianism with feminist politics and the construction of a women's culture. Amanda Udis-Kessler observes, "The place of women's culture would become important when lesbians defended what they defined as 'their culture' against bisexuals, claiming that the difference between lesbian feminism and bisexuality was the difference between a way of life, a political commitment, and an entire culture, on the one hand, and a set of sexual experiences on the other" (1996, 55). This is to say that whereas those lesbian feminists inclined to separatism defined sexuality as a component (albeit a central one) of a larger social and political community, bisexual women were seen as failing to be fully committed, thus their continued willingness to be sexually involved with men. Recognizing this construction, Clare Hemmings suggests that within it "bisexual women are only political when they are 'temporary lesbians'" (1995, 47).

The critical question, of course, is how gender can and should interact with sexuality. Although separatist lesbian feminists do not understand sexual identity as pre-given and therefore fixed, they do understand sexual desire as so thoroughly rooted in gender politics that for a woman to desire a man is to betray feminism, and therefore women's interests as women. Moving outside of this narrative of identity requires asking new questions that, as Shane Phelan recognizes, can serve to enlarge lesbian communities by fostering political discussion instead of exclusionary gatekeeping (1994, 97). Such practice is important for lesbian politics not only because it might help to bridge differences between women who identify as bisexual and those who identify as lesbian, but also because it would help to increase discussion between lesbians who identify gender as a central form of power and those who identify gender as one among a number of different forms of oppression. For those in the latter category, working with men may be necessary for furthering antiracist, anticlassist, pro-sex agendas.

The political positions that come from understanding identity as fixed, whether by nature or political affiliation, are ahistorical in two ways. First, they deny that as society continues to change, people will develop new and different understandings of sexual identity. Second, they ignore the historical forces that led to the present dominance of essentialist models of identity. In the process, the reality that gender, race, and class understandings beneficial to those with power and privilege were consolidated by the ideological assertion that heterosexuality was natural and should be directed into the nuclear family is ignored. Thus the possibility of exploring interconnections between race, class, gender, and sexuality is lost. The loss of gay liberationist perspectives, including those connected to the meaning of gay identity and the role of family in society, is connected to losing the voices of those within gay and lesbian communities who do not have other kinds of privileges. Losing these voices is to continue a destructive pattern in gay political life. Allan Berube observes: "It's a mistaken idea that gay community or gay studies can stand alone as 'gay.' They were all made possible by the past civil rights, ethnic, and women's struggles, and by those who enjoyed many forms of institutionalized power and privilege. The white, male, middle-class separation of 'gay' from these other struggles and histories is one of the many predictable outcomes of a larger process of Americanization that I know too well from my family's class and ethnic history" (1997, 60). The construction of "homosexuality" arose as part of the construction of white, middle-class privilege along with the reinscription of male gender privilege.

Despite the dominance in our society of either the ideological assertion that homosexuality is natural and normal, or the opposite ideological assertion that it is unnatural and abnormal, the relative uniqueness of dichotomous categories "homosexual" and "heterosexual" in human society is clear to anthropologists. Bisexuality, Rebecca Ripley notes, is normal in much of the world. What is abnormal is for individuals to be able to choose not to marry. This analysis leads her to conclude that "the gay struggle is less about freedom to fuck than about freedom not to marry" (1992, 93). By this she means that because within many cultures homosexuality is not a category of being, homosexual acts continue to be understood simply as acts. If monogamy is not a central value of marriage within a particular culture,[9] an individual who combines marriage with same-sex sexuality will not be judged as immoral because of the homosexual experiences. Bisexuality is common, but only within the social constraint that one must enter into marriage. As Ripley points out, this has particularly negative consequences for women, since nonmonogamy is less likely to be tolerated for women than for men. Thus, how one's same-sex acts will be judged is a function of overall social position within society; multiple aspects of identity play a role in determining how, if, or under what circumstances same-sex sexuality will be judged negatively.

If sexuality enters into the judgments made by others and into one's own definition of identity as a result of social and cultural factors that have little direct connection to sexuality, then building a queer movement requires an understanding of how some of these other factors enter into constructions of self and other in our society. Brenda Marie Blasingame's (1992) analysis of bisexuality in black communities helps us to do this. Research indicates that black men are more likely than white men to practice bisexuality. For example, Cochran and Mays report that "black men are more likely than white men to be classified as bisexual (30 percent versus 13 percent) rather than homosexual (70 percent versus 87%)" (1995, 435). Contrary to the dominant construction of bisexuality as more common than homosexuality in black communities because of homophobia (Cochran and Mays 1995, 435), Blasingame argues that bisexuality may be more common for black people than for white people because sexual identity is less important to the core sense of self. Catherine Saalfield's experience of coming out provides some evidence for the importance of sexual identity to a white woman: "When I came out as a lesbian," Saalfield writes, "I became aware of what makes me so different from other people, and the naming of this difference made me comfortable. Identity (and by extension, community) became very important to me. I was no longer a person who felt she didn't have one (or the other)" (Saalfield and Nakagawa 1997, 241).

Because racial/ethnic identities are more likely to be central to the definition of one's self if one is a person of color in the United States, one can have greater freedom sexually because he or she feels less need to embrace a fixed identity in order to have a sense of belonging within a community (Blasingame 1992, 51). Blasingame's argument leads to the conclusion that we have no real sense of how common bisexuality might be, particularly within white communities, because social conditions and identities that are seemingly unrelated to sexuality and sexual identity have a powerful influence on whether an individual desires a unitary understanding of sexuality to feel like a human being who is part of a community. Bisexual identity, and differences in the percentage of individuals within different social groups who identify as bisexual, reinforces the idea that sexuality can be chosen and variable. As a result, it calls into question a fundamental assertion of those who argue that because sexual identity is fixed, lesbians and gays deserve rights, including marriage rights. At the same time, some bisexual theorists indicate that other assumptions underlying the social preference for monogamous marriage are undercut by bisexual identities.

Can Queers Be Mature?

The construction of relationships and sexuality by those who advocate gay marriage as central for gay and lesbian health suggests that by finding an individual partner, people can create stable lives that will, if both partners are honest, last for many years. Some bisexual writers, however, argue that this narrative of living happily ever after is flawed, and that bisexuality can be critical for revealing the presumptions implicit in it. In her critique of the romantic story of monogamy, a story based in the idea that one desires a single sex, Susanna Trnka writes, "It's not that bisexuality automatically makes a person nonmonogamous, but that bisexuality often brings nonmonogamy up as an issue. The knowledge that there isn't one person out there who is perfect for you, that for some of us there isn't even one type of person (male or female) you're looking for, makes the search for a partner all the more difficult" (1992, 107). Yet it also makes the need to negotiate relationships and to make choices within them all the more important. That is, it requires that one exercise agency in making decisions about sex and relationships. It is agency that leads to nonmonogamy, however, that advocates of marriage see as a particularly strong threat to society.

A central tenet of Western liberal capitalist society is that a mature adult should be not just heterosexual, but also monogamous. This assertion of the moral superiority of monogamy rests on a number of foundations, each of which can be connected to the capitalist economy. It may be, as Friedrich Engels (1978 [1884]) asserted, that the underside of the official story of heterosexual monogamy has always been female prostitution, but it nevertheless remains the case that middle-class norms required that the underside remain policed and hidden from the view of society. George Chauncey (1994) argues that it is was primarily because of the desire of nineteenth-century middle-class reformers to enforce heterosexual monogamy that gays became a target of the state. Despite the source of antigay police activism in a social discourse of monogamy, many gays and lesbians advocate monogamy and identify the ability to form and sustain monogamous relationships with individual and group maturity.

One place in which this construction has been highly visible is debate and discussion about AIDS. In the analysis of many both in the dominant culture and in gay communities, gay male emphasis on sexual freedom and nonmonogamy made gay men themselves culpable in the spread of AIDS throughout gay communities. Others have expended considerable energy arguing that it is particular sexual practices, not nonmonogamy, that spreads AIDS (Altman 1987). A similar argument exists in relation to gay politics in general. Lehring provides a particularly compelling example of this as he discusses his students' reactions to gay liberationist writing about family: "The liberationist agenda which sought to change the social order, challenging the institution of heterosexuality, and confront the cultural and social practices that make heterosexuality 'compulsory,' was dismissed by my students as the rhetoric of an 'immature' political movement" (1997, 185).[10] A mature movement, according to these students, is one that accepts sexual identity as a fact and works to become part of the institutional structure of society. Such a movement would certainly accept monogamous marriage as a desirable practice.

The perspective of these students is not unique. Many, including those in the gay community who wish to oppose radical gay critiques, focus on the visibility of sexuality in the politics of individuals and groups to argue that their analyses and actions are immature. An example of this can be seen in Bruce Bawer's opposition to the tactics of the radical direct action group "Lesbian Avengers." In his critique of picketing by members of the group outside a New York City middle school in response to the defeat of the Rainbow Curriculum, Bawer uses language that is revealing: "What they should be seeking is not simply to achieve visibility, but to banish ignorance about, and thus fear and hatred of, homosexuality. Among other things, heterosexuals should be made to recognize that being gay does not exclude the possibility of being a mature, responsible adult. Instead, however, the Lesbian Avengers managed to reinforce the notion of gays as reckless and infantile" (1993, 182). One may dispute whether this particular action was effective, but to choose to identify handing balloons to children that read "Teach Lesbian History" as "reckless and infantile" is indicative of far more than a debate over strategy. Rather, it indicates the extent to which questions of political analysis and political strategy are often reduced in gay politics to questions of maturity. If one shares Bawer's perspective, these activists should simply grow up, recognize the necessity of social institutions such as marriage and the family, and work to gain inclusion in those institutions. Anything else is a sign of immaturity. This tendency to attack activists and leaders using the language and constructions of the dominant culture is, according to David Jernigan, a continuing problem within gay organizing: "Within the gay movement, the internalization of gay and lesbian stereotypes by gay and lesbian people has impaired our ability to recognize and support leadership. Attacks on leaders have been endemic, and have often come in the same language used as that of external oppression. Leaders have faced charges of immaturity, of puerile fascination solely with things sexual, of being untrustworthy, of not really being committed to gay people, of not being 'really gay' or being 'too gay'" (1988, 34).

The standard applied to judging maturity in these instances comes not from critiquing the values of society, but from accepting them and demanding that gay leaders live up to them. The critical issue to Bawer, as well as to Eskridge and Sullivan, is not how human beings can have the freedom to exercise greater agency in making sexual and relationship decisions, but how human beings who already have an essential sexual identity can best be encouraged to channel their sexual desires into institutional structures that can control the chaos of untamed sexual desire. Marriage is central to their answer. "Marriage," Sullivan writes, "provides an anchor, if an arbitrary and weak one in the maelstrom of sex and relationships to which we are all prone. It provides a mechanism for emotional stability and economic security" (1996, 183). The understanding of marriage from which Sullivan draws is not, however, one based in nature; it is a construction of human relationships that was consolidated in the late nineteenth century.

Ideologically, monogamy is the preferable form of human sexual relationship because within a monogamous relationship human beings learn to control their desires and direct their energy into useful social purposes. In fact, the social privileging of heterosexual monogamy was part of an early twentieth-century attempt to control and civilize European immigrants, and to control and encourage white middle-class women to reproduce. It was a social norm heavily connected to the middle-class desire to encourage the development of private family life, a life away from the public space of the street. By forming such isolated family units, men would be influenced by the pro-social desires and needs of their wives; workers would be more hesitant to strike, both because they would be less connected to one another and because they would feel greater responsibility to their wives and children; ideal consumer units would be created; and parents would be able to support their increasingly costly children. In cases of divorce the custody of these costly children was now awarded to their mothers, a policy that Carol Brown (1981) sees as central to the construction of a new form of patriarchy. Within this patriarchal construction, women were accorded rights by the state and benefits from the state not as individuals, but as mothers and as caretakers of others.

The understanding of men, women, and family necessary to meet these social needs was very different from the Victorian family that preceded it. Within that social understanding, women were constructed as asexual, moral beings who needed the protection of husbands, while children—still seen as the property of fathers—were taught by their mother until, if they were boys, their father introduced them to the public world (Bloch 1987). Children, in this time period, remained an economic resource for most families. These norms changed because industrialization and the resulting urbanization necessitated the creation of new family norms. Sex was to be located and regulated within this new family. Mark Poster notes, "A gospel of thrift was applied to semen as well as to money. The act of sex, with its connotations of lust, rapture, and uncontrolled passions, was the epitome of unbusinesslike behavior. The bourgeoisie defined itself against the promiscuous proletariat and the sensual nobility as the class with virtuous self-denial" (1978, 169). Thus, the monogamous family idealized by many today is not a form of family that has any "natural" advantage; it is a form of family that enforces multiple social values, each of which was beneficial for developing capitalist industrial society.

The process of institutionalizing a social preference for marital monogamy, at a time when the lessening of other constraints provided people with an alternative, resulted in the construction of a psychological discourse that harmed and continues to harm lesbians and gays. Central to this discourse was the idea that heterosexual, married, monogamous life indicated that one was a mature human being who had developed a properly gendered sense of self and recognized that this self would be enhanced by being joined to another, different kind of being—that is, a person of the opposite sex. Within this relationship, sexual desire would be channeled in proper directions. Weston observes that many are unlikely to see gay or lesbian relationships as a model because they see heterosexual relationships—with their assumed unification of opposites—as intrinsically more interesting. She notes, "To the extent that heterosexuals view lesbian or gay lovers as two like halves that cannot be reconciled to make a whole, gay relationships seem to yield a cultural unit deficient in meaning (which, as any good structuralist knows, must be generated through contrast)" (1991, 137). The construction of men and women as opposites has multiple roots, from psychological research that continues to seek differences between them, to psychoanalytic theory that sees "opposite sex" parents as necessary so that children can come to understand their own sex/gender identity, to the very real differences between men and women that persist in the labor market. The psychoanalytic discourse is particularly important because, as Weston notes, it played powerfully into ideas of lesbians and gays as narcissistic, self-centered, and immature (1991, 156)—that is, as people who essentially desire ourselves rather than coming to accept and appreciate gender difference.

Although the understanding by gay theorists of a settled, monogamous life as more mature does not rest on the creation of a whole through the unification of opposites, it does preserve the goal of monogamy as a means by which sexual energy (through the union of romance and sexuality) can be controlled and directed into more useful goals. Thus, with modifications, central aspects of the original bourgeois construction remains. Additionally, these theorists argue that the acceptance of a stable, secure gay identity is an important element in maturity. Paula Rust discusses the extent to which this conception of sexual identity development denies bisexual experiences. Her research on the identities of bisexual women suggests that many women do not ever reach a stable understanding of their sexual identities. Instead, their understanding changes as the circumstances of their lives change. To some this might indicate that these women remain confused and immature. Rust, however, reaches a different conclusion: "Bisexual women's frequent identity changes do not indicate a state of searching immaturity, but a mature state of mutability." When identity is understood in this way, " 'coming out' would not be a process of essential discovery leading to a mature and stable identity, but merely one story constructed around one of the myriad identity changes we all go through as mature adults attempting to maintain accurate self-description in a changing social environment" (1996, 66). If identity formation is about adapting to a changing social environment, we can best understand how the identification of monogamous relationships with maturity arose by exploring in greater detail the historical forces that led to the consolidation of the middle-class nuclear family. It is this narrative of appropriate private life that has so influenced the way in which many lesbians and gays represent gay life, judge one another, and make judgments about our own behavior. What is most important about this particular understanding of family is that its development helped to consolidate not only the primacy of monogamous heterosexuality, but also interwoven gender, race, and class systems of power.

The Consolidation of "Family"

The history of norms of sexuality in the United States is indicative of the extent to which sexual constructions are connected to the needs of society at given moments and to the needs that these forces foster in individuals. The construction of homosexual and heterosexual identities came with consolidation in the larger society of middle-class norms, embraced by those who understood their development as necessary in order to foster social integration in an era of urbanization, instability, and fears of race suicide. The idealization of marriage, Julian Carter writes, was one important element in narratives of progress from early in the twentieth century: "In the first forty years of the twentieth century, scores of people wrote about modern marriage as a triumph of evolution. In such accounts, 'primitive' reproductive arrangements developed, across ages of natural selection, into romantic and sexual love between spouses. . . . As such studies forged connections between Anglo-Saxon civilization, evolutionary progress, and normal marital sex, they also linked sexual perversion to primitivism and savagery" (1997, 155). At the same time, these norms consolidated the dichotomous understanding of gender that underlies the construction of heterosexuality as a mature outcome of sexual development.

The mid to late nineteenth century was a time in American history when men's and women's lives were more separate than in prior times when household production and interdependence were more common. They were also more separate than they would be in the future when companionate marriage based on romantic attachment and sexual satisfaction became the desired norm. The interplay between gender conformity, sexuality, and family norms as companionate marriage was constructed is somewhat clear: men's and women's essential psychology was viewed as different, though complementary, in such a way as to make heterosexuality a necessity for the creation of complete couples. Creating and maintaining relationships that embodied romantic love and sexual desire directed energy into the private sphere of the family. Equally important, it provided a rationale for addressing what had been a serious social concern—an increased number of educated, middle-class women who were choosing not to marry and not to give birth.

In the period immediately prior to the consolidation of the companionate marriage as "normal," women chose in extraordinarily large numbers to forgo marriage and childbearing. Trisha Franzen reports that "at the most basic demographic level, the generations of women born between 1865 and 1895 had the highest proportion of single women in U.S. history." Not only were these women single, but they could also be "respectable": "The unmarried state was respectable for both working-class and middle-class women. In the public's view, less privileged women were objects of concern as 'women adrift,' while they viewed middle-class, educated women as 'social housekeepers.' In addition, among feminists and progressives, turn-of-the-century independent women were the vanguard of women's struggle for equality" (Franzen 1996, 5). Whether or not any, many, or most of these women who chose not to marry were lesbians has been a source of much discussion, but for our purposes how they saw themselves or how we could label them is less important than their existence as women able to build primary connections with other women (D'Emilio 1983, Rich 1980). At the same time, the number of unmarried men was also high, and as Chauncey documents in regard to New York, there was a thriving gay subculture. The circumstances that gave rise to an ideology that defined single women and men increasingly as "sick" and dangerous are instructive for us today because they reveal the complex ways by which gender, sexuality, race, class norms, and privilege were woven together through the creation of norms of family. Many of the middle-class women of the late 1800s and early 1900s were able to survive independently because they played important roles in fostering "virtue" among the lower classes, in part through the development of government policy (Sklar 1993). One component of virtue was sexual control, a value that had to do with both middle-class thrift and with changing demographics.

Although fostering virtue in the wider society was important, it was less important for the native white middle class than giving birth. While white middle-class women were giving birth to fewer children in the late 1800s, large numbers of immigrants continued to enter the country and rates of reproduction were higher among immigrants, blacks, and the native working class than for the white middle class. Spreading the middle-class value of sexual restraint to the working class was one answer to growing fears of "race suicide." This would only be effective, however, if combined with increasing pressure on white middle-class women to marry and give birth to more children. President Theodore Roosevelt expressed these desires: "By 1906 [Roosevelt] blatantly equated the falling birth rate among native born whites with the impending threat of 'race suicide.' In his State of the Union message that year Roosevelt admonished the well-born white women who engaged in 'willful sterility'—the one sin for which the penalty is national death, race suicide" (Davis 1981, 209). A critical element in encouraging women to refocus their energy on the family was the reconstruction of images of women and sexuality. A new image of women as desiring sexual satisfaction in the context of marriage replaced the asexual, morally virtuous image of women that had guided Victorian ideology.

The development of hegemonic family centered around companionate heterosexual relationships had a particularly devastating effect on women who often did not have the economic resources to choose not to marry. The attack used against women who were choosing to not marry was that they were too androgynous—that is, not accepting of their proper place as women. "Linking orgasms to chic fashion and planned motherhood, male sex reformers, psychologists, and physicians promised a future of emotional support and sexual delights to women who accepted heterosexual marriage—and male economic hegemony. Offered such an alternative, only the 'unnatural' woman, they argued, would continue to struggle with men for economic independence and political power" (Smith-Rosenberg 1989, 272). Whereas in many cultures, gendered behavior is not necessarily linked to heterosexuality, by the early twentieth century this link was part of dominant discourse within European and American middle classes.

The rise of companionate marriage and the institutionalization of the (hetero)sexual family required not just a redefinition of femininity, but also a new understanding of masculinity. The understanding that developed served to reinforce the threatened masculine identities of middle-class men. Chauncey's history of gay New York indicates that the gay male identity that developed in the early twentieth century was connected to a common fear among middle-class men—fear of loss of masculinity—that resulted from the growth of an industrialized and urbanized society in which physical labor became increasingly uncommon for them. In the late 1800s, middle-class men more often worked in bureaucracies where they were dominated by bosses and verbally attacked by working-class men—that is, men whose physical labor confirmed their own masculinity (Chauncey 1994, 112).[11] Given these fears, middle-class men, unlike working-class men, felt a need for confirmation of their masculinity. Heterosexual marriage provided one such means of identity confirmation.

As in much of the rest of the world, homosexuality was not an identity among men of color and white ethnic lower-class men in early twentieth-century New York. These men could easily have sex with both men and women without their masculinity being called into question. Among middle-class men, however, for whom changing economic roles brought on fears of loss of masculinity, their core identity came increasingly to revolve around their family relationships, and their role within the family. For those middle-class men who did not capitulate to the social pressure to marry and have children, a new homosexual identity developed. Thus the roots of gay identity may be traced back to the development of social constructions of masculinity and femininity intended to secure the hegemonic power of the white, native-born middle class.[12]

Given the relationship between gender, sexuality, marriage, and motherhood that developed in this time period, it should not be surprising that many of the conflicts that continue to divide gays and lesbians have to do with gender, class, and race, as they interact with sexuality. These are not conflicts that will go away if we are able to more commonly view them through a historical lens that indicates the ways by which they came to be connected. Yet without such a historical perspective, we are in danger of continuing to see each of these conflicts as isolated and disconnected from the others. What historical understanding can help us to appreciate is that the construction of the sexual family was a critical element in bringing together discourses that worked to enforce systems of power in relation to class, gender, sexuality, and race. Central to this discourse was the construction of a series of binary understandings—such as those between homosexual and heterosexual, married and unmarried, and masculine and feminine—that have had obviously negative impacts on gay and lesbian communities.

At the same time, the racial binarism (white/black) and the class binarism (poor/middle class) were constructed in relation to a particular understanding of family life. These binarisms also remain central to splits within lesbian and gay communities. One way of seeing this is to look at the impact that these divisions have on private relationships within gay and lesbian communities. Although sexual relationships outside of committed relationships may cross class lines and race lines with some frequency, tensions remain as a result of these differences. In her discussion of lesbian relationships, Dunne points out that the lesbians to whom she spoke are highly aware of the destructive impact of economic inequalities in a relationship, particularly when these inequalities foster dependency. The result is that lesbians sometimes work out strategies that allow them to overcome this inequality,[13] but more often relationships with economic imbalances simply do not last. Dunne notes, "None of the respondents [in her study of lesbian couples] was in a relationship at the point of interview which was seen as problematic in terms of economic imbalance. This may be because, when partners recognize an imbalance of economic power and are unable, or unwilling, to take steps to counter the problem, the relationship is short-lived" (1997, 197). The imbalance of power, though recognized as a problem in a way that is often masked in more status-defined marital relationships, remains a problem that is not faced within the relationship. In fact, building relationships across lines of power may require political attempts to reduce power differentials between people.

The challenge of interracial politics and relationships remains a source of division with gay communities. Gregory Conerly notes that although it is possible to bring a gay identity and a black identity together in multiple ways, two have been prominent. One involves identifying primarily as gay, thus focusing one's energy (sexual and non-sexual) in predominantly white gay communities. The other involves identifying primarily as black and focusing one's energy in black communities even if this means denying homosexual desire and experience. These two essentialized identities, Conerly argues, lead not to constructive discussion about how sexuality and race interact in the lives of individuals, but rather to in-fighting that denies both the strengths and limits of all understandings. An alternative goal would be to recognize that multiple understandings of identity are important, while not resorting to a relativistic position from which no judgments can be made about any construction of black lesbian/gay identity. "Even if it were possible to give all black lesbigay identities equal validity and weight," Conerly suggests, "it would not be desirable because there are some constructions of black lesbigay identity that should be discouraged, such as those rooted in internalized racism or homophobia. The goal, then, is to have multiple non-oppressive black lesbigay identities that take into account the diversity that exists between us" (1996, 142). Of course this also requires that white gays and lesbians be challenged to confront racism.

Stereotypic images of black sexuality—images constructed to reinforce white sexual and family norms and white economic power—play an important role in fostering the division that Conerly notes within black communities, as well as divisions between white and black lesbians and gays. After observing that in the 1980s blacks were generally welcome at night in places where gay men were sexually active, Essex Hemphill notes:

> Open fraternizing at a level suggesting companionship or love between the races was not tolerated in the light of day. Terms such as "dinge queen" for white men who prefer Black men, and "snow queen" for Black men who prefer white men, were created by a gay community that obviously could not be trusted to believe its own rhetoric concerning brotherhood, fellowship, and dignity. Only an *entire* community's silence, complicity, and racial apathy is capable of reinforcing these conditions. (1992, 40)

Hemphill warns us of the extent to which dominant social constructions influence relationships, and that although gays and lesbians may explicitly advocate equality within relationships, the overall lack of concern with racism in gay communities (particularly gay communities that fetishize black sexuality) makes interracial relationships difficult.[14] Combating the sexual and family stereotypes that give rise to fetishizing the sexuality of people of color requires not that gays and lesbians seek to enter into family, but rather that we challenge norms that are antithetical to the relationships of many lesbians and gays and to positive views of gay/lesbian/bisexual and heterosexual people of color.

The difficulty of challenging these norms for lesbians and gays, women, the lower class, and people of color is that each of these groups comes to understand successful integration into power as requiring adaptation to and acceptance of dominant norms of family and sexuality. In speaking about the impact of this desire for acceptance by the black middle class, Cathy Cohen identifies the strategy as one that harms black lesbians and gay men: "We need only look around to see the great efforts many black leaders and academics engage in to distance themselves from those perceived to be participate in 'inappropriate immoral sexual behavior.' Examples of such distancing efforts are evident not only in the absence of sustained writing on black lesbians and gay men by black authors and academics, but are also found in the counter-experience of unending writing and policy attacks on the 'inappropriate" and 'carefree' sexuality of those labeled the 'underclass' and more generally black women on welfare" (1996, 378). The distancing in which some gays and lesbians engage in relation to those who are non-monogamous, nongender-conforming, and publicly visible as sexual beings is the same kind of distancing intended to gain entrance into middle-class acceptability.

Choosing Children

In relation to gay theorists such as Sullivan or Eskridge, the desire to see gays and lesbians accepted within the framework of dominant institutions is explicit. Often, however, the language lesbians and gays draw from to describe and justify the decisions that we make and the judgments that we make of others is less explicit, even though it may still draw from and reinforce dominant discourses. One area where the question arises of how, or whether, one is making choices or fulfilling natural desires is in how we think about and justify decisions to have children. As the number of lesbians choosing to have children in the context of lesbian relationships has increased, this question of whether one should have children and what children mean in terms of identity has fostered conflict within lesbian communities. In part, this is because the language lesbian mothers often use to assert their right as well as their desire to parent and to counter social approbation is a language that stems from what have come to seem like "commonsense assertions," at least to those who use them. This appeal to "commonsense," however, has serious social and ethical implications. One point often made by the lesbian mothers with whom Fiona Nelson (1996), Phyllis Burke (1993), and Laura Benkov (1994) spoke is that in order for a family to be complete, it is necessary that a couple have children. For example, Benkov discusses the desire to have children as a natural desire, almost a necessary part of adulthood, particularly in the context of a maturing couple relationship: "It [the Massachusetts foster care controversy] all began when a gay couple acted on one of the most profound human desires: a wish to be parents" (1994, 86); "things were clicking into place for them, and having children together seemed like a natural next step" (1994, 243). Burke, in a book that connects parenting to radical political activism, understands her parenting as coming from "a deep maternal urge." "Before Jesse's conception," she writes, "I did believe that it was acceptable, perhaps even noble, to deny myself and my partner the full range of human experience because we were a detested minority" (1993, 6). The understanding asserted by these women is fairly straightforward: as lesbians come to value ourselves, we will begin to allow ourselves to satisfy the "natural" desires allowed traditionally to heterosexual women.

The gender-specificity of this understanding is clear in the ideas of the women interviewed by Lewin: if one is a woman, the desire to mother is natural; to be a mother is to be a more mature and responsible human being than to be a "childless" woman. Many lesbians, she reports, see the fact that they are mothers as confirming that they are "women," thus it is not surprising that the language they use to discuss maternity draws from dominant discourses. In fact, many of these women believe that they have more in common with heterosexual mothers than with lesbians who are not mothers. Lewin notes, "Lesbian mothers, like other mothers, select elements of their narratives from a circumscribed repertoire, a language of caring and nurturance, a language that makes motherhood supersede and engulf other aspects of identity" (1993, 183). What goes unexamined in these discussions is the social pressure put on some women to have children, and the social pressure put on women to have these children in the context of secure couple relationships that ideally contain the resources necessary for the couple to support the child with minimal external support.[15]

Nancy Polikoff (1987), like Benkov, notes that the increase in lesbian mothering[16] in the 1980s coincided with an increasingly challenging political environment, one in which women could feel most acceptable by retreating into the private world of family and motherhood. The desire to retreat may be traceable to the realization that lesbian communities will be sites of political conflict, rather than conflict-free "homes." Polikoff evaluates this retreat differently than Benkov, seeing in it the potential for division between lesbians. In discussing the increasing tendency by many lesbians to define motherhood as most central to their lives, Polikoff writes, "I also believe the perception that one's interest as a mother supersedes one's interest as a lesbian is politically devastating" (1987, 52). It is devastating both because it serves to reinforce dominant norms, by reinforcing divisions between women who choose to mother and those who do not, and because it provides a refuge from a confrontational but necessary public, political world. Irena Klepfisz also recognizes the desire to create private family as connected to the inability to construct safe, alternative spaces, and suggests that pressure has developed for lesbians to mother children. "The message communicated to me," she writes, "was that I—a woman alone, without a partner, without children—was enigmatic at best, superfluous at worst" (1987, 64). This is a message that came to her not just from heterosexual men and women, but also from lesbians.

Such conflict between lesbians raises serious questions about how lesbians can and do justify their decisions to have children. Appealing to the desirability of completing one's relationship with a partner by adding a child, or suggesting that one's life as a woman is not complete unless one has a child, serves not only to create conflict between lesbians who are mothering and those who are not, but also to reinforce a privatized understanding of family. Although the presence of lesbian mothers undoubtedly also challenges other social stereotypes—for instance, the notion that lesbians are not capable of being proper women or that children raised by lesbians and gays are likely to suffer negative emotional consequences—these values can be challenged even if lesbians justify their childbearing and child rearing choices in a less essential language. That is, by constructing childbearing and child rearing as an act of agency, rather than as the result of natural biological desires or relationship needs, the conflicts that arise over mothering between lesbians could be refocused, while also not continuing to support understandings of women and family that are embedded in discriminatory and oppressive social institutions.[17]

Finally, we need to understand that these constructions can easily lead lesbians, like heterosexual women, down a road that increasingly requires medical intervention and control. The social consequences of accepting the normalcy of couples (particularly financially secure couples) having children is apparent both in everyday discourse, such as that through which others question Klepfisz's choices, and also in the highly profitable and growing reproductive technology industry. As feminist authors such as Janice Raymond (1993), Kathryn Pauly Morgan (1989), and Linda Williams (1989) have noted, this industry thrives because social pressures to have children, particularly children who are biologically one's own, are so great that women are willing to undergo highly invasive, often not very successful procedures in order to try to have a child.[18] Janice Raymond writes, "Infertile women especially are portrayed as desperate for children. One woman, in responding to an article in *Ms.* magazine, related that the classic comment whenever anyone discovers she is infertile is, 'Have you ever thought about adoption (or in vitro or surrogacy)' as though simply getting a child will somehow solve the problem. It is assumed that in order to be a whole family, we must desire and seek to obtain a child" (1993, 5). Developing a more complex understanding of mothering can help us challenge the power of science and prevent us from feeling compelled to use whatever technology is available to make us complete women and couples.

Beyond Rule-Based Monogamy to Judgment

Whereas conservatives, including gay conservatives, assume that marriage and family life are the ideal way to satisfy multiple human needs for love, sex, friendship, parenting, and caring for the elderly, many gays and lesbians (among others) create and continue to create multiple structures to perform these many functions. Although the conservative story of family indicates that if family is functioning well the best thing that political life can do is to protect the sanctity of the private sphere, the story of private life and ethical decision making that is embedded in the decision making of many gays, lesbians, and bisexuals suggests an alternative: Given that social and political understandings are always part of family life, and private life in general, we might be better served by making these understandings and values visible so that the issues people confront in meeting human needs are explicitly part of political discussion and debate, as well as personal decision making, as individuals attempt to define relationships with others.

If monogamy is understood as a choice rather than as an indication of the ability to form sexually and ethically mature relationships, it is possible and useful to ask new questions about the values and decision-making processes that are part of either choosing or rejecting monogamy. Many gay couples would argue that it is a great challenge to engage in the process of defining a relationship that exists outside of hegemonic norms, one that allows both partners to define and meet their needs. Gay theorists such as Steven Seidman (1992) and Jeffrey Weeks (1995) have theorized ways of considering moral and ethical obligations within sexual relationships that provide grounds for judging relationships. What is critical to both Weeks and Seidman is that in a situation where conventional standards are lacking a new freedom exists, but it is a freedom that requires careful moral evaluation. For gay men, the reality of AIDS makes the necessity of an ethical framework in sexual decision making particularly apparent.

One impact of the AIDS pandemic is to make clear the embeddedness of personal decisions in public discourses and practices. Although an individual may feel that s/he is exercising individual choice in choosing a sexual partner and making decisions about sexual activity with that partner, community norms and practices influence both choices. The difficulty that Seidman sees gay communities facing as they respond to AIDS is that the place of sex within the community has never been clear. On the one hand, he argues, there has been a romanticist strain within gay male communities that copies hegemonic heterosexual culture's emphasis on monogamy and love in intimate relationships. Such relationships are understood as necessary in order for the whole self to be recognized and satisfied. For romanticists, an adequate response to AIDS would require that individuals protect themselves by choosing to have sex only in the context of monogamous relationships, with each partner aware of the HIV status of the other. Romanticists are also likely to favor marriage and family rights, seeing these as providing gays and lesbians with the entrance into social institutions that allow for the development of "wholeness." At the same time, gay communities have contained libertarians, or those committed to permitting and encouraging all mutually agreed upon sexual expression, even when this sexuality becomes commercialized and in part defined by the ability of some to profit. These positions are not unique to gay male communities; in fact, they are also central to debates among lesbians and feminists over sexuality (Seidman 1992, 9–143).

Seidman argues that a crisis such as AIDS highlights the inadequacy of both positions as guides for sexual decision making. The romanticist/libertarian divide, as well as the other divisions discussed in this chapter, exist because gay and lesbian decision making has taken place in a society that has little, if any, understanding of how ethics and politics are linked. Romanticists are unable to recognize that as historical forces promote change in society, people's sense of identity and their ethical judgments will change as well. It is ironic that gay romanticists ignore this reality since without such changes in self-definition and ethics, gay romanticists would not exist. Yet there do need to be grounds for judgment other than simply the consent of those involved, since differently situated people may well consent to practices not from desire but from lack of meaningful choice. Thus, just as extending marriage to a more freely chosen contract does not guarantee greater freedom, neither does an ethic that judges sexual decision making on the basis of consent.

The inability of either ethic to be effective in addressing AIDS makes this theoretical argument more compelling. Whereas the romanticist understands friendship, sexuality, and romantic love as ideally linked, the fact that this was not the norm for many gay men in the 1970s meant that the ethical standards of romanticists were inappropriate and ineffective for many in the gay community. Since romanticism was the dominant ethical construction, it discouraged the development of alternative means of judging that may have been more compatible with practice:

> In this regard, studies show that a typical gay male pattern in the 1970s subculture involved long-term intimate, loving relationships that would be desexualized, with sexual expression centered in casual sex with multiple partners. The key point is that a sexual ethic needs to be attentive to significant variation, by which I mean differences in meaning, expectations, and intimate arrangements that would have to be considered in understanding any specific population. This is an important issue. In order for a sexual ethic to avoid authoritarian implications, its descriptions and judgments of a group's prac-

tices must be expressed in language capable of being understood and contested by that group. (Seidman 1992, 193)

One response to the typical gay male pattern of the 1970s, as we have seen, might be to judge those who participated in this culture as overly sexual and immature. But this position is unlikely to save lives in the face of a disease such as AIDS. A sexual ethic that has the power to be effective in the face of this crisis, and in the face of social change in general, must be capable of allowing for experimentation and change in how individuals and communities understand personal life, while still providing grounds for judgment. The implication, as Weeks clearly understands, is that private and public visibly interact with one another: "The links between the social and the personal are constantly being defined and redefined, while at the same time, the power relations in the domains of everyday life are being made visible, and the spaces for individual inventions of self are being expended" (1995, 32). The key is to have a guide for action that allows for such experimentation.

Such a guide, as Weeks agrees with Seidman, will not be found in the glorification of individual choice. This would ignore the influence of social forces on the acting agent. Instead, Seidman suggests that the concept of responsibility is necessary to modify consent: "This means assessing the morality of acts by situating them in their specific social historical context, and analyzing them not only in terms of whether they involve choice or intentionality, but in terms of these consequences. The concept of responsibility, like the idea of consent, compels us to view acts in relation to the meanings of those engaged in the acts, as well as in terms of their effects" (1992, 200). Thus, a critical element in sexual ethics is considering not simply whether both parties have consented to particular acts, but also what we can expect the outcome of our actions to be. Although Seidman reads Weeks's earlier work as denying the importance of consequences,[19] it is clear in *Invented Moralities* that Weeks does see consequences as critical. Similarly, Weeks argues that concern with consequences most effectively leads to a sexual community able to continue to have sex while also protecting itself from AIDS:

Safer sex became a means of negotiating sex and love, of building respect for self and others, in a climate of risk and fear. From this point of view, safer sex was a way of recovering the erotic, not a defensive reaction to it, based on the minimization, if not complete elimination, of risk in relationships of mutual trust and responsibility. I take this as a powerful example of the ways in which a responsibility for the self requires a responsibility to others, in a web of reciprocity that takes for granted a small concession of absolute freedom to do as you desire guarantees a wider freedom. (1995, 181–182)

Such responsibility toward both self and other is understood by Weeks as central to what he calls an "ethic of love." In fact, both Weeks and Seidman understand that an effective response to AIDS in personal, sexual relationships requires an empathic, responsive engagement with the other. This engagement may result in sexual partners choosing to form a monogamous relationship, but it also may result in the partners agreeing to other sexual arrangements intended to enhance safety. What is important is not that these individuals follow particular, externally defined rules, but that they acquire knowledge and engage in processes that allow them to make informed judgments.

Because this ethical approach will produce different outcomes, it is inevitable, as Seidman recognizes explicitly, that conflicts will arise between individuals and within communities over sexual ethics and sexual decision making. Since individuals will always make judgments and act based on their own understanding of values and cultural traditions, "the morality of sexual practices should then be almost always a matter of conflict or contestation" (1992, 202). These conflicts will be played out politically, as conflicts over sex education are currently. They are conflicts, Seidman argues, that require a basic level of respect for current sexual practices, and a desire to understand their importance to practitioners. They are also conflicts through which individuals can grow as ethical thinkers, thus enhancing their ability to participate in the debates so necessary for democratic society. The connection between defining one's sexual identity and politics is also discussed by Mark Blasius, who argues that "constituting and reconstituting oneself through erotic relations and a way of life, or ethos, with others thus allows for the emergence of a new ethic—an invented autonomy like the drag queens' assertion 'I am what I am'—and a consequent new relationship of the self to politics" (1994, 220). We cannot, however, engage in these processes of defining new relationships between the self and politics if we channel all desires into current institutional structures.

Asking that people engage in judgment by considering social context and expected outcomes provides the basis for an alternative perspective on how one can build ethical relationships. This is a perspective that asks individuals to do more than follow the rules of society—it asks instead that s/he recognize a complex set of factors in order to make a decision about what is best for her/himself and others. Gay and lesbian life suggests the possibility of realizing this alternative understanding of relationships, one that is based not solely on individuals accepting social roles (and sometimes acting deceptively in order to appear to be meeting the demands of these roles), but on working to negotiate relationships based on considering cultural norms, one's emotional needs, and the emotional and material needs of others. In the process, new roles are both developed and called into question when they fail to satisfy.

This is a moral understanding that is not only justified by gay practice; it also gains support from feminist theorists. For example, Joan Tronto (1989) argues that in moving away from a perspective on women's morality that constrains women into "feminine" roles, it is important to recognize the centrality of care to what has been discussed as women's moral voice, and to bring this voice more forcefully into social discourse. Blankenhorn's work, following in a long tradition of theorists who believe that individuals should not—or perhaps cannot—learn to exercise judgment, denies that individuals possess the ability to engage in the form of ethical decision making theorized by Seidman, Weeks, and Tronto. He believes, instead, that morality in society is dependent on internalizing rules, a process that is theorized as most effective in the sexual family and as done more completely by men than by women. Thus, the ethics of relationships that gays and lesbians sometimes live suggests that there are other possibilities that may be more compatible with freedom and democracy.

The challenge is to understand the norms embedded in concepts of marriage and family well enough to recognize that these norms are often sources of conflict not just between gays/lesbians and heterosexuals, but within gay and lesbian communities. Although recognizing the extent to which these norms are connected to conflicts within gay politics is important, once we recognize the power of these norms we have taken only one step in the development of a political movement that attempts to move beyond this narrow and limiting vision of normality. A further step involves analyzing the social conditions that are necessary to allow people to have the freedom to build relationships in ways that meet both their own needs and the needs of others. Thus, as we develop a vision of family and private life, we need to ask how this vision may reinforce narratives used to control others—that is, the narratives of Otherness that allowed for the consolidation of middle-class dominance.

At the same time, as we draw on gay and lesbian relationships to develop models of alternative ways of organizing private life, it is important to note that lesbian and gay relationships fail in ways that need further analysis. For example, just as the potentials illustrated by current lesbian and gay relationships can demonstrate the extent to which humans can exercise agency in building relationships, the reality of violence within gay and lesbian relationships should serve to remind us of the complexity of human relationships, particularly when idealized relationships are removed from public attention to the extent that they are in a society that glorifies the nuclear family.

The prevalence of violence in gay or lesbian relationships is hard to estimate precisely, though the research that has been done suggests that violence is as prevalent in gay and lesbian relationships as in heterosexual relationships (Renzetti 1992). Research indicates that dependency is a primary and irreconcilable issue in gay and lesbian relationships that are violent. What is interesting, however, is that economic dependency, though somewhat important, is much less central in homosexual relationships than in heterosexual relationships. What stands out as an indicator of violence in lesbian relationships is the power of emotional dependency (Renzetti 1992). The presence and cause of violence in lesbian relationships can tell us much about identity, insecurity, and the pressures that result from a social ideology that encourages individuals to rely on a single person for intimacy, security, and nurturance. Renzetti argues that this is a particular problem for lesbians, since female socialization attempts to mold women into people who will be concerned primarily with maintaining relationships and caring for others (1992, 31–33). Thus, lesbians may be more inclined than gay men both to form monogamous relationships and to become dependent on their partner within a monogamous relationship, a dependence that can come to threaten one's sense of self and lead to violence. This finding is important in relation to debates over the extent to which gays and lesbians should emphasize marriage, because research on lesbian dependence suggests not that institutionalizing the couple relationship through marriage would help to lessen battering, but that social pressure on lesbians to marry and dedicate themselves completely to one another might further contribute to abuse within lesbian relationships. This is exactly what can result from social pressures to see marriage as central to one's identity. Combating violent relationships, whether those of lesbians and gays or those of heterosexuals, may require a reduction in the social isolation created at times by either marriage or fear of oppression. This is, again, a social and political issue.

Rethinking Family

In his discussion of black gay men in Harlem, William Hawkeswood notes that in this community the language of family does continue to be central in discussing fellow gay men (1996, 201n38). Yet here the term "family" refers not to the dominant understanding of family, but rather to a counternarrative of family that has a long history in black communities. In commenting on the use of "sister" and sisterhood within white feminist communities, Pat Alake Rosezelle notes that this term was appropriated from the Civil Rights Movement and black communities. Within these communities, she suggests, the use of familial language both conveyed respect for political allies and signified the alternative family patterns that were so central to the survival of black communities. In communities without this understanding, Rosezelle suggests, the language of family has less chance of fostering political ties since it naturalizes connections rather than highlights their political nature. Further, the language of family can work politically just as it does in personal life to mask power differences (Lugones 1995, 136).

One alternative to trying to build a political community that understands itself as a family is to build a political community of friends. "There are no rules specifying the duties and rights of friends," Lugones notes. "Rather, in friendship one is guided by concern for the other in her particularity. This is an aspect of friendship that cannot be up for reconstruction without losing the meaning of the term, as one would lose the concept of sisterhood if one were to think *apart* from family" (1995, 148). Yet because she does not believe that feminists are capable of building such ties across the social boundaries of racist, capitalist, patriarchal society, Lugones argues that the relationship of "companera" is the best that can be hoped for because this term connotes a less unconditional relationship (1995, 138). Given this history of family and the divisions that hegemonic family norms foster within gay and lesbian communities, perhaps it is time for those of us outside of communities with a history of alternative family life to stop using the language of family politically, thus challenging these ideas: (1) there is an essential connection between people because of sexual identity; (2) families are essentially places of emotional closeness, rather than socially defined institutions in which power operates; and (3) that familial connections are preferable to other kinds of close, nurturing commitments. At the same time, we might stop using the language of family to justify our personal relationships, instead working to foster friendship in our personal lives and companera relationships in our political lives. Liberal political strategies will not foster such an understanding of political identity. The critical question is whether there are political understandings that might provide guidance for building companera relationships.

3

Radical Democracy and Queer Identity

I n the previous chapters, I argued that a liberal, rights-based approach to change is unlikely to increase the freedom of many gays and lesbians, as well as heterosexuals, because this political strategy provides no means of confronting dominant cultural understandings, particularly those connected to family, that limit freedom. Given this, we need to consider whether there is an alternative political strategy that could be pursued by lesbians and gays seeking to enhance freedom in private life, while also fostering ethical evaluations such as those discussed in the previous chapter. The goal of such a political strategy would be to provide the social support necessary to allow people greater freedom in private life while also trying to increase feelings of security. In conceiving of what such a strategy would need to accomplish, Jeffrey Weeks's observations about what families do currently provide a useful reminder. Families are important because they serve as mediating institutions that "connect the public and private, provide sociable human contact, value systems and socialization, and act as a major source support and practical help" (1991, 153). He reminds us that there are many other relationships that serve this same purpose but that, unlike the sexual family, these relationships are either not institutionalized or not provided with social support and recognition. Once we recognize this, he concludes:

> The real challenge lies not in attempting to find alternatives to the family, nor in attempting to make the term family so elastic that it embraces everything and nothing. On the contrary, the more dangerous and difficult task lies in the attempt to forge a moral language that is able to come to terms in a reasoned way with the variety of social possibilities that exist in the modern world, to shape a pluralistic set of values which is able to respect difference. . . . It does not mean that "the family" is redundant or that it can contribute nothing to individual and social well-being. But a true pluralism must begin with the assumption that happiness and personal fulfillment are not the privileged prerogative of family life. (1991, 155)

The political strategy necessary must be one that addresses material needs while also challenging dominant constructions.

Urvashi Vaid argues compellingly that gay and lesbian politics need to be transformed, seeing the goal of transformation as the recognition that fighting for civil rights will create not equality, but "virtual equality." "In this state," she tells us, "gay and lesbian people possess some of the trappings of full equality but are denied all of its benefits. We proceed as if we enjoy real freedom, real acceptance, as if we have won lasting changes in the laws and mores of our nation" (1996, 4). In order to achieve equality that is more than virtual, she argues, gays and lesbians must return to and expand upon the liberationist goals that were part of gay and lesbian analysis at the movement's inception. Vaid advocates a strategy based on building cultural power more than political power, cultural power that could provide the basis for broad coalition politics with the possibility of transforming social institutions. This is an analysis of gay and lesbian politics with which I largely agree; I do, however, believe that combining her activist insider's perspective with the insights of political theorists can help us to develop an even stronger understanding of gay politics in general, and gay and lesbian family politics in particular.

Despite my substantial agreement with Vaid, I believe that the politics she advocates may be more usefully thought of as radical democratic, rather than liberationist. In choosing this language, I am cognizant of Phelan's (1994) argument that "liberation" has implications that may not be appropriate given that the common understanding of liberation in our society is that it allows us to be free from power. A liberation movement, then, would work to create a society in which power does not operate. Phelan notes that although "the idea of liberation expresses the desire for release and for self-determination, it offers no real help with questions of how we should live" (1994, 119). Further, she suggests that within a context where invisibility is a primary problem, as it is for lesbians, the antidote cannot be release from power; the real antidote is engagement with power, or "increasingly visible entry into and transformation of a system not defined by or for lesbians. This visible entry is inseparable from the project of power" (1994, 120). In trying to envision what this entry requires, we need a framework that recognizes the power of identity, while also recognizing that identity must be understood not as an essence, but as the result of historical, social, economic, and political forces. With this recognition, it is possible to build political projects that bring together multiple identity groups to create interconnected social movements. This understanding underlies the radical democratic theory that I will discuss, along with the possibility of family issues as central to such a radical democratic politics. This framework has the power to guide gay and lesbian activism in a manner that would base political involvement not simply on our identities as gays and lesbians, but rather on dialogue with others in a way that recognizes "gayness" as only one facet of complex identities, and as a facet of identity that is not definable outside of practice. Such a perspective is particularly useful for addressing family issues.

I privilege a radical democratic perspective because it is a framework able to address the questions about the construction of self raised in the previous chapters. If we understand that the self is constructed through power relations, including the institutionally-based disciplinary powers that Foucault (1995) discussed and the status relationships reinforced through marriage, we need an understanding of political activism that is able to theorize how people's identities can be both drawn from and transformed by activist politics. Such an understanding of identity contrasts with the image of identity as fixed or stable. Successful activism, or activism that challenges institutional structures and cultural norms, will transform the identities of those involved, as well as the identities of others in society. That is, radical democratic theory understands that social movements do not simply organize people with pre-given identities; they also play a role in constructing, deconstructing, and reconstructing identities.

Political actions that reveal and challenge the ways by which everyday exercises of power define self in society are often negatively received because overtly transgressing social norms reveals to others that people have made choices; they can no longer assume that they are simply acting "naturally." Writing about movements that seek to transform identity, Allen Hunter observes:

> As women, people of color, or gays and lesbians empower themselves and expand democracy and liberty, men, whites, and heterosexuals have to be disempowered as the kinds of men, whites, and heterosexuals who had oppressed them. Marxists did not seek to change capitalists, but to defeat them as a class; liberal politicians do not seek to change interest groups, but to set the terms for compromise. Identity politics, however, demands much more of both subordinate and dominant groups: It asks for major and subtle changes in definitions of ego and other, self and community, difference and hierarchy, and conceptions of the good life. Second, although identities are often narrowly defined, they are constructed through the articulation of many structural, institutional, and cultural practices. (1995, 330)

Hunter points out clearly the challenges of political activism that moves beyond the liberal framework, challenges that gay and lesbian activists who wish to transform cultural norms must face. The question, then, is how do we most effectively face these challenges? To explore the complications of pursuing a nonliberal but democratic political agenda and thus better understand what alternatives to a liberal family agenda exist, and to evaluate their potential, we must first discuss social theory that argues for the importance of constructing social movements in ways that recognize identity as complex and changing.

The Limits of Gay and Lesbian Identity Politics

As we have seen, essentialist understandings of gay identity have often been embraced by gay liberals. Interestingly, this understanding of identity has also been embraced by many with more radical goals. Sexual identity understood as relatively fixed and natural has also been a tenet of gay and lesbian identity politics. In this case, the fixity of identity enables activists to argue that gays formed a different culture, one that the dominant society ought to recognize and value, rather than to argue that the inclusion of gays into dominant institutions would civilize gays. This assertion of identity and culture draws from and copies racial understandings of politics and identity, resulting, Phelan argues, from the power of black politics: "The impact of civil rights and Black Power movements on the U. S. political imagination made them ripe for imitation. . . . The large component of cultural nationalism in radical gay/lesbian politics is the result of this 'racial' articulation" (1994, 60). In addition to racializing sexuality through constructing it as essentially part of the self, a racial/ethnic model of gay and lesbian life requires the construction of ethnicity, as Josh Gamson notes:

> Gay and lesbian social movements have built a quasi ethnicity, complete with its own political and cultural institutions, festivals, neighborhoods, even its own flag. Underlying that ethnicity is typically the notion that what gays and lesbians share—the anchor of minority status and minority rights claims—is the same fixed natural essence, a self with same-sex desires. The shared oppression, these movements have claimed, is the denial of freedoms and opportunities to actualize the self. In this *ethnic/essentialist* politic, clear categories of collective identity are necessary for successful resistance and political gain. (1996, 396)

A well developed critique of ethnic/essentialist[1] politics, one developed by both social theorists and activists inside gay politics, calls into question the usefulness of pursuing this strategy if radical change is desired.

To a number of theorists, the tendency of groups to break away from universal visions in order to embrace their own identity is deeply troubling for both theoretical and practical reasons. Theoretically, some critics—including Judith Butler (1990) and Shane Phelan (1994)—correlate the adherence to identity categories with the modernist understanding of identity as unified and noncontradictory, an understanding that they associate with maintaining the power of the privileged through refusal to admit that human beings are not self-made but, rather, are produced by social forces that are neither natural nor noncontradictory. To reinforce an understanding of identity as unified around a single aspect of our experience through identity politics is to accept an understanding of the self and definitions of naturalized social reality that make systemic change difficult, if not impossible.

Another way of critiquing identity politics is to examine the activism and change that this form of political organizing has produced. This exercise leads some theorists to conclude that activism growing out of essentialist identity movements is not really political. Stephen Bronner states this position: "As 'political' expanded, the 'political' was robbed of any determinate meanings. Symbolism became confused with programmatic action and, in the process, it became impossible for the movement to gain a sense of ideological coherence or enforce discipline" (1991, 105). Others see identity politics as apolitical because identity politics ends up producing pluralist interest groups that do nothing more than bargain to strengthen their own position within the political and economic system. In this sense, those engaged in identity politics may understand the importance of transforming culture, but the overall impact is the same as that which comes from liberal politics—demands for distributive justice. Stating perhaps an extreme version of this point, Todd Gitlin argues that whereas there had been a common commitment to universalist values among civil rights and antiwar activists, all that remains to unite activists today is a common enemy: "A good deal of the Cultural Left felt its way, even if half-jokingly, toward a weak unity based not so much on a universalist premise or ideal, but rather on a common enemy—that notorious White Male. Beneath this, they had become, willy-nilly, pluralists, a fact frequently disguised by the rhetoric of revolution hanging over from the late sixties" (1993, 176). The common enemy is all that remains because identity politics assumes a unity and fixity of identity that is not real and that explodes as soon as an identity group tries to define what is essential. The result is that identity groups are constantly fracturing into smaller and smaller groups with more and more intricate definitions of identity. As this process continues, the anger and conflict that arise with each successive split makes it difficult for groups to agree on any programmatic goals. All that is left is the "common enemy."

L. A. Kaufman suggests another means by which identity politics can foster rather than challenge dominant values, in this case the values of consumer society. The tendency within identity politics for self-transformation to be equated with political change, Kaufman argues, perpetuates dominant values: "Yet perhaps the most striking aspect of this broad transformation of identity politics into this broad, fragmented anti-politics of lifestyle is the extent to which the values it promotes—individual solutions to social problems, attention to lifestyle, choice—mirror the ideology of the marketplace" (1990, 78). Rosemary Hennessy extends this line of thought by alerting us to the possibility that even if participants reject a unified understanding of identity in a social movement, they have not necessarily created a progressive political movement: "By refiguring the self as permeable and fragmented subjectivity but then stopping there, some postmodern discourses contribute to the formation of a subject more adequate to globally-dispersed and state-controlled multinational consumer culture which relies upon increasingly atomized social relations" (1993, 6). Individuals who continually feel threatened because of the social devaluation of some aspect of their identity, or who feel increasingly frag-mented, are perfect targets for advertisers who will sell a comfortable lifestyle, whether a "normal" lifestyle like that offered to gays in IKEA advertisements that show a male couple buying furniture, or alternative lifestyles for which corporations continually produce and market new products.

David Evans's (1993) analysis of the entry of gays and lesbians to citizenship both supports the argument that identity politics is limited as a political strategy and encourages us to see that the state, by provid-ing limited protection to gays and lesbians, encourages a shift from politics to consumption. Evans argues that gays and lesbians are admit-ted to citizenship only in a limited way, as "sexual citizens." This form of citizenship does not bring political rights, it accords consumer rights: "Sexual citizenship involves partial, private, and primarily lifestyle and leisure membership" (1993, 64). The state neither guarantees nor tries to guarantee that other citizens will not judge a lesbian or gay individual as immoral, and therefore subject her or him to regulation and punish-ment. Instead, the state merely provides minimal protection, enough to guarantee that gays and lesbians have private lives in which they can act as consumers, and thus offers protection and rights only to the extent that they allow businesses to target new consumers. When politically useful, these lifestyle groups become the target of moral purity cam-paigns, or as Vaid's discussion of virtual equality indicates, the target of centrist politicians, such as Bill Clinton, who want money and votes. Privileged citizens tend to reject state policies that might actually help those excluded on the grounds that these policies offer something spe-cial, thus violating norms of equality.[2]

In general, because gay/lesbian identity politics bases political orga-nizing on the assertion that there is a gay or lesbian identity, it is not a politics that can easily move beyond the binary identity divisions so central to Western cultural understandings. One consequence for gay and lesbian identity politics, as well as the identity politics practiced by other groups, is that if those who are gay, or women, or people of color assert their separate identity, there is little that those who are straight, male, or white can do in response. It is, therefore, a form of social activ-ism that does not lead to political engagement over complex issues. Rather, it leads to the formation of, to use Bernice Johnson Reagon's concepts, separate homes with barred doors (1983). The narrow defi-nition of "home," as poet and activist Pat Parker suggested in her poetry, can become so restrictive that literal homes become the only place of safety, particularly for those who recognize that their own identity does not fit neatly into any of the identity boxes:

> I told my booking agent one year
> book me a tour
> Blackberri and I
> will travel this land
> together
> take our Black Queerness
> into the face
> of this place and say
>
> Hey, here we are
> a faggot and a dyke, Black
> we make good music
> & write good poems
> We Be—Something Else.
>
> My agent couldn't book us.
> It seemed my lesbian audiences
> were not ready for my faggot
> brother
> and I remembered
> a law conference
> in San Francisco
> where women
> who loved women threw tomatoes
> at a woman who dared
> to have a man in her band.
>
> What is this world we have?
> Is my house the only safe place
> for us?
>
> (1985, 20–21)[3]

The limits of identity politics organized around an ethnic/essentialist model of gay/lesbian identity has become clear to many theorists and activists in the past few years. One result of questioning the feasibility of building gay or lesbian identity movements is the development of queer theory and activism, a strategy employed to try to reverse the fragmenting and consumer tendencies of the past. "Queer," in this formulation, moves beyond a fixed notion of gay and lesbian identity. As Steven Seidman understands it, "Queer theory has accrued multiple meanings, from a merely useful shorthand way to speak of all gay, lesbian, bisexual, transgendered experiences to a theoretical sensibility that pivots on transgression or permanent rebellion. I take as central to Queer theory its challenge to what has the dominant foundational assumption of both the homophobic and affirmative homosexual theory: the assumption of unified homosexual identity. I interpret Queer theory as contesting this foundation and therefore the very telos of Western homosexual politics" (1996, 11). Arlene Stein and Ken Plummer basically agree with this formulation of queer theory, but also point out that one result of this new theorization is "a rejection of civil-rights strategies in favor of a politics of carnival, transgression, and parody which leads to deconstruction, decentering, revisionist readings, and an anti-assimilationist politics" (1996, 134). The critical question that remains, however, is whether such a strategy can foster significant political change.

Deconstructing Norms: Activist Parody, Irony, and Humor

Just as a primary impetus to queer theory was a recognition of the intellectual necessity of moving away from unified understandings of identity, a primary impetus for queer activism is activists' recognition of the practical necessity of building connections between lesbians and gays, white lesbians/gays and lesbians/gays of color, bisexuals and lesbians/gays, and transsexuals and lesbians/gays. Queer activists intend "queer" to convey commonality, while not denying difference. The political action in which queer political groups engage, with Queer Nation being the most prominent example, is transgressive. Activists intended to challenge the naturalness of identity categories, including lesbian and gay identity, by employing a combination of anger and humor. Alex Chee comments in relation to Queer Nation, "Queer Nation/SF is as angry as it is funny" (1991, 16). The relatively rapid decline in commitment to and visibility of Queer Nation alerts us to the possibility that there are significant risks in employing these two mechanisms as a political strategy. Before directly considering transgressive activism as an alternative strategy in relation to family, I want to explore the link between transgression, humor, and anger in more detail.

Political actions designed to combat destructive binarisms employ tactics intended to reveal the extent to which people often view natural identities as social roles, which can be played in combinations that appear odd or unnatural within an essentialist framework. Despite the different languages theorists use to discuss how activists can challenge unitary understandings of self and cultural binarisms, we can make connections between the practices advocated by a number of theorists, and we can begin to see both the strengths and limitations of such politics. Kathy Ferguson argues that irony is critical for political activism because of the competing understandings of subjectivity trying to dominate the landscape of cultural critique. Since neither the competing forces within subjectivity nor the competing concepts of subjectivity are reconcilable, we need something to help us cope with the loss of unitary subjectivity: "Without an ironic stance toward the contrary pull of needed incompatibilities, despair or rigidity are likely" (1993, 164). In order to explore the implications of this idea, I want to connect it to the advocacy of parody and humor discussed by Butler, to Lugones's recommendation that we practice the art of "curdling," and to Phelan's positing of laughter as a critical force.

Central to Butler's understanding of the importance of parody is the idea that since we produce gender through the repetition of cultural practices, it is possible to destabilize the subject "woman" by interrupting these practices. In discussing the potential of drag to challenge gender, Butler writes: "*In imitating gender, drag implicitly reveals the imitative structure of gender itself—as well as its contingency.* Indeed part of the pleasure, the giddiness of the performance is in the recognition of a radical contingency in the relation between sex and gender in the face of cultural configurations of causal unities that are regularly assumed to be natural and necessary" (1990, 137–138). Interrupting the naturalness of social meaning opens up the possibility of resignification.[4]

At the same time, by interrupting daily life, it is also possible to help people to see the ways by which hegemonic norms are constructed (invisibly) in everyday life. We can see such an attempt at revelation in some of the strategies of Queer Nation, which are designed to challenge understandings of normalcy by "performing" roles that the dominant culture defines as abnormal, and through this performance, revealing the hidden content of everyday life. In analyzing the actions of the Queer Shopping Network of New York and the Suburban Homosexual Outreach Program (SHOP) of San Francisco, Berlant and Freeman write:

> Whereas patrons of the straight bar at least understand its function in terms of pleasure and desire, mall-goers invest in the shopping mall's credentials as a "family" environment, an environment that "creates a nostalgic image of

[the] town center as a clean, safe, and legible place." In dressing up and step-
ping out queer, the network uses the bodies of its members as billboards to
create what Mary Ann Doane calls "the desire to desire." As queer shoppers
stare back, kiss, and pose, they disrupt the antiseptic asexual surface of the
malls, exposing them as sites of any number of explicitly sexualized exchanges—cruising, people watching, window-shopping, trying on outfits,
purchasing of commodities, and having anonymous sex. (1993, 210–211)

By interrupting the normal and using parody to bring to the surface
both the hidden values of American society and alternative values,
Queer Nation attempts to create more space for alternative understandings by displaying the extent to which heterosexuality is everywhere,
despite the fact that most heterosexual people do not recognize this
reality.

In part, the success of Queer Nation strategy is contingent upon
those in the "audience" being able to laugh with Queer activists. Theorizing from his own observations concerning the need for certainty and
control felt by modern individuals, William Connolly suggests that
laughter must be a necessary part of coming to accept the contingency
of life, the contingencies of our own identities, and the limits of individuals. Laughter is one indication that we have learned to live our
identities in a more contingent way. We might, he suggests, find ourselves "laughing in a way that disrupts this persistent link between ethical conviction and self-reassurance, while affirming the indispensability
of ethical judgment in life. Such laughter pays homage to fugitive
elements in life that exceed the organization of identity, otherness,
rationality, and autonomy" (1991, 181). Shane Phelan (1989) also understands humor as critical for political change, in particular, for cor-
recting the tendency of lesbian feminist identity politics to focus on the
creation of a true, unitary lesbian identity. The process of confronta-
tion as lesbian feminists recognize other differences among themselves,
Phelan asserts, will only succeed if lesbian feminists recognize that identities are not fixed, and if this recognition leads to a healthy regard for
emotion and play. "The opposite of oppression in this sense is, not truth
or respect, but humor or lightheartedness—the humor that sees all
categories, all explanations, all identities as provisional" (1989, 156).
Phelan believes that with such an understanding of identity, identity
politics can come together with a somewhat revised liberal politics to
encourage us to see each other as different, yet deserving of respect. It
is clear, however, from Phelan's analysis of lesbian feminism that humor
has not played the desired role. Yet because humor in political activism

is generally connected to anger, it may be more difficult to make political gains through such actions than theorists have recognized.

Connolly implies that the ability to laugh may itself be a product of culture—that is, it may exist as a constituted element of subjectivity—but he does not develop this point in much detail. This is a critical omission given the centrality of humor, laughter, and irony in theories of social change. It is clear that irony and humor do not come easily when questions of identities are perceived to be in conflict. Thus, the theorization of irony or humor as a mechanism that helps us to conceive of subjectivity as less fixed must itself be based on an understanding that human beings have a natural capacity to mediate conflicts using these emotional techniques, *or* it requires that we theorize the social and political context in which they are most likely to produce positive results. This requires that we have an understanding of how the threat that arises from deconstructive politics can be minimized.

Maria Lugones's conclusion to "Purity, Impurity, and Separation" helps us to understand better the complexity of employing parody and humor as social activism. She understands identity as multiple and uses the term "curdling" to refer to a stance that explicitly rejects understanding oneself as "pure" in relation to any particular identity, suggesting that curdling behavior is behavior with an awareness of multiplicity: "When confronted with our curdling or curdled expression or behavior, people will often withdraw. Their withdrawal reveals the devaluation of ambiguity as *threatening* and is thus also a metacomment" (1994, 479). An examination of either gay and lesbian politics or feminist activism makes it clear that even when humor is understood to be a critical tool for deconstructing hegemonic discourses and revealing the complexity of identity, it has been very difficult for people to confront heterogeneity within movements, or curdling, with humor and critical reflection rather than with anger and withdrawal (Lehr 1993). Rather, these struggles have had a persistent and disturbing tendency to lead to the breakup of organizations and groups. Although such breakups may not be entirely negative in terms of organizing, they do call into question the possibility of sustaining social movements that put a primary emphasis on deconstructing identity.

The ability to feel humor as activists deconstruct social norms through symbolic politics requires that there be perceived commonality between oneself and those who are challenging a social norm. Without such a sense of commonality, the audience for the actions is likely to feel the action as a threat. This is the case because such deconstructive acts are inevitably expressions not simply of humor, but also, as Chee recognized in relation to Queer Nation, of anger. In general, the deconstructive humorous/ironic/parodic actions advocated by Butler, Phelan, Lugones, and Connolly are very much about the expression of anger. The ability to laugh may be important in not taking oneself and one's position too seriously, but it is impossible to ignore the reality that people engage in critical, parodic actions because they understand social forces as oppressive. If anger is necessarily part of transgression, then one needs to be able to identify the target of anger. Without an explicit analysis of the centrality of structural forces, the target of anger is likely to be understood solely as those who are privileged.

Yet because no single identity ever motivates activist planning, it is likely that conflict will arise in analyzing and formulating actions within a movement. For example, one of the conflicts that arose in Queer Nation concerned the slogan "Bash Back," which is certainly an expression of the rage that arises from the frequency of queer bashing. The response, however, was one that angered some women: "'Bash Back' is a slogan and campaign that alienated a lot of women last summer; women have been dealing with violence and aggression all their lives" (Kate Arthur, qtd. in Chee 1991, 19). These women felt that fighting violence with the threat of violence was a masculine response, one likely to be neither effective nor desirable for women.[5]

This situation illustrates a question that Nancy Fraser has raised in relation to Butler's work: "How does one determine whether a resignifying process is desirable? In opting for the epistemically neutral 'resignification,' as opposed to the epistemically positive 'critique,' Butler seems to valorize change for its own sake and thereby to disempower feminist judgment" (1995, 68). On one level, Fraser's question leads us to the necessity of accounting for self-reflection and judgment within movements. That is, how are decisions made? Is it legitimate within the decision-making process of a particular group to bring "marginal" aspects of identity to the center? Despite the intentions of Queer Nation, the identity that drove much of the organization's activism was the identity of white, middle-class, gay men (Berlant and Freeman 1993, Chee 1991). Conflicts arose when multiplicity was introduced into conversation. Thus, it is important to ask whether activism focused on transgression *can* tackle deconstructing more than one binary at a time.

On another level, Fraser's question can lead us to consider how actions are received. That is, regardless of the intent of the actor, those viewing actions can judge them as justified critique, as a reassertion of some dominant values, or as an unreasonable attack on social norms. For the moment, I want to focus on the question of how acts are received. Lugones's recognition of the possibility of withdrawal is, of course, only one possible course of action for those threatened by resignifying practices. It is, perhaps, a response most likely for those who are somewhat supportive of the goals being pursued. Anger and violence are alternative responses. Karen Foss's (1994) discussion of folly and the political campaigns of Harvey Milk helps us to expand our discussion of deconstructive political action by reminding us that wider social forces influence reception. Foss discusses Milk as playing a role that fits closely to that of the fool in traditional societies.[6] Her discussion is particularly interesting because the fool, as she discusses this role, demonstrates that things are never exactly as they seem, and that such demonstration occurs primarily through reversal and laughter. There are a number of points that Foss makes in relation to the fool that can be useful for helping us to better understand deconstructive or transgressive politics. First, she points out that the fool is particularly important when society is forced to confront transitions that lead to encountering the mysterious, life, and death. It is our desire to control these forces that Connolly identifies as central to modern society's inability to positively conceive of difference. Foss also suggests that the role "fool" is important because "it is simultaneously outside of and in society. . . . The function of folly is to show members of society the borders of their worldview, and by bringing to consciousness taken-for-granted assumptions about what reality is, folly reinforces existing norms, values, and meanings of society" (1994, 10). Thus folly challenges society to live up to its values, as much as it challenges a wholesale rethinking of these values. She argues that it was Milk's ability to act the role of the fool that allowed him to become what was "previously unspeakable"— a gay politician. In the process, he was able to bring together groups that had not identified common interests in the past. Yet, he could not use this technique in a way that did not arouse anger: "The natural divisiveness that is inherent to folly, too, may help to explain Milk's assassination. Perhaps the opposition set in place by the mirroring of alternative realities cannot be completely overcome by laughter. The divisiveness of folly may not be overcome so much as it is covered up or ignored in favor of a happier attitude" (1994, 22–23). She continues by suggesting that the very divisiveness that makes folly necessary is indicative of a dangerous and conflictual world—one where folly can be important but cannot overcome the potential violence, and may arouse it.

Foss's reminder of the violence that is always possible need not mean that it is impossible to use folly or laughter as a tool of social and political change. Milk's success indicates the flip side of folly: Milk was a smart politician able to make connections in relation to issues that helped bring diverse groups together to form an electoral coalition. Although folly was part of Milk's strategy, there was also a positive political program that recognized the different needs of different constituencies and was able to build connections between these groups. Perhaps we need to understand folly and laughter as potentially most successful when they are being employed in relation to a political issue that can, with political analysis, bring people together to fight for common, though shifting, goals. In this understanding, identity concerns may be important for bringing people together, but because these concerns lead to questioning institutional structures and making institutional demands, they prompt action that is not purely directed to challenging cultural norms. This allows for the possibility of alliance building.

Elizabeth Wilson reaches a similar conclusion in her critique of transgressive politics. In fact, she ends by commenting that "we have to have an idea of how things could be different, otherwise transgression ends in mere posturing. . . . It is therefore not transgression that should be our watchword, but transformation" (1993, 116). There have certainly been moments in gay and lesbian politics where transformation and transgression have come together in powerful, productive, and humorous ways. We may see the successes that ACT UP (AIDS Coalition to Unleash Power) had in addressing complex issues that involved not only gay men but also women, communities of color, and IV drug users, among others, as the result of a complex combination of political analysis, humor, and interruption intended to challenge normalcy, transform policies (either state or business), and build intentional coalitions (Lehr 1993). One example of an ACT UP demonstration that illustrates this success is the interruption of Wall Street in 1989. This action succeeded[7] because it played on and challenged stereotypes of gay men that make the possibility of being both gay and a stockbroker seem impossible. At the same time, by stopping business on Wall Street and challenging Burroughs-Wellcome's pricing policies for AZT, the demonstrators had a clear goal aimed at a specific institutional target. The goal was not only important to gay men, but to the multiple identity groups affected by AIDS (Crimp and Ralston 1990). Although political activism such as this can be effective, another action—the 1989 STOP THE CHURCH action of ACT UP—shared many of the same characteristics (passing in order to gain entrance and targeting an institution that needed to be challenged to benefit multiple identity groups) but was less successful and, in significant ways, failed. In relation to this demonstration, Crimp and Ralston write that "media coverage was extensive, distorted, and negative. The immensely powerful Cardinal O'Connor was portrayed as a martyr" (1990, 138). This leads Crimp and Ralston to suggest that "STOP THE CHURCH taught us the necessity of applying rigorous political analysis to our choice of targets, with the goal of productive change uppermost in our minds" (1990, 140). Activists need to target institutional structures in ways that are understood by both other activists and onlookers as humorous and important, not as a threat to cherished values. Yet it is not clear that this lesson, which I will argue is particularly important in relation to family politics, has been learned by queer activists.

The inability of queer activism to sustain political activism for more than a short period of time is somewhat discouraging since groups such as Queer Nation were trying to build an understanding of identity that was not fixed. In fact, an important goal of these local direct action groups was to build a movement that would foster unity among people who understood their queerness in different ways. Despite this, Vaid observes, "In the end, direct action neither produced new divisions among us nor contributed new understandings to help us to resolve the old splits of political ideology, race, gender, and class. Instead direct action reinforced them" (1996, 105). The reinforcement of these splits occurred despite the adoption of the language of "queerness," a language intended to bridge difference. The queer activism that Vaid, as well as others, critique is problematic because it was political action that focused most centrally on challenging cultural norms. One problem that resulted from this focus was that activists had little basis upon which to judge what actions were most desirable, that is, most likely not to be felt as threatening and thus provoke reflection instead of anger. After all, if the goal is to challenge the normal, it is difficult to judge actions that upset normality. The fact that countering dominant images was a primary goal meant that queer activism never had to set forth a positive vision, one guided by ethical positions. Rather, as Vaid points out, queer activism was often guided by what would win media attention. Yet winning media attention on a regular basis is difficult without engaging in practices that are likely to only win not support but approbation.

This kind of political activism is particularly difficult in relation to family because in the lives of many people, the family plays a role that simply cannot be abandoned without major social transformations. The family is an institution that people are fighting to maintain because they feel that their individual survival depends upon the institution. Fears about the breakdown of family are for many people materially-based fears, since family connections continue to be a primary means of assuring that care is provided for children, the incapacitated, and the elderly. Jane Humphries made a point in the early 1980s that can help us to understand the political implications of these fears: although feminists, particularly Marxist feminists, were able to develop theoretical arguments about how feminists and the working class had a common interest in abolishing the family, it might have been more fruitful to examine the tensions that existed between the largely middle-class feminists and working-class people. In particular, she went on, the working class had resisted the erosion of family, seeing the maintenance of family as critical for their survival (1982, 199). David Greenberg and Marica Bystryn recognize the challenge that current economic threats to family life pose for gays and lesbians: "Anxiety over the family's threatened status thus makes lifestyles that appear to be inconsistent with the perpetuation of the traditional family salient and subjectively threatening, especially in the lower middle class, where family members are especially vulnerable" (1996, 102). Thus, gay and lesbian political activism cannot simply threaten the family if it is going to gain broad political support; it must also be able to address material fears. It is, therefore, imperative that the lesson of STOP THE CHURCH be understood in relation and applied to family issues if gays and lesbians are to create political challenges to dominant constructions of family.

The complexity of identity, rather than making the possibility of changes in how we think about family and personal life more difficult, can help to make the goal of building political alliances more feasible. As Humphries and Greenberg and Bystryn suggest, working-class families that feel threatened may respond to conservative messages that changing moral norms are responsible for their family problems. But these same working-class families may well be inclined to accept gay and lesbian children, whom they love and whose support and incomes can help them to get through tough times. Joanna Kadi observes that "within working-class families where members love and respect each other (and I'm *not* saying this describes all working-class families), caring for kin is linked to a deep distrust of 'the system'—the capitalist system that exploits us and benefits the rich. Our love for each other is tempered and steeled by our exploitation and our need to stick together. We're all we have, so we must stay connected" (1997, 32). The contradiction between supporting political programs that they hope will allow them to regain a sense of financial security and the harms that these programs can cause to valued family members is critical for framing an alternative political discourse. The interesting question is how activists can recognize and use this conflict to build support for a positive political program that moves beyond transgression.[8] Radical democratic political theory provides one possible answer to this question.

Developing a Radical Democratic Approach to Politics

Josh Gamson observes that there was something of a standoff in the 1990s between gay and lesbian civil rights activists and queer activists, with each side accusing the other of using ineffectual tactics. In his evaluation, an evaluation supported by the analysis in this chapter, both sides were correct. Gamson sees this as revealing something important about American society and points out a central paradox that political theorists and activists must face: "In the contemporary American political environment, clear identity categories are both necessary and dangerous distortions, and moves to both fix and unfix them are reasonable" (1996, 410). Only by directly confronting the state can we create a strategy that neither falls into the pitfall of reinforcing identity categories by asking for protection, nor is so focused on deconstructing those categories that political action is purely symbolic. The task for an analysis of family is to understand how state policy constructs "family" and how we can resist these policies in ways that are both material *and* symbolic. Given the impact of separation of public and private life in liberal ideology, it may seem odd to those who live in a liberal society that creating families we choose can only come about by challenging and transforming the state and our understanding of politics and citizenship, yet there are good theoretical and practical reasons to believe that this is the case.

The possibility of confronting domination, and playing a larger role in constructing the conditions under which we live is, according to sociologist Alain Touraine, a focus of social movements that is only beginning to come into play in post-industrial society. This occurs, he argues, because (1) we are increasingly less concerned with constantly expanding material production and more concerned with making choices about how we will live; (2) we are inclined to reject universalist claims set forth by the state in favor of local knowledge; and (3) the visible power of the state in not only the economic realm, but also the cultural realm, means that the state itself is felt increasingly as a source of domination, and therefore a power that needs to be challenged and resisted (1988, 77). The very possibility of organizing for something other than state intervention intended to foster economic growth opens up a new focus of political organizing: happiness. Touraine explains:

> In mercantile societies, the central locus of protest was called *liberty* since it was a matter of defending oneself against the legal and political power of merchants and, at the same time, of counterposing to their power an order defined in legal terms. In the industrial epoch, this central locus was called *justice* since it was a question of returning to workers the fruit of their labor and of industrialization. In programmed society, the central place of protest and claims is *happiness*, that is, the global image of the organization of social life on the basis of the needs expressed by the most diverse individuals and groups. (1988, 111)

The difficulty for political organizing is to construct a movement with the power to bring together enough force to challenge the power of the state to affect both economic institutions and cultures.

A radical democratic conception of political action and political change focuses on the question of how political power can be obtained and used. Proponents of radical democracy are aware that the use of power always means that new categories of control and power are created, but they understand these new categories not as fixed, but as themselves subject to debate and reformulation. As a result, citizens cannot become passive consumers; they must be political agents willing to engage in the process of debate and willing and able to reformulate their sense of their own identity. Chantal Mouffe states one version of this vision:

> To belong to the political community, what is required is to accept a specific language of civil intercourse, the respublica. These rules prescribe norms of conduct to be subscribed to in seeking self-chosen satisfactions and in per-

forming self-chosen actions. The identification with those rules of civil intercourse creates a common political identity among persons otherwise engaged
in many different enterprises. This modern form of political community is
held together not by a substantive idea of a common good, but a common
bond, a public concern. It is therefore a community without a definite shape,
a definite identity, and in continuous reenactment. (1991, 77)

Political activism, then, focuses not on demanding that rights be extended, but rather on demanding that they be redefined, since guaranteeing rights for those previously excluded requires new understandings
of the rights constructed around exclusion. Zillah Eisenstein (1994)
makes a similar point when she argues that a democratic state should
recognize that women have a right to control their bodies. She does
not conceptualize this right in a classical liberal sense, but rather in a
way that is more compatible with radical democratic understandings.
Drucilla Cornell agrees, suggesting that social recognition of the importance of reproduction requires an understanding not of equal rights,
but of "equivalent rights." Equivalent rights are rights defined not abstractly, but in relation to the differing roles that people play, whether
by choice or because of biological difference (1992, 292–293). Since
rights are based on the roles that people play, these rights would change
and would be subject to political dispute.

A number of theorists (W. Brown 1995, Epstein 1990, Hennessy
1993) critique the vision of radical democracy set forth by Mouffe
(1991, 1992), and by Laclau and Mouffe (1985), for failing to adequately
connect the transformations in rights that they discuss to necessary
changes in the economic system. For example, Hennessy makes the following criticism: "Throughout the various complexities of [Mouffe's
and Laclau and Mouffe's radical democratic] theory, power is primarily presented as a matter of discursive struggle over equal rights.
While the democratic impulse of distributing power equally among the
people lies at the heart of emancipatory movements, like feminism,
socialism, or anti-colonialism, any notion of power that ignores the
relationship between equal rights and the ways divisions of labor or al-
locations of resources effect social equality re-enacts the liberal project
of political reform" (1993, 26). Regardless of whether this is in fact an
accurate critique of Mouffe, and Mouffe and Laclau,[9] it is an important reminder that we cannot think about family issues from a radical
democratic perspective without exploring the role that the family plays

in relation to the division of labor and the allocation of economic resources.

Fraser (1995), Cooper (1995), W. Brown (1995), and Phelan (1994) each point out the necessity of having a positive vision to guide critique and activism. For each, it is necessary to try to move beyond identity by creating a public sphere, one dominated with a political discourse through which people define the terms for making political judgments, rather than by discourse intended to gain the protection of the state or to resist dominant cultural images. In Brown's formulation, "Such judgments require learning how to have public conversations with each other, arguing from a vision of the common ('what I want for us') rather than from identity ('who I am'), and from explicitly postulated norms and potential common values rather than from false essentialism and unreconstructed private interest" (1995, 51). Phelan adds to this that such discussion needs to occur not only between communities, but also within them. This is most likely to occur when we "get specific," that is, when we create communities that seek to understand the specific social forces that have led to their existence (Phelan 1994).

To engage in this kind of community formation means that the process of constructing lesbian and gay communities requires that discussion over understandings of identity be explicit, thus helping community participants understand the grounds upon which exclusion and inclusion in the community are based. This means, in turn, that the community must understand itself as constructed, not as naturally given. The ability to engage in such discussions, Phelan observes, is contingent on genealogic explorations of the communities of which we are part, helping us to understand why these identities have come to be so necessary and meaningful to us. For example, gays and lesbians might ask why the sex/gender or race of sexual partners, as opposed to the many other characteristics of human beings that can be eroticized, are central categories through which we establish identities and make judgments about people in our society. "Getting specific," she comments, "provides the link between identity politics and broad-based movements for social change by bringing identities out of their isolation and into a world of multiple locations and discourses. In consequence, we move beyond (but do not dispense with) community to alliances; we move from identity to justice" (1994, 97). Without such historical perspective, as my discussion of the divisive power of family values within gay and lesbian politics indicates, it is difficult to build a community that has political goals, much less political goals that enable the community to enter into alliances.

Vaid provides an example of the kind of political organizing that results from citizens seeking to create conditions for their own freedom by building alliances with others. She notes that one place where lesbians and gays have been under attack is on the streets. Gay and lesbian people could respond to such attack by seeking police protection and trying to control the availability of weapons. Another response, as she points out, is to see increased police protection and state regulation as only having the possibility of being effective when combined with citizen initiatives intended to create safe spaces. Communities are most likely to accomplish this goal, Vaid suggests, when they move beyond identity politics to build connections with others who are also commonly targets of street violence. She asks: "What if we allied in our neighborhoods with all others who fear violence to understand the construction of violent people, and to expose conditions like alcohol, drug addiction, insecurity, and economic anxiety that contribute to violence? What if we all worked together to develop neighborhood-based education, organizing, and intervention strategies?" (1996, 208). She goes on to suggest that the task gays and lesbians face is the transformation of straight culture (1995, 209). This is a task that I believe requires us to look critically at the family, since this institution is so powerfully implicated in the construction of identity.

Radical Democracy: Agency, Alliance, and a New Idea of Family

Implicit in the critiques of identity politics, liberal rights, and my own position on gay and lesbian marriage is the assumption that structural change is necessary for guaranteeing freedom. This does not mean that identity concerns cannot and will not play an important role in social movements that work to build analyses of structural constraints on human freedom, including sexual freedom. In this regard, Jeffrey Weeks's discussion of sexual identity is important for helping us to understand an alternative to the limited identity politics critiqued above. "Identities are troubling," Weeks observes, "because they embody so many paradoxes: about what we have in common and what separates us; about our sense of self and our recognition of others; about conflicting belongings in a changing history and a complex modern world; and about the possibility of social action in and through our collective identities. And few identities are so paradoxical as sexual identities" (1995, 86). Weeks's consideration of these paradoxes leads him to the conclusion that identities are "necessary fictions." They are necessary because we need to have a sense of belonging in order to resist domination (1995, 99). They are fictions because they are historical and social, not natural or essential.

If we come to believe that our identities are natural, we create an understanding that oppresses others. We can see this dynamic in multiple ways. The model of identity formation that developed to trace the "life cycle" of gays and lesbians, with its assumption of sexual identity as a pre-given that unfolds until a coherent identity is created, is one that denies bisexuality as an identity that may not be stable. Minnie Bruce Pratt's recent writing provides an illustration of how those who construct categories designed to resist oppression can, through these categories, oppress others. Her comparison of seeking to attend a women's music festival with her transgendered lover and seeking to cross the Canadian border with her lover makes clear the extent to which the nationalist definition of belonging in counter-hegemonic politics is parallel to the hegemonic nationalisms that counter-movements try to resist. She suggests an alternative formulation: "I stay on the sandy road that runs between the two encampments [the "Trans Camp" and the main camp], at the boundary of womanhood. I don't want *woman* to be a fortress that has to be defended. I want it to be a life we constantly braid together from the threads of our existence, a rope we make, a flexible weapon stronger than steel, that we use to pull down walls that imprison us at borders" (1995, 184–185). In the process of braiding this rope, we will create categories of identity, but we need to recognize that the categories we create are no more natural than those we resist; they are fictions. It is the fictional nature of identities that makes them potentially radical, because as fictions it is possible, under different circumstances, to rewrite, or rebraid, them. As we consider the fictional nature of our identities, it might be useful to try to stop thinking of ourselves as subjects and begin to understand ourselves as agents. This distinction is important, Patricia Mann argues, because to see ourselves as speaking from a subject position, or even multiple subject positions, already assumes that there are narrative subject positions, and that the problem we face is figuring out how to combine these predetermined subjectivities. In a world with unstable identities, she suggests "that we think more about the quality of our actions, or in the terminology of social theory, upon our *agency*" (1994, 4). Mann challenges us, for example, to think about how we might understand the conflicts faced by a woman who is a soldier and a mother. If we think in terms of subjectivity, an individual might consider herself a mother or a soldier, and form her sense of self around whichever identity seems most salient at a particular moment. But, Mann argues, neither the subject position "mother" nor "soldier" is, or has ever been, unified:

> It is misleading, for example, to refer to the "multiple subject positions" of a soldier-mother, insofar as this implies that there are several traditional subject-positions that such a woman can attempt to combine. This route leads us back to the thicket of binary oppositional characterizations of the roles of mothering and soldiering. It is more compelling, as well as more analytically precise, to think in terms of the "multiple agency positions" we occupy. (1994, 171)

The distinction Mann draws is important in that she is arguing that hegemonic discourses interact with material reality to produce agents who often have no clear sense of subjectivity from which to act. That is, they do not fit easily into any subject position, thus necessitating judgment in order to act. The dominant discourses of mothering and soldiering each draw on a different, and conflicting, hegemonic discourse. The challenge for us as agents is to exercise judgment and act in ways that challenge both constructions, ultimately working to refigure what it means to be mothers and soldiers: "With the categories of interpersonal agency and engaged individualism, we can begin to move beyond issues of women's formal entrance to military participation and explore the substantive social and symbolic ramifications of sending solider-mothers and soldier-fathers to perform dangerous military assignments" (1994, 172). Being forced to consider sending these soldiers, instead of teenage boys, to fight can, she argues, lead to different decision making about war and peace.

The position taken by bell hooks (1989) in relation to feminism might help us to further develop both why the agent/subject distinction is important and how we can enhance our understanding when we consider gender as it interacts with race. hooks points out that many women of color have been hesitant to claim the subject position "feminist" even though they support what may be called feminist goals. The identity "feminist," which both results from and helps to further the "unmoorings" that Mann (1994) discusses, has been defined too exclusively in relation to the needs/experiences of middle-class white women. Thus it is unable not only to reflect the needs, desires, and experiences of women of color, but it is also unable to provide a theoretical discourse capable of confronting the material realities faced by women of color, particularly those who are also poor. It is not, then, simply a question of the subject position "feminist" being inadequate; it is that the inadequacy of the subject position leads to a politics able to confront only a small range of political questions. Political agency is restricted. hooks argues that for women of color attempting to expand the range of politics, it makes little sense to identify as a feminist, or even as a black feminist, suggesting an additive approach to subjectivity. Rather, it is more useful to support feminism, opening up the possibility that this support, when combined with support for other political positions, will lead to new options, and with these new options, to new understandings of agency.

Yet it is also the case that hooks does not wish to stop talking about identity; instead she posits new ways of talking about it, ones more compatible with working to form political agency. Her suggestions are consistent with those of a number of other theorists who see identity politics as a trap but do not believe that we can simply stop talking about subjectivity or identity and have it go away as a compelling means of self-identification. hooks writes: "To challenge identity politics we must offer strategies of politicization that enlarge our conception of who we are, that intensify our sense of intersubjectivity, our relation to a collective reality. We do this by emphasizing how history, political science, psychoanalysis, and diverse ways of knowing can be used to inform our ideas of self and identity" (1989, 107). As I discussed in the previous chapter and will further develop in the next chapter, history and politics can indeed help us understand how ideas about the family shape our identities. However, it is useful to also consider how these forces shape the possibility of agency, rather than subjectivity.

Stuart Hall and David Held (1990), in an analysis similar to that of hooks, choose to use the term "ethnicity," rather than "identity," to highlight the fact that identity is relational: it changes as social, cultural, and historical forces change and as our view of "others" changes. Ethnicity is important, however, because people need a position from which to think and speak: "We need a place to speak from, but we no longer speak about ethnicity in a narrow and essentialist way. *That* is the new ethnicity. It is a new conception of our identities because it has not lost hold of the place and ground from which we can speak, yet it is no longer within that place as an essence" (1990, 20). It is continually being redefined, as a result of interaction. Kathy Ferguson agrees: "The placements of identity descriptors shift, sometimes unpredictably. Through the interactions, practices, confrontations, and accidents of history or circumstance, different positionalizations are mobilized, put on temporary alert. They come to the fore and do their work, but always with the persistent jostling of their own histories and of the contending positionalizations against which they are deployed" (1993, 167). Because of this constant jostling for position Ferguson prefers to talk about "mobile subjectivities," rather than multiple subjectivities. We might take part of this language and again rethink the terminology that we wish to use to discuss radical democratic actors: perhaps the key point is that radical democratic citizens are mobile agents, that is, people who are constantly challenged to judge and to act in situations where different understandings of self and subjectivity are mobilized and often in conflict. As Patricia Mann observes, changes in the economy and changes resulting from feminism have made this especially true in the family, where people often need to act in ways that are counter to their sense of "male family identity" or "female family identity" (Mann 1994, 6–7). It is these moments of conflict that demand judgment, and that reveal social problems in need of political remedies.

To talk about agents as mobile is not to suggest that they are fragmented or, perhaps more importantly, to celebrate fragmentation. Maria Lugones argues that fragmentation contains the implication that wholeness is possible and desirable, and thus is a continuation of Enlightenment reasoning in its "generation of a subject who can occupy a vantage point from which unified wholes can be captured" (1994, 463). Multiplicity (or mobility), on the other hand, "affirms a complex version of identity politics and a complex version of groups" by recognizing heterogeneity (1994, 475). Additionally, it confirms the need for individuals to act, to resist the "logic of purity." As we begin to think about the consequences of this understanding of agency for political activism, we should note that mobile agency can help us to think through some of the conflicts that arise when lesbians and gays use the language of liberalism to justify family relationships. In fact, one might argue that when we begin to understand the potential challenges that a liberal politics of gay family can pose, we can begin to see that liberal political change in family politics has a radical potential. By recognizing this radical potential, it is possible to build a movement that intentionally addresses the complex issues raised, and therefore may feel less threatening to those who are dependent upon family for daily survival.[10]

By highlighting the contradictory roles that queer people create when we enter families, we can perhaps identify some of the challenges that queer families pose for dominant understandings of family: How do we understand lesbian nonbiological mothers who live with a child's biological mother? Are lesbian partners mothers or fathers in those relationships? Can a lesbian be a father? Similarly, how do we understand the roles played by two male parents? Are they fathers, mothers, or some of each? What roles do transsexual mothers/fathers play? Do they change as an individual's legal sex changes? Can one be a mother one day and a father the next? If a child has three or more parents, how do we identify them? Can we understand them all as mothers or fathers? Does this language make sense? What do these oxymoronic subject positions, but completely possible agent positions, reveal about conflicts within family that must be subject to social and political questioning? How can understanding the history and the challenges to dominant norms in these agent positions help us to rethink family in ways that will avoid the pure threat of transgression? That is, can we create a narrative of family that understands the incomprehensibility of these subject positions as rooted in systems of domination, systems that oppress not only gays and lesbians but also many heterosexuals? Further, can we answer these questions in ways that help to deconstruct norms offensive not only to those who claim lesbian and gay identities, but also others harmed by the dominant discourse of ideal family? Can we move beyond these fictions to create a more effective language? A gay/lesbian queer family politics that fails to tackle these complex questions is a politics that leaves dominant understandings largely intact, and therefore, one that will also have difficulty creating alliances.

If we explore politics and culture over the past twenty years, it becomes clear that the Right has done a much better job of creating "necessary fictions" in order to mobilize activism than has the Left. The Right makes its claims with religious and historical arguments, that is, by suggesting the naturalness of some ways of living compared to the perversions of others. These arguments have been successful with a significant segment of the American public and the Supreme Court. By deviating from previous decisions in which the Court had ruled that a

history of discrimination was not adequate grounds for continued discrimination, *Bowers v. Hardwick*[11] relied on just this logic. Sullivan and
Eskridge make rational and, to those who are open to persuasion, perhaps compelling arguments about why both this deviation from precedent and decisions that deny marriage to gays and lesbians violate
constitutional principles and rest upon faulty religious and historical
reasoning. These rational arguments are unlikely to persuade those
convinced by the Right that gay rights, along with single parenting
(particularly by women who receive welfare benefits) and sex education,
will lead to the downfall of Western civilization. We might see the narrative that the Right has created as a fictional narrative of Western identity, and as including a normative sexual identity that powerfully asserts
the "Others" who need to be controlled while also being flexibly employed in order to gain support in any given political moment. Homosexuals are, as Wilton states, centrally located within this narrative:
"For a politic which attempts to structure the social arena around the
idea of a nation as a family, the idea of the homosexual as the enemy
within—the embodied challenge to the naturalness of familial ideology—is a necessary fiction. If homosexuals had not existed they
would have had to invent us. And invent us they have done, cleverly
cobbling together a veritable Frankenstein's monster, howling in the
outermost darkness around the embattled hearth of the Happy Heterosexual Family" (1995, 191).

In this context, the effort of the Religious Right to mobilize African-
Americans to support their cause by fighting gay rights becomes understandable, in spite of the Religious Right's very real history of opposition to black civil rights (see Vaid 1996, 340). The Right's strategy is
one that conveniently ignores history to portray the Religious Right as
supporters of black civil rights who do not wish to see the impact of
black gains weakened by an extension of civil rights law to "unnatural"
gays and lesbians. In the process, the Right is able to draw on fears of
sexual deviation so powerfully built into black institutions as a result
of the sexualization of racism (Cohen 1996, West 1993). As Suzanne
Pharr notes, this strategy has a chance to succeed because those on the
Left, including gays and lesbians, have been unable to build the connections necessary to counter the Right:

> Many people talk about how the religious Right splits communities off from
> each other. I don't believe they do the splitting; instead, they simply work the
> splits that are already there. For example, because of the deep-rooted racism

in the lesbian and gay community—in which white people disregard and marginalize lesbians and gay men of color—the religious Right finds it easy to accentuate and increase that division community-wide. (qtd. in Cagan 1990, 72)

Lee, Murphy, and Ucelli (1990) echo Pharr in their discussion of the debate over New York's Children of the Rainbow Curriculum. This debate provides additional evidence of the power of the Right to use stereotypes to maintain splits between communities. In each case, gays and lesbians were defined as rich, white, powerful, and not in need of recognition through public policy.

The ability to counter the fictional narrative of American identity promulgated by the Religious Right requires the recognition, contrary to Sullivan's argument, that fighting political battles for rights alone is inadequate. Such fights, as Vaid notes, need to be combined with cultural battles. It is particularly important that these cultural battles be fought with an understanding of the importance that dominant constructions of acceptable family and sexuality play in politics and policymaking. This lesson is important for gays and lesbians interested in increasing their own freedom, but it also important for others. Cerullo and Erlien, writing about how welfare rights can best be defended, recognize the necessity of constructing a counter-narrative that can connect various family and sexual issues: "If the cultural assumptions about female sexuality, 'normal' families, proper relations between men and women, and 'good' mothering are not challenged, any defense of welfare rights will be inadequate" (1986, 251). Indeed, it is only by understanding connections between rhetoric intended to further anti-gay agendas and rhetoric intended to justify welfare cuts that gays and lesbians will be able to offer an alternative rhetoric of family and personal life. Before developing such a rhetorical and political strategy, however, it is important to better understand how current social problems are connected to changing (or what many might suggest is really deteriorating) families. Only with this knowledge is it possible to frame an alternative rhetorical and political discourse with a radically different understanding of how family and private life might be understood, and therefore with a radically different perspective on the family and personal rights necessary in our current political and economic environment.

4

Social Problems and
Family Ideology

I ncreased anger and violence in society are often topics of
discussion in American politics. Recently, politicians argued
that as a result of "get tough" policies, the crime rate is
decreasing and the problem of violence is in decline. It
will decline further, some politicians and theorists such as
Blankenhorn argue, if the traditional family is reconstructed.
Despite this political posturing, it is difficult for lesbians and
gays, as well as other frequently-targeted groups, to feel that
the United States is becoming safer, or that further institutionalizing an "ideal" form of family will make it safer.
Indeed, the frequency of antigay hate crimes is rising. "According to a report issued by the National Coalition of Anti-
Violence Projects, the incidence of violence against gays and
lesbians increased 6% in 14 major cities in 1996" (Condon
1997, 29).[1] Additionally, terrorism—whether the bombing
of gay bars, abortion clinics, or black churches—has become
a disturbingly regular part of our landscape. The confluence
of anti-abortion actions and the bombing of a gay bar in At-
lanta suggests that the social understandings that lead to
such violence is, at least some of the time, connected (Gover
1997, 41–42). The rhetoric contributing to these acts of violence can be challenged through the creation of an alternative discourse of family and private life, which can attempt
to forge the building of a broad alliance and work to clarify
the ways by which the social discourse of traditional family

that some seek to reassert harms multiple social groups, in part by re-inforcing the idea that those who do not live in the sexual family are inferior and undeserving. The ability of gays and lesbians to play a role in constructing such an alternative narrative requires that we reject making arguments about our worth as citizens on the basis of our ability to copy, albeit with some modification, the sexual family.

At the same time that violent attacks occur with some regularity, le-gal attacks on the equality of many citizens are also part of political rhetoric and are built into state policymaking. The attempt to define policies and programs that combat discrimination not as equal rights, but as special rights, is central to this state-sanctioned violence. Again, such targeting is directed against people of color, immigrants, women, and gays and lesbians. The political construction of appropriate family serves to reinforce the targeting of each of these groups. Gays and lesbians who are concerned about antigay violence and the linkage be-tween these hate crimes, other violent crimes, and legal, often offi-cially sanctioned antiminority rhetoric and action can benefit from an analysis that explores the connection between social constructions of "appropriate" family, "appropriate" masculinity, and anti-equal rights rhetoric.

The ideology of the heterosexual nuclear family as the means of raising good citizens has a fascinating history in relation to analyses of social problems. The problems that theorists, often writing from dif-ferent political perspectives, identify with changes that challenge the ability of a male parent to play a role in child rearing cover almost every social ill. Writing in the early 1960s, Dr. Benjamin Spock suggested that American problems such as the high number of prisoners of war taken in Korea and these prisoners' demoralized response to imprison-ment, as well as juvenile delinquency, were the result of maternal over-protectiveness (Ehrenreich and English 1978, 255). Yet the advice, in-cluding his own, that led mothers to this tendency was developed by child rearing experts challenged to theorize how mothers could raise children with little paternal involvement. Spock suggested that one al-ternative was for the mother to play up her feminine role (Ehrenreich and English 1978, 248–250). Betty Friedan (1963, 270) picked up on the dangers of exaggerated maternal femininity and paternal absence by citing sources who argued that as the demands of the white collar world removed middle-class men from the family, women became increas-ingly isolated. They fought this isolation by becoming more involved in their sons' lives, with boys becoming increasingly effeminate and in some cases homosexual.[2] Writing almost at the same time as Friedan, but about a very different group of "fatherless" boys, Daniel Patrick Moynihan (1965) identified a lack of male role models in black families, or the "matriarchal structure" of the black family, with increased welfare dependency. Francis Cress Welsing, writing in the 1980s, identified a lack of male role models in black families with homosexuality, a condition that she believed was a white-imposed attempt to control black people by spreading a sexual identity that precluded reproduction, and would therefore decrease the black population (Hemphill 1992). Blankenhorn associates a lack of male role models with increased crime, incest, domestic violence, teen pregnancy, and the poverty of women and children. It appears as if multiple social ills, including male effeminacy, male aggressiveness, and male homosexuality, can be explained by the same cause: maternal over-involvement and paternal absence. What is common to all of these theories, in addition to indebtedness to Freudian and post-Freudian psychoanalytic theory, is an understanding of gender as dichotomous, thus precluding women from socializing children, particularly male children, without the help of a male (or in Blankenhorn's case, without at least the memory of a deceased father). Further, and despite the reality that men raise children by themselves, these theorists' writing suggests that they do not believe men can perform the feminine role of nurturing children. In fact, they never discuss this issue.

One way for gays and lesbians to address these arguments is to accept some of the basic premises while demonstrating that two men or two women are equally capable of forming a sexual family that is close enough to the (hetero)sexual family to be virtually interchangeable. In making this argument, many elements of the idealized family ideology can be preserved, even while the gender and sexuality premises are rejected. Yet there are multiple ways in which the maintenance of this model in gay discourse will work to reinforce not only the divisions within gay and lesbian communities as discussed in chapter 2, but also divisions between gay communities and other communities that could be allies in constructing a radical democratic movement oriented around family issues. The alternative to this strategy of inclusion is better understanding of the values embedded in the sexual family so that those harmed by the current ideological construction can construct an alternative discourse. This chapter will focus on four narrative strategies that gays and/or lesbians have used in discussing and justifying their desire to create families. The first two involve social benefits presumed to come from gay marriage, specifically that more children would be raised in two-parent families and that gay marriage would tame gay men. The second two strategies focus on how gays and lesbians justify the choice and means used to have children. By drawing on the dominant language of family, gays and lesbians, often despite their intentions, create conditions that make the development of a radical democratic movement around family issues less likely, while simultaneously restricting the extent to which gays and lesbians can exercise agency in creating conditions that might better meet human needs.

Two-Parent Families: Necessity or Ideology?

As we have discussed, central to the dominant norm of family is the desirability of a male and female who live together in a marital relationship while parenting children, or creating what Fineman calls the sexual family. Arguing that lesbian and gay male couples could play both of these roles requires separating the role from the gender of the person who plays it. Andrew Samuels (1995) makes the argument that since mothering and fathering are social roles rather than essential characteristics, men can be "good enough mothers" and women can be "good enough fathers." That is, it is possible to accept that there are different roles that parents play in socializing children, but to argue that if gender characteristics are socially constructed, rather than essential, there is no reason a lesbian cannot be a father or a gay man cannot be a mother.

Although this argument begins to justify a right of gays and lesbians to have and/or nurture children, it has two limitations. First, because it begins from the assumption that gender is not natural or essential, it is not likely to persuade those who believe that men and women are different and that civilization is threatened when we fail to recognize these differences. This position informs Jean Bethke Elshtain's rejection of gay liberation (Elshtain 1981).[3] Christopher Lasch and Blankenhorn use this idea to reject the possibility that men and women can take on more androgynous roles. One can, of course, respond to this point by arguing, as Eskridge does, that there is no empirical evidence to suggest that children raised in two-parent gay households have more problems than children raised in two-parent heterosexual families.[4] But, as long as the responses that gays and lesbians provide continue to assert the superiority of two-parent families, rather than to identify and address other social issues that may be more foundational than family structure to social problems, it will be difficult to achieve many goals, such as understanding how to address the problems that many gays and lesbians will face in raising children, constructing the grounds upon which political alliances can be built that enable us to have greater freedom in defining the conditions of our private lives, and theorizing alternative means of decreasing antigay/lesbian activism and violence.

Two-parent families only make sense as a practical necessity if children are born into families isolated from larger community networks. That is, if it is possible for children to be exposed to and interact with a diverse array of human beings as they are nurtured to adulthood, the theoretical justifications generally put forth for needing two-parent homes lose their power. This is particularly the case if the community provides not only exposure to multiple role models, but also takes responsibility for supporting the child. This point is well-developed by Judith Stacey in her recent critique of ideological assertions of the superiority of two-parent families: "Most children from both kinds of families turn out reasonably all right, and when other parental resources—like income, education, self-esteem, and a supportive social environment—are roughly similar, signs of a two-parent privilege largely disappear" (1996, 60). If this is the case, there is no reason to argue that gay and lesbian two-parent families are better than single-parent families. Instead, it is useful to understand the social conditions that would provide the support and stability necessary to allow all families, regardless of how many parents are present within them, to function to the best of their ability.

Although we might be able to argue that with greater social rights two-parent gay or lesbian households would well be able to meet the needs of children, this is an argument that has costs for gays and lesbians. First, it ignores the reality that gay and lesbian couples, like all couples, sometimes break up.[5] When this happens, many of the children born to these two-parent couples will live in single-parent families that would lack social support, just as single-parent families do currently. Second, the argument made by some theorists that gay family equality would increase the number of children born into stable two-parent families—because more children would be born into *stable* relationships while fewer would be born into heterosexual relationships entered into by socially coerced gays and lesbians—ignores the reality that many of the children of parents who might at some point in their lives identify as gay, lesbian, or bisexual will continue to be born to many of these people when they are in heterosexual relationships. Although central to Eskridge, Bawer, and Sullivan's arguments is the assertion that recognizing gay marriage will decrease the number of children born to gays in heterosexual relationships, this argument presupposes two points, both of which are disputable. First, it suggests that granting marriage rights will have the power to combat significant antigay messages. Second, and more critical in the long term, it assumes that sexual identity is fixed. Since many of the children living in single-parent gay homes live with lesbian mothers, and since lesbians are more likely to reject an understanding of their sexuality as fixed early in life, there is little reason to believe that recognizing gay and lesbian marriage will reduce the number of children born into heterosexual relationships to the extent that these authors assert and desire.

The more important reasons, however, to rethink justifying gay and lesbian marriage and parenting by privileging two-parent families are ethical and political. The glorification of two-parent families is not a neutral, innocent discourse; it has been a central discourse in blaming African Americans for not making greater economic strides in the United States, and as a result for the failure of black communities to raise "appropriately" masculine men. This, of course, was central to Moynihan's analysis of welfare and to Cress Welsing's analysis of homosexuality in black communities. Despite the careful analysis of Carol Stack (1974) over twenty years ago and of other sociologists such as Patricia Hill Collins (1990) since then, it remains almost a commonsense notion in American life that black families remain disproportionately poor because they are disproportionately single-parent families.

The current struggle over reducing social welfare expenditures focuses on programs designed for women and children and associated with single mothers. Reducing expenditures is coupled with a moralizing discourse that denies a connection between the poverty of women and children and economic structures and political decisions. A number of feminist theorists have discussed how social welfare programs that are primarily directed toward men differ from those that focus on women: those for men, such as unemployment insurance, are based on an understanding that men have earned the right to state support; those for women are based on an understanding that women who are dependent on the state, rather than on husbands, have failed (see Abramowitz

1988, Fraser 1989, Pearce 1990, Sapiro 1990, and Solinger 1992). This discourse, rooted in the historical fears of race suicide, portrays women who need the support of social welfare programs as irresponsible, particularly sexually irresponsible. Rickie Solinger points out that following World War II, white women were less likely than black women to be single mothers needing state support because social norms encouraged white unmarried pregnant women, understood not as biologically flawed but as neurotic, to give their babies up for adoption—an option that was possible because white babies were a valuable commodity.[6] "The biological stain, however, remained affixed to black unwed mothers, who were often portrayed by politicians, sociologists and others in the post-war period as unrestrained, wanton breeders, on the one hand, or as calculating breeders for profit on the other" (Solinger 1992, 9). Thus, women were encouraged to take actions that would provide children for good households while being discouraged from any dependency that cost the state money. At the same time, racist stereotypes received confirmation because of social policy.

The importance of family and sexuality to racist stereotypes is noted by Collins, who after discussing the controlling images of black women as mammy, matriarch, welfare mother, and the Jezebel notes: "Taken together these four prevailing interpretations of Black womanhood form a nexus of elite white male interpretations of Black female sexuality and fertility. Moreover, by meshing smoothly with systems of race, class, and gender oppression, they provide effective ideological justifications for racial oppression, the politics of gender subordination, and the economic exploitation inherent in capitalist economies" (1990, 78). The image of "welfare mothers" draws upon and reinforces these racist stereotypes to create a powerful image of "failed women"—women whose children may deserve some minimal level of public support but who themselves deserve condemnation. Teresa Amott writes, "Much of this debate [about welfare] focused on the 'long-term dependent,' a phrase that echoed the simultaneously emerging discussions of a black 'underclass' characterized by criminal behavior and out-of-wedlock births and thus functioned as a code word for black" (1990, 290). This debate, and the (re)construction of welfare as a problem of black culture and community life, arose at a time when white families were increasingly experiencing exactly the problems (high rates of divorce, poverty among women and children, and of out-of-wedlock births) that in the

1960s led to a view of black families as inadequate. This is not coincidental: black women and men in the dominant ideology of the United States are symbols of sexual looseness. Thus, when fears of reproductive sexuality become great, black women are a target for policymakers and opinion makers—a target that serves to warn others of the consequences of exercising sexual agency in ways that are outside of the dominant ideology. This targeting should be familiar to gays and lesbians, who also serve as a symbol of unregulated sexuality and make an easy target in times of changing sexual mores.[7]

The retrenchment of racism makes possible the continued denial of the need to rethink work and family life as we know them. Even moderates, such as Bill Clinton, choose to define the current social problem as "rethinking welfare as we know it," primarily by putting in place work requirements. Given the racially and sexually stratified labor market, any policy that focuses on replacing entitlement programs with work will disproportionately harm black women. As Amott points out, in 1987 almost one-third of black women working for wages lived below the poverty line, compared to 17 percent of white women (1990, 293). Nancy Rose argues that mandatory work programs have historically been racist and sexist. These programs are appealing in the 1990s, she argues, because they help to increase the supply of "low-wage labor, disproportionately women of color," and, in part, because policymakers no longer perceive unions as having the strength to resist policies that help to depress wages (1993, 336). Workfare programs may be most significant because they bring together liberals and conservatives. In other words, the language of welfare reform has become a fiction with the power to build a political alliance. "This 'New Consensus,'" Philip Neisser and Sanford Schram argue, "uncritically accepts the denial implicit in contemporary welfare policy discourse and hastens to regiment the poor to accept the inadequacies of the emerging post-industrial economy and reorient themselves to finding the means to survive within it. In the process, the 'New Consensus' promotes work and family even as the policy remains inattentive to the deterioration of conditions that make them possible" (1994, 18).

While this discourse of blame has been developed and promulgated, the reality that many African American children are successfully raised in single-parent families goes ignored. So, too, do the support systems within communities that have allowed for this success. One element of these systems rarely mentioned in any detail is the role that lesbians and gays play in nurturing children, even if the children are not biologically their own. In discussing the role of "othermothers" in the lives of black children, Collins cites one example indicating that she sees lesbians living in close connection to a partner's children as playing this role, which she understands as critically important to the survival of both black children and black communities (1990, 128). Similarly, William Hawkeswood notes in his discussion of the roles black gay men play in Harlem life that "the support these gay men receive from women when they [gay men] have trouble with men is reciprocated with financial assistance, baby-sitting, or 'father' role playing. In many instances, gay black men acted as 'fathers' to their sister's children. These men are probably the 'uncles' in Stack's *All Our Kin* (1974)" (1996, 103).[8]

The ability to recognize the role that these men and women play is contingent upon understanding children as influenced not only within the "private" world of the nuclear family, but also by people in the more "public" world. The fact that gays and lesbians play important roles in the lives of children requires that we look increasingly at what raising children within gay communities says about the need for support from friends and how the children of gay/lesbian parents define these friends. We also need to understand in more detail the lives of lesbians and gays who have chosen to remain in close proximity to their families of origin to raise their own children with support from these families or play a central role in nurturing the children of relatives or friends. The network of support that allows for the growth and development of children is more complex than what conservatives, whether heterosexual or gay, care to see. Because they view two parents who live together as the ideal for children, neither conservative faction is inclined to ask—rather than ignore or vilify—how social policy might better recognize and respect these extended relationships. The privacy of the home becomes a rationale for failing to ask more complex questions about social relations and social support. Yet, these are the questions that gays and lesbians should ask, both to better recognize and support the relationships that many form, and to diffuse the power of a discourse that rests on and supports a gender division and an understanding of "appropriate" sexuality that continues to cause great harm to lesbians and gays as well as to people of color, particularly African Americans.

The Threat of Untamed Men

Another central component of the sexual family is the idea that men will be better citizens if they live in intimate connection to women. This leads to a social ideology that identifies men who are not socialized by women as one of the biggest threats to civilization—that is, although women are less powerful than men, they can through love entice men into behaving in a manly way that is economically productive and does not threaten overall social structures. Sullivan refutes the idea that women, as opposed to the institution of marriage, are responsible for this civilizing role and quotes Hadley Arkes on the more dominant ideology:

> It is not marriage that domesticates men; it is women. Left to themselves, these forked creatures follow a way of life that George Gilder once recounted in its precise and chilling measures: bachelors were twenty-two times more likely than married men to be committed to hospital for mental disease (and ten times more likely to suffer chronic disease of all kinds). Single men had nearly double the mortality rate of married men and three times the mortality rate of single women. Divorced men were three times more likely than divorced women to commit suicide or die by murder, and they were six times more likely to die of heart disease. (qtd. in Sullivan 1996, 108)[9]

Randy Shilts's portrayal of the thinking of some gay men in the beginning of the AIDS crisis draws from and reinforces this interpretation of male behavior unconstrained by women. Joe, one of the men who becomes a central figure in *And the Band Played On*, comments that "promiscuity was rampant because in an all male-subculture there was no one to say 'no'—no moderating role like that a woman plays in the heterosexual milieu. Some heterosexual males privately confided that they were enthralled with the idea of the immediate, available, even anonymous, sex a bathhouse offered, if they could only find women who would agree. Gay men, of course, agreed quite frequently" (1987, 89). Given the fear that men who are not under the supervision of women will behave badly, it is not surprising that in considering the values embedded in monogamous heterosexual models of family life, fostering and maintaining gender division and complementarity become quickly apparent. The middle-class model of family life that was developed with industrialization was premised on the idea that women would have primary responsibility for socializing children. Many asserted that because men and women are different kinds of moral thinkers, each would have an appropriate sphere in which to exercise their moral judgments. Heterosexuality, particularly through marriage, joined these two essentially different moral ways of thinking and judging.

The differences between the sexes was both assumed and, many feminists have argued, determined by the family structure of the heterosexual nuclear family. Yet the social forces and understandings of gender that made the nuclear family workable for many—at least through the 1960s—have changed, leaving many men wondering why they should make any commitment to the family at all. Interestingly, conservative authors who see multiple problems with families because of the freedom that heterosexual men have to opt out of family life are struggling to figure out how to get men involved again, at the same time that authors such as Eskridge and Sullivan are arguing that gay male life—a life that they see as uncommitted, overly sexual, and irresponsible—can be tamed simply by allowing gay men to marry. How, we may ask, can gay authors put so much faith in the family to tame and control gay men while heterosexual conservatives are arguing that even marriage and fatherhood are failing to contain the antisocial desires of men? In fact, authors such as Blankenhorn can and do cite the instability of gay male life as an indication of the need for women to socialize men into a socially positive masculinity. Despite the impasse over the question of whether women or marriage are necessary to socialize men, in the end both groups of authors share a basic assumption: men cannot be moral citizens and community members without some variant of the sexual family.

Since the institutionalization of the sexual family, however, there has been tension between masculine men and good family men. The two came together in the understanding that a good man would provide the economic support for his family. If he did this, he was guaranteed a private realm in which he could be dominant, and in which public concerns with nonmonogamy and violence would be generally ignored if such things were not practiced too publicly. It is not clear, then, that men—whether gay or straight—socialized into the hegemonic norms of masculinity actually understand and practice masculinity, in private or public life, in a way that is compatible with freedom and nonviolence. To develop faith that men can move outside of these norms of masculinity and family life requires an analysis of masculinity and current social problems that focuses on public institutions and structures. That is, it requires a nonessential understanding of masculinity based on the assumption that since institutions and cultures construct masculinity (and femininity), they are changeable. This is, however, exactly what the gender essentialism of these two sets of theorists—conservative heterosexuals and gay men who promote marriage to increase monogamy—prevents them from seeing. Neither set of theorists questions social institutions enough to see men as potentially nonthreatening. Further, because masculinity is not called into question in their writing, these gay theorists do not recognize the role that dominant constructions of masculinity, reinforced by the family norms that the theorists seek to copy, play in antigay violence.

As with the discourse of mothering and failed mothers, the discourse of failed fathers does not take into account the relationship between economic structures and men, as individuals or as fathers. We are today in a situation both similar to and different from that of the late 1800s. The similarities should give us pause: we are again living in a time when the dominant understanding of "masculinity" is being challenged because of changes in economic production and fears that too few men are located within stable family arrangements. There are also, however, important differences. The impact of men's changing role is being felt more by working-class men, who are being displaced as industrial production declines. Thus, unlike at the previous turn of the century, the men whose masculinity appears threatened as the twentieth century closes are not primarily middle class. Instead they are men who have neither the power nor the privilege necessary to redefine norms; they do, however, have the power to resist changes that feel threatening. Despite the greater security of middle-class men, their masculinity is also threatened as they find themselves unable to support families on their incomes alone. In fact, throughout society, it is no longer clear what role, if any, men are to play in the family. Patricia Mann argues that as men have lost the ability to see their wives as extensions of themselves, they have also lost a clear understanding of their personhood:

> When a man ceases to identify with his family as a creative projection of himself, the services that he has traditionally been expected to perform for the family take on a new set of meanings. If the family can no longer be seen as an extension of the male self, then in acting on behalf of the family, the man is acting on behalf of distinct others. If he accepts the liberal dichotomy between freely "acting for oneself" and only acting for others in the face of some sort of coercion, a man may begin to feel enslaved by family obligations, coerced by society or his wife into sacrificing his own interests on behalf of others. (1994, 54)

This tendency to feel coerced may be most clearly present when re-lationships end. We know that large numbers of men either refuse to pay child support at all or do not pay the proper amount, a defiance that E. Anthony Rotundo suggests "is consistent with a radical form of male individualism that considers family responsibility to be a quiet form of tyranny" (1987, 73). It is necessary for us to examine how this erosion of traditional male responsibilities, built very heavily into social under-standings of masculinity, has come about and what its consequences are both for particular groups of men and for the family. Given the em-phasis on civilizing men that Eskridge, Blankenhorn, and Lasch have voiced, this can clearly create problems for society: if men are no longer able to feel masculine through their families, can society civilize them? Is it possible for men to act "civilized" without women being controlled within the institution of the family? Finally, we might ask whether men can be "civilized" in a way that is less violent, since many men have been able to exercise violence in private life with little, if any, social interven-tion or condemnation.

Dominant Masculinity's Challenge to Men

As the family/household system was institutionalized in the early twen-tieth century, patriarchy was transformed. In part, a system of public male power was firmly established to oversee those women not directly connected to an individual man. Even as this occurred, the state contin-ued to work with other interests—including employers, unions, and sometimes groups of women—to support policies that encouraged the formation of private, independent, male-dominated units. Establishing the norm of the father as the family wage earner necessitated a guar-antee that there would be some jobs paying enough for this norm to be achievable as part of the American Dream, even though the dream re-mained impossible for many, and it had to be possible to limit em-ployment in these positions to men. State policy, union-management agreement, and sometimes the political activism of women made pos-sible the restriction of such jobs to men.[10] By exploring the origins of this system, the limits that it places on just arrangements within fami-lies, and the challenges that families face currently as the system is breaking down, we can increase our understanding of the difficult task faced by men and the state in the 1990s and taken advantage of by the Right to call into question affirmative action, gay rights, and other policies that, in the end, have little to do with the threat to masculine identity that white, working-class and middle-class men experience. As I develop this argument, I will focus primarily on working-class men. One of the arguments made about the lack of radical activism in the United States is that since the working class has not been excluded from the franchise, and since unions have been able to strike relatively good deals for some (largely white) segments of the working class, working-class people have not felt the need to engage in radical political activism. The decline of union power and working-class security may provide some hope for politicizing working-class men. However, thus far the politicization that has occurred has been largely conservative, a phenomenon that we can best understand by exploring how social changes have fostered masculine insecurity.

The idea of the family wage is, of course, that by paying a man enough money to support his family, it is possible for his wife to maintain the home, raise children, and provide a place where, unlike in the world of work, average working-class men can feel a sense of power. Unions and management promoted the family wage in the early 1900s. When combined with protective legislation, which was, as we have seen, also supported by some women, labor market segregation and the payment of lower wages to women was institutionalized. Overall, as Boris and Bardaglio observe, "The family wage had a dual function: it bolstered men's power over women and children, and it facilitated the efforts of capital to segment the labor force along gender lines" (1983, 81). This division of labor has had a significant impact not only on women (by defining them as primarily responsible for the private sphere and by segregating those women who worked outside the home in low-paying jobs) but also on men, whose masculine identity has become problematic as filling the role of provider has become increasingly more difficult. Economic change has also made it more difficult for males to establish and reinforce a masculine identity in the workplace. Aronowitz (1992) notes that Fordism, which helped to institutionalize gender roles by making labor more secure, began to gain dominance in the pre–World War II period with consolidation coming in the 1950s. This managerial strategy was dependent upon stable wages, the ability to buy on credit, and the development of advertising—all of which promoted consumerism. Within this system, he notes, workers valued labor because it enabled the laborer and his family to purchase goods. Any idea that work could have an intrinsic meaning was increasingly lost, a process accelerated in the post-industrial era. Thus, masculine identity was not connected to pride in craftsmanship, which declined with mechanization, but to wages and the goods that these wages enabled families to purchase.

As a result of these changes, three characteristics became central to masculine identity within the family household system: being the breadwinner, being heterosexual, and exerting power. The family household system builds on the assumption and enforcement of heterosexuality to create the conditions whereby men can be breadwinners and can have power at least in the household. Power in the workplace is more elusive for most men, although the working-class male culture does build masculine identity around physical power and risk. This is certainly an understanding of masculinity with considerable benefits for maintaining the economic system, and considerable costs for the men themselves. The values of the dominant masculinity were present even when men attempted to rebel against the system. Thus Paul Willis (1981) found that the rebellion of working-class "lads" led them to an understanding of physical labor that fit nicely with the needs of industry. Stan Gray's exploration of the sexual integration of a Westinghouse manufacturing plant also points to the centrality of physical labor in working-class men's masculine identities. Despite the scorn directed toward working-class men, Gray writes, "The men can say we are better than them all in certain ways: we're doing men's work; its physically tough; women can't do it; neither can the bankers and politicians. Tough work gives them a sense of masculine superiority that compensates for being stepped on and ridiculed" (1987, 225). This was true to such an extent, Gray observes, that men did dangerous work to reinforce their masculinity (1987, 219–220). Deindustrialization poses a threat even to this ability to maintain a sense of oneself as masculine. The advent of the post-industrial era, as Aronowitz discusses, meant that the secure labor of the past had declined, leaving technologically displaced workers with unions that were unable to negotiate for anything other than protection for the few workers able to maintain their union jobs. Although theoretically unions could work to challenge gender/sexuality norms in positive ways, the realities that they must confront make this difficult. For example, gay and lesbian organizing within unions is made more difficult as unions lose power and are forced to put their energies into maintaining membership, rather than fighting for benefits and challenging their own members to expand their understandings of gender and sexuality. R. W. Connell notes that although working-class men's lives often provide a solid foundation for challenging hegemonic masculinity, this possibility does not have any collective mechanism by which to become something more than personal protest: "As the United Steelworkers of America (in Canada) and the Builders Labourers Federation (in Australia) have shown, such a response *can* come from male-dominated unions. But in an age of union decline, it is difficult to see how a wider response will develop" (1995, 117–118). In fact, the collective response to the gender change that is occurring in the United States seems to be coming through organizations such as The Promisekeepers that wish not to challenge gender roles and conservative understandings of sexuality, but to reinforce them.

For workers themselves, there is either no leisure time because part-time minimum-wage labor requires working more than one job, or job insecurity creates the need to make oneself indispensable, or there is leisure time available but nothing with which to fill it in a privatized world where workers increasingly lack the resources even to consume. One consequence is that men who lose their jobs lose a critical sense of their identity. Lillian Rubin notes, "Ask a man for a statement of his identity and he'll almost always respond by telling you what he does for a living. The same question asked of a woman brings forth a less predictable, more varied response, one that's embedded in the web of relationships that are central to her life" (1994, 104). Her reports of interviews reinforce the impact that job loss has on families and on relationships between women and men:

> A woman notes: "I don't mind working; I really don't. In fact, I like it a lot better than being home with the house and kids all the time. But I guess deep down I still have the old-fashioned idea that it's a man's job to support his family. So, yeah, then I begin to feel—I don't know how to say it—uncomfortable, right here inside me . . . like maybe I won't respect him so much if he can't do that." (1994, 109)

> A man who has been laid off reports: "It's not just the income; you lose a lot more than that. When you get laid off, it's like you lose a part of yourself. It's terrible; something goes out of you." (1994, 110)

The overall impact in these families is higher divorce rates, increased problems resulting from alcoholism, and increased violence. It is interesting, as Amott (1993, 83–112) and Stacey (1996, 35–36) note, that although conservatives often blame women for the decline of family, women are generally laboring more to maintain and support families, while men have, and sometimes exercise, the ability to opt out. Thus, social ideology blames women for challenging a gender system that "worked," while social policy attempts to coerce women into the secondary labor market and to coerce men into providing support for families, even if this means that they have to take jobs that they view as inferior and as a threat to their identity.

The contradiction between reinforcing cultural norms of masculinity—which suggest that men should be able to support families and should exert physical power—in a society where physical labor is less necessary and the ability to support a family is less possible, is explosive. Working class white men feel the current deconstruction of masculine identity, but it has already been experienced by working class black men, thus giving us a sense of how devastating the inability to live up to hegemonic masculinity can be. For young black men, the earlier loss of industrial labor produced communities debilitated by anger that has no outlet, other than the community itself. Cornel West observes: "Sadly, the combination of the market way of life, poverty-ridden conditions, black existential angst,[11] and the lessening of fear of white authorities has directed most of the anger, rage, and despair toward black fellow citizens, especially toward black women, who are the most vulnerable in our society and in black communities" (1993, 18). This has not only destroyed nuclear families, but has also harmed larger community institutions that often rest on the labor of women and sustain black Americans. bell hooks (1984) and Patricia Hill Collins (1992) each note that the extended family as a support network no longer has the force that it once did. West agrees, noting that local-level institutions must be able to provide a sense of self-worth and self-esteem if the destructive anger is to be checked. Certainly racism plays a major role in destroying the self-esteem of young black men, but gender constructions that glorify a masculinity that is less and less possible also play an important role (Segal 1990).

Aronowitz recognizes an increasing trend in this direction for white male youth as well. The result of the loss of industrial jobs is that young men are increasingly members of communities, "constructed out of their exclusion. Their culture is rife with rituals neither of protest nor passivity, but of hostile and aggressive despair" (Aronowitz 1992, 245). Jay MacLeod writes, "As boys, the Hallway Hangers [a group of White high school-aged men living in a public housing project] can inhabit a subculture that receives a good deal of validation from the dominant culture. . . . Lacking in nearly every category that defines success in America, the Hallway Hangers latch onto and inflate the one quality they still have: their masculinity" (1987, 142). Racism, sexism, and homophobia are among the values of the dominant culture embraced by these young men and by the young men discussed by Lois Weis (1990) and Fine et al. (1997). Both Weis and Fine et al. convey the extent to which young men who in the past would enter industrial production but now are neither prepared for any alternative nor able to establish a sense of self that is not based on seeing themselves as superior to "Others." This is not unique to working-class men, yet when combined with the frustrations of a hopeless future, it has an explosiveness increasingly visible in the public sphere.

Weis, writing in 1990, argued that white working-class youth were a natural constituency for the New Right to target. Her argument is supported by political polling data indicating the critical role that white working-class men (and to a lesser extent women) have played in forging an electoral coalition that has put more Republicans in office, while encouraging the Democratic Party to retreat from progressive politics. These are men who, as Rubin's interviews show, blame immigration and affirmative action for job losses. "In an expanding economy," Rubin notes, "opening the door to those who have been shut out may stir the apprehension of the in-group, but so long as they are not themselves at risk, their discomfort is tolerable. When the economy contracts and jobs become scarce, it's another matter. Then, each time the door swings open for those who were formally left out—a woman, an African-American, a Native American, and so on—it slams shut on a white man who until then had assumed the privilege of both whiteness and maleness without even knowing it" (1994, 211–212).

Although I have focused on the impact of these changes on working-class men, it is a mistake to think that middle-class white men have also not become more conservative as they try to maintain privilege. Middle-class men may still get well-paying jobs, but they generally are not the sole providers for their families; thus, they are also unlikely to get a clear sense of masculine identity. The reactions of the young middle-class white men is no less conservative than that of their working-class counterparts. One place where this is clear is on college campuses. After discussing the movement to the right of both college men and women in the 1970s, Paul Loeb notes, "By 1993, 30 percent of college women considered themselves liberal and 18 percent conservative, a gap of nearly two to one, with the balance saying they were middle of the road. For men, conservatives led by a 29 to 23 percent majority. The difference between men and women was a staggering 18 points" (1994, 212). As he goes on to note, these figures would be even more skewed if "we exclude the considerably more liberal minority males (and as the student gay movement has become more active, gay males)" (1994, 212). Further, the recent decline in the number of men enrolling in liberal arts institutions has become a source of concern. As Arthur Levine, president of Columbia University's Teacher College, comments in a recent *New York Times* front-page article, "It's worth thinking about what it means if our broadest education, the liberal arts, is increasingly being reserved for one sex" (Lewin 1998, 38). Some young men who in the past would have gotten a broad-based liberal arts education are now choosing to try to preserve white, male privilege by focusing their education on technical fields such as engineering and computer science; that is, those fields that remain "masculine." Since we know that liberal arts institutions define broadening how young people think as a central component of their educational mission, this should be a serious concern to those interested in furthering progressive agendas.

The fears of men whose masculinity and privilege are threatened have been mobilized to oppose affirmative action; they are also used to mobilize antigay sentiment and to mobilize support for antigay rights measures. Harris notes that in Colorado, "The 'Christians' exploited the fear of affirmative action for gay people to get straights to vote for Amendment 2" (1996, 6). Equally important, young men hear messages about how others are a threat to them and act on these messages in the streets.

If one manifestation of the hopelessness and fear that spread throughout society with declining economic opportunities for men is the desire to oppose or repeal legislation extending civil rights to gays, another is hate crimes. Violence directed toward gays and lesbians in public spaces, including college campuses, is one element of increased hate violence. It has never been possible to create exclusive enclaves untouched by the problems dominant in the larger society; this should be clear at a time when antigay violence has increased. Unless citizens confront the rigid gender separation, the class separation, and the racial separation of American life through political action that builds alternative understandings of people's roles in society and alternative systems of support, particularly for youth, this violence is unlikely to decrease.

Theorists such as Blankenhorn construct such violence not as an indication of the necessity of engaging in potentially positive change, but as indication of the breakdown of "tradition" and "family."

This construction, however, is one that fails to recognize the changes in society that are coming about as the economy changes. A form of family that developed out of the fears and challenges of industrialization cannot address the fears and challenges of post-industrialism. Yet the norms of family to which theorists such as Blankenhorn continue to appeal, and that are embedded in Eskridge and Sullivan's hope of civilizing men, arose as a result of fears of social instability (connected to fears of race suicide and class conflict) and resulted in the destruction of working-class public life, ethnic life, gay life, and middle-class women's freedom. This should alert us to the reality that change is not linear and progressive. From this historical vantage point, it is not surprising that one component of post-industrial society's attempts to address its current fears is a backlash against people of color, women, and gays and lesbians.

Parenting without Reproducing/ Reproducing without Sex

As we begin to recognize that many of the constructions to which gay and lesbian authors appeal in justifying our right to freedom in private life are embedded in pre-existing, relatively conservative understandings of what families are and what they do, it is important to keep in mind that one of the most significant challenges to traditional family politics revolves around the separation of sexuality from reproduction. As we have seen, the family as an institution developed in such a way that socially sanctioned sexuality was justified on the basis of its role in reproduction. Legal decisions through the 1970s reassert this connection, suggesting that privacy rights are largely connected to the link between sexuality and reproductive decision making. The assertion of their capacity to reproduce has been central to the delegitimization of lesbian and gay sexuality and relationships. Similarly, cultural norms that understand children as valuable regardless of the marital status of their parents, and that therefore understand marriage as an unnecessary prerequisite for childbearing in black communities, have left black people more vulnerable to the intrusion of the state and to a discourse that identifies the impact of racism and class division not on the institutional structures of the United States, but on black people's sexual and reproductive behavior.

The problem society now faces is that many people's reproductive behavior has little connection to their marital status or to a sexual relationship that exists within a marriage. Scientific discoveries and the decriminalization of many older methods of birth control, combined with ever-new ways to fertilize an egg, have made sex without reproduction easy, even for heterosexuals, and reproduction without sex easy, regardless of sexual orientation. This ever changing reality poses significant ethical questions for us as a society, ethical questions that lesbians and gays are playing a part in both defining and answering in our everyday practices and discourse. What we may not always remember as we engage in everyday decision making or as we justify decisions is that the practices in which we engage and the language that we use to justify those decisions have the potential to reinforce social divisions. This is particularly true because fears of white European Americans becoming a minority in the United States—fears that in recent years have focused on denying social support to immigrants—remain a part of mainstream American discourse. Such fears may open up the possibility for white European American gays and lesbians to draw upon them (whether intentionally or unintentionally) to argue for parenting rights, but doing so would make building political alliances extremely unlikely. As a result, it is critical to examine very carefully how lesbians and gays discuss parenting and reproductive technologies.

The quick, though varied, responses of contributors to *The Advocate* to the cloning of Dolly the sheep is indicative of gay fears and hopes regarding the issue of reproduction.[12] These fears and hopes are connected to the difficulty of parenting for gay men, and for lesbians they are connected to fears of male power, even when reproduction is removed from sexual intercourse. At the moment, gay men who wish to parent a child or children outside of a heterosexual relationship have three options: adoption or foster parenting; contract pregnancy or surrogacy; and co-parenting with a woman, women, or mixed group of men and women where one of the women in the group gives birth. Lesbians who do not wish to give birth themselves also have the options of adoption, foster parenting, and co-parenting. Each of these options raises interesting ethical and political questions that go to the heart of the problem of building a radical democratic movement centered around family issues.

One argument that gay people who wish to adopt might make is that there are many children who need homes. However, the obstacles for lesbians and gays who wish to adopt are formidable: despite the fact that adoption and foster parenting by gay people are legal in most states, it is not easy to find an adoption agency or state agency that sees either a single gay or lesbian person, or a gay or lesbian couple, as desirable parents for most children. As a result, when adoption or foster parenting is possible, the children most likely to be available to gays and lesbians are mixed-race children, disabled children, or older children of color from the United States, and adoptees from poor or war-torn countries around the world.[13] Those children most likely to need homes are children of color. Yet, for the white middle-class gays and lesbians most likely to pursue legal adoption, attempting to adopt these children is fraught with political and ethical questions and controversies.[14]

Some black social workers have been vocal proponents of minimizing or banning the adoption of African Americans by European Americans. There are multiple arguments that these social workers make: (1) that black children should be raised in African American communities; (2) that the reason there are more African American children who are adoptable stems from racist policies that do not provide the support necessary to allow parents to raise their own children; and (3) that social service agencies do not make an effort to find black parents who could, with some help, provide good homes for black children. The first of these points is contested, even within black communities (Bartholet 1994, n. 28). The second, however, seems to be increasingly difficult to dispute as politicians argue for restrictions on welfare benefits that would make supporting children even more difficult. The overall question that this controversy raises concerns the ways by which as a society we encourage particular people to relinquish custody of children in the name of providing greater opportunities for those children. That is to say, this controversy raises serious ethical questions that continue to divide communities from building political alliances with one another.

It is dangerous for gays and lesbians to see children who become adoptable as a result of social inequalities and discrimination as benefiting from gay parenting, while failing to vocally call into question the policies that create the need for the adoption of these children. This is particularly true if my analysis is correct that a counter-narrative of family and private life with the power to challenge the narrative of the Right requires an understanding of the construction of nuclear families as embedded in the construction of whiteness, middle-classness, and heterosexuality as norms. Rather than helping to reinforce the social and economic conditions that make these children adoptable to begin with, it is more useful to challenge those conditions. The ideology that justifies taking away the benefits necessary for some (particularly single-parent) families to nurture children for whom they would provide care in other circumstances also justifies policies, like those in Massachusetts and Florida, that make it impossible for gays and lesbians to adopt legally, which in turn makes it possible for private adoption agencies to legally exclude gays and lesbians from consideration. As long as there is a "preferred and privileged" family form, neither single mothers who need social support nor gays and lesbians who would like to play a central role in the lives of children will be able to obtain the social support that they need. Further, these same privileged constructions will discourage the formation of political alliances that seek ways to make nurturing roles more available to those socially defined as undesirable.

The possibility that gays or lesbians could join heterosexuals in having biologically-related children by using surrogacy may be equally problematic. There are interesting parallels between the ways proponents of marriage and proponents of contract pregnancy use the words "choice" and "freedom." Both see freedom as residing in the ability to agree to a contract. Thus, a woman who has agreed to contract pregnancy has exercised free will and, many would argue, is legally accountable for fulfilling the terms of the agreement. Mary Lyndon Shanley suggests the possibility and necessity of questioning this understanding of contract pregnancy:

> Starting our analysis of contract pregnancy from women's experience compels us to see how some forms of liberal theory have ignored or misunderstood what it means to be "free" and "autonomous" as physically embodied and gendered beings. Contract pregnancy sheds important light on the necessity for any adequate account of human freedom to attend to the conditions under which we form, sustain, and develop within relationships—including sexual and reproductive relationships—that are central to human existence. Contract pregnancy raises issues that are important not only for children, mothers, and fathers who are directly touched by them, but also for all those concerned with the meaning of new reproductive practices for the common life we shape together through public discourse and law. (1995, 157)

Most importantly, Shanley argues, it is necessary that we examine the labor and the care involved in contract pregnancy. When we focus on these aspects of the pregnancy, the ability of a woman to contract away rights to parent a child becomes questionable.

In her rejection of contract pregnancy as an ethically acceptable practice, Shanley uses Carole Pateman's arguments concerning contracts, marriage, labor, and contract pregnancy. Just as women have been taken advantage of in the marriage contract in order to guarantee that the labor of care is provided with minimal social expense, contract pregnancy asks that a labor of care be provided with minimal acknowledgment of the connection between the use of one's body and one's sense of self. "The forfeiture of self involved in contract pregnancy," Shanley observes, "is an extreme instance of the diminution of the self involved in many labor contracts" (1995, 164). The woman is understood, within contract theory, to be able to make a binding agreement even though she has no way of knowing in advance what kind of relationship she will form as the fetus develops within her body. Her labor of care, even a labor as intimate as pregnancy, is completely alienable from her body. The damage that the conflict between this social ideology that encourages women to see adoption and surrogacy as appropriate actions and the reality that some women confront is apparent in the reflections of a woman considering abortion quoted by Carol Gilligan. Although the woman is talking about her reaction to giving a child up for adoption, her feelings about a prior pregnancy indicate the strength of connection that a woman can build with a fetus, even when she does not intend to mother the child: "Having previously given up one child for adoption, she finds that 'psychologically there was no way that I could hack another adoption. It took me four and a half years to get my head on straight. There was just no way I was going to go through that again'" (1982, 85).[15]

In further considering the potential harm to alliance building that can come from using reproductive technologies in a society constructed around vast inequalities, Janice Raymond points out that surrogacy is likely to be another means by which to exploit poor women, especially women of color. Reflecting on the surrogate birth of a child in her family, Uma Narayan remarks:

> As I turned the family gossip over in my mind I made further connections that fueled my moral unease about gift surrogacy. I knew from conversations with workers at Indian adoption agencies that many Indians, higher-caste Hindus in particular, had reservations about adoption since adoptable children were un-

likely to be of the right caste. I was reminded of arguments here in the United States about how it was the shortage of adoptable *white* infants that made commercial surrogacy attractive to so many couples. (1995, 177–178)

This attractiveness can happen because surrogacy is a means by which white parents can have a white child nurtured in the body of a woman of color. As Raymond notes, the availability of technologies such as egg harvesting allow women to carry children to whom they have no genetic relationship, thus opening up the possibility that black women can carry white children, and allowing white potential parents to bypass the decreased availability of adoptable white children.

Gay men are, of course, more likely than lesbians to use surrogacy to have children. For evidence that this method of having children is desirable in gay communities, one need look no further than *The Advocate* to find an advertisement for a surrogacy program that works with both gay individuals and couples ("Advocate Marketspace" 1998, 69). Although some women agree to surrogacy arrangements for reasons having nothing to do with monetary benefits, the danger of surrogacy being a "means to exploit poor women" cannot be forgotten. Thus, although this possibility is not caused by gay men wishing to have children, the gender, race, and class privilege of some gay men means that unless arguments for surrogacy recognize the need to create social conditions in which women are able to meaningfully choose to enter into contract pregnancy agreements, the inequalities could well be reinforced. Within our current society, this is ethically and politically problematic.

Justifying the Right to Have Children

In the chapter 2, I discussed the impact that lesbians having children can have within lesbian communities. In addition, how the decisions that lesbians make about having children are discussed and justified can create external divisions as well. In justifying their own choices, lesbian mothers often set forth an ethical standard of reproductive decision making not just of lesbian mothers, but of all mothers. Choosing to have a baby, lesbian mothers assert, is a right that women should have. Yet it is not an unqualified right, as Fiona Nelson indicates in her discussion of lesbian mothers in Canada: "Almost every woman I spoke with mentioned that there are right, or acceptable, reasons for having a baby and wrong, or unacceptable, reasons for doing so" (1996, 34). Although she did not find agreement about the particular reasons that are considered to be right or wrong, the mothers generally agreed that right reasons are selfless: one should have a baby "not for one's own sake but for the sake of the baby" (1996, 34). This language suggests that lesbians raising children is particularly positive because lesbians must consciously choose to become pregnant.

The emphasis on rights and choice in this context, as in discussions of marriage, raises questions that I believe we should consider before accepting this formulation: Is it always necessary for people to "choose" to have children in order for them to love those children? [16] Do we wish to establish an ethical standard for giving birth that asserts choosing pregnancy as necessary? If so, under what conditions would the choice be deemed rational? How might this standard of judgment reinforce arguments made by conservatives about childbearing by teens or poor women? How does it fit with attempts to use the law to control the lives of pregnant women (generally poor women of color)? Does it say anything about the obligations of the wider society? What does it mean for a woman to choose to have a baby in a society that views women who choose not to give birth as odd? Do people have significant choices about having children in a society that does not provide either incentives or encouragement for nonparents to play important roles in the lives of children? What would it mean for girls and women to be able to make reproductive choices? [17] As the discussion of lesbian mothering in chapter 2 indicated, one change that would be critical is to challenge the assertion that mothering is necessary in order for women to be proper adults. Yet as we have seen, the understanding of many lesbian mothers reinforces, rather than challenges, this cultural understanding.

These questions are important, not because the choice to have children if one wants them and is prepared for the responsibility lacks value, but because the prerequisites of meaningful choice are absent from our current social circumstances for so many women. To assert "choice" and "unselfishness" as primary criteria for judging both ourselves and others as fit parents is a dangerous practice that can work to reinforce efforts to limit childbearing for poor people and people of color while encouraging reproductive technology developments for those who are deemed to be unselfishly choosing to have children. As Angela Davis notes, it is simply not adequate to see abortion as necessary purely because the social conditions in which a woman lives are so inadequate that she feels she cannot give birth to a child. In a society that truly cared about justice, the recognition of this problem would lead us to ask how social relations need to be changed so that individuals can make meaningful choices (1981, 204–205).

One of the clearest situations in which we can see judgments of self-ishness and inadequate choice being made is in relation to alcohol/drug use and pregnancy. In the name of protecting unborn children, the state has increasingly taken punitive measures against pregnant women, with such actions focused on those who are poor (Bower 1995, Young 1995). Lisa Bower notes that this current construction of dangerous mothers is racist in a way that echoes the past and is necessary for the construction of "good mothering," as well as "bad mothering," in the present:

> In the fetal harm debates, Africanism, understood as stereotypic views of blackness connected to substance-abusing women of color, functions 'meta-physically' to reaffirm white maternal identities that have been seriously eroded. A concern with fetal harm, like contemporary debates about family values, single mothers, and homosexualities, is a reaction to the unsettling of 'natural' categories of sexed, gendered identities. One question animating these diverse debates is how to (re)configure white maternal identities once they have been undermined by technological changes, medical discourses, and ironically, by feminist and legal rhetoric that redefined women's roles in-dependent of mothering. (1995, 147)

The questions that lesbians must face if we are to further a radical democratic understanding of family is how to justify reproductive de-cision making without drawing from and helping to reconfigure moth-erhood as central to the identity of white women and without con-structing poor women as necessarily inadequate if they choose to give birth. Moving outside of the liberal framework of individual rights to a framework that recognizes and challenges the complex interweaving of race, class, and sexuality in discourses of appropriate mothering is an important part of the process of reconceptualization. In fact, such a re-conceptualization is an important guide for developing a narrative of family that avoids the divisive impacts discussed in this chapter.

Toward a New Narrative of Family and Private Life

The danger of arguing for greater freedom in private life is that unless the social inequalities that restrict choice for many are broken down, the available options will remain highly restricted. For those concerned with meaningfully increasing freedom, this poses a critical question: If we wish to enhance freedom in personal life, how can we develop a narrative of family and private life that recognizes and confronts the ways by which social inequalities constrain freedom for many? Lesbians and gays might ask a more narrow version of this question: If we would like to construct an understanding of family that provides grounds for connecting gay/lesbian demands to those of other communities, how can we think about family and private life?

Reconsidering what family does in our society may be one way to begin to answer these questions. As the discussion thus far indicates, a central function of family is providing care for dependents, either through direct laboring in the household or by bringing economic resources into the home, with these two functions divided in gender-specific ways. Those families under public scrutiny, and therefore seen as "deficient," tend to be those where there are either inadequate monetary resources or where a private arrangement violates gender norms. One way of understanding why these two "transgressions" are such a serious threat to society is to consider what the ideology of the gender-divided, privatized family tells us about how the labor of care is provided in our society.

Within liberal perspectives, such as those dominant in the United States, decision making about family is relatively simple. Although one's decisions are private, they are also presumed to be guided by a rule-based ethical and moral system that recognizes marriage and monogamy as central for the lives of mature adults. There may be some room for questioning the norms of marriage or how children are reared, yet there is little room for questioning the construction of marriage as an indication of mature adulthood because this norm rests not on political values open to debate, but rather on the higher plane of religious and ethical beliefs. This seeming contradiction between privacy and the dominance of Christian morality is possible because, as Joan Tronto argues, liberalism rests upon an assumption that values are prior to and separate from politics. This is one of three "moral boundaries" that constrain political discourse in our society, since these "widely accepted social values constitute the context within which we interpret all moral arguments. Some ideas function as boundaries to exclude some ideas from moral consideration" (1993, 6). In addition to the separation between morality and politics, Tronto identifies the requirement that moral judgments be made from a position of disinterest and distance and the separation of public and private life as the moral boundaries defining political discussion in our society. She argues that these boundaries need to be redrawn, though not completely broken down, to bring women's voices more centrally into moral thought and to enhance freedom and democracy in both public and private life. As a result of moral boundaries, there are within dominant discourses few grounds for questioning the dominant moral rules.

The boundaries that Tronto identifies rest in significant ways on the family ideology that some gays and lesbians seek to embrace by gaining entrance into marriage and family. By assuming that individuals are equal moral decision makers and denying the interrelationship between political and social context, and political and moral judgment and agency, the liberal political order has been able to ignore that individuals are not equal moral decision makers because status remains critical, even if it has shifted from being legally inscribed to being socially enforced. Critically, both forms of socially constructed and enforced inequality have significant impacts on the labor that individuals perform. Thus, the ability to compete as free and equal citizens was, and is, precluded. Of equal importance is that this restriction was integral to the creation and maintenance of labor market segregation that confers radically different wages and benefits to different groups of workers. Outside of the agricultural labor market, the labor of people of color, as Tronto discusses, is primarily channeled into providing direct services, that is, into jobs of providing "care." It is not surprising that in addition to women (whose care work in families is seen as natural), those who most often provide care directly in the "private" sphere of the family are illegal immigrants—or people who have no rights. Again, as white, middle-class women gain more equal status, the labor of care assigned to them in the sexual family is transferred to others, most often women, who lack equal status. Both care and people defined not as free individuals, but as people with lower status, are devalued within the dominant ideology and institutional structures.

If we saw the responsibility of providing care not as a family responsibility or as a responsibility that should be executed in the private world by those who lack power, but as a social concern, we would have to evaluate individuals and society in new ways. Tronto suggests that in a society where care was a more public concern—that is, a society with different moral boundaries—the central moral question that we would ask of ourselves and others would be different. Instead of asking if I am (or we are) living in accord with the moral precepts of my (our) society (or even in accord with universal moral precepts), we would need to ask, How do I (we) best meet my (our) caring responsibilities? How we evaluate our caring requires that we consider not just how we think we are acting, but also how others for whom we are caring receive our action. Thus, responsiveness is a central component of the practice of caring. "Responsiveness," Tronto tells us, "suggests a different way to understand the needs of others rather than to put ourselves into their position. Instead, it suggests that we consider the other's position as that other expresses it" (1993, 136). To make the question that Tronto poses central to our individual and social moral thinking requires a major shift in how we think about and debate political issues. In fact, a politics of private life that began with this question would look very different from current political debates. In the next chapter, I will argue that this perspective on care has much to offer as we consider how gay and lesbian adults can more positively influence the lives of children. Yet we can also see that such a perspective offers assistance in confronting some of the problems discussed in this chapter.

Analyzing the social response to fetal harm, Iris Marion Young reveals the contrast between social policy based on care and social policy that grows out of a liberal, individualistic understanding of choice. Because policy is formulated in accord with the latter perspective, even when "help" (rather than simply punishment) is offered, it is biased:[18] "The problem with the confessional talk typical of drug therapy, as well as most other therapies, is that it tends to be depoliticizing and individualizing. It enlists the patient's own complicity in her adjustment to existing institutions and relations of privilege and oppression by encouraging her to construct her self, or her family, as the source of her pain and problem. This self-reflective exercise diverts her from locating her life in the context of wider social institutions and relations of solidarity and resistance" (1995, 121). It also diverts the focus of others to either engaging in or resisting a politics of individual blame and responsibility, rather than asking how social circumstances and institutions need to be changed to decrease drug addiction, including the drug or alcohol addiction of pregnant women and how programs that focus on treating pregnant substance abusers could construct treatment in ways that are empowering.[19]

Young clearly recognizes that adopting a genuinely caring approach requires political discussion and debate because it requires that those who receive care have a significant voice in the process (1995, 125–126).

This kind of politics is, however, very different from that which is restricting the rights and freedom of lesbians, gay men, people of color, and women. It is different because a foundational assumption is that people are capable of making decisions about their own lives but that in order to define and enact these decisions, they require social support. Thus, within a framework defined by care, rights are important, but it is equally important that an individual actually be able to exercise those rights. This perspective differs from that with which we live currently in powerful ways. Workfare policies are one element in the development of what, following Rosalind Petchesky, we might call a privatized state. Petchesky talks about the formation of this kind of state as she attempts to understand contradictory policies of the 1980s that simultaneously reduced social welfare spending while, through the passage of the Hyde Amendment, restricting federal financing for abortion. The Supreme Court, in upholding the Hyde Amendment, made it clear that having a "right" did not mean that the state had any obligation to provide the means necessary to actually make use of the right. These policies, Petchesky argued, were part of a larger political attempt to restrict rights in ways that reprivatize much decision making, but this privatization does not free individuals. "It is corporate privatism—in the service of business, church, private school, and patriarchal family—that is intended, not individual privacy. Moreover, it is put forward in the name of a particular class—white middle-class Christians—whose relationship to 'private' institutions is one of ownership" (1990, 248). This is a privatism that appeals to conservative communitarian ideas of tradition and community. In this community, political debate is less important than moral purity, because conservative communitarians see social problems as easily dealt with if individuals control their desires. Thus, individuals may technically have rights, but they lack agency.

One way of highlighting the contrast is to consider how a social issue such as AIDS could best be confronted. In the corporate privatist perspective, AIDS would be seen as an indication of the impossibility of enhancing individual freedom without the restraining influence of the church and the family. Thus, AIDS would be fought through campaigns suggesting to individuals that they should say "no" to sex and drugs. A care perspective would encourage us to formulate different responses based more on empathic engagement, leading us to understand that there are many factors influencing people's agency and behavior. The importance of empathy for care is understood by Diana Tietjens Meyers, who argues that although individuals need to construct moral ideals for themselves, these ideals change as we come into contact with others who have different moral ideals. The presence of cultural pluralism, she notes, helps each individual to develop his/her moral ideal by "encourag[ing] people to examine and reexamine their values" (1994, 129). Moral decision making and political decision making, then, create a complex process of critical reflection, action, and interaction with others. It is a process that encourages us to bring the multiple components of our identities into discussion with one another, just as we enter into discussion with others. Once we begin to engage in this process, simple precepts can no longer appear as adequate solutions to complex social problems. Instead, in relation to an issue such as AIDS, we are forced to ask how people can more safely engage in practices critical to their sense of self, even while we ask how we can better provide services for those who wish to change behaviors or those who simply need care.

Tronto notes that we can see care being provided to people living with AIDS in multiple ways—through paying taxes, giving money to service organizations, providing direct and personal care—with some of these ways being less bureaucratic and more direct, and requiring greater degrees of responsiveness and empathic engagement. The provision of care is fullest, however, when these different aspects of caring for people living with AIDS are most integrated. Thus, the ethic of care can be useful in helping us to judge the extent to which the provision of services is adequate, given the needs that those who require services express. "Because care forces us to think concretely about people's real needs, and about how these needs will be met," Tronto notes, "it introduces questions about what we value into everyday life" (1993, 124). AIDS has demanded that gays and lesbians face such questions, with this questioning sometimes leading to internal conflict, while at other times leading to anger over the construction of AIDS within the dominant culture. Such anger has been a powerful force in political organizing designed to contest the definition of needs set forth by the dominant scientific and service discourses, while also attempting to assert new definitions and obtain the resources necessary to meet these newly-defined needs. Weeks observes that the attempt to bring these different goals together can result in new models for social policy whereby professionalized groups and governmental agencies can work with communities to serve individuals (1991, 129).

The critical question facing groups harmed by the dominant ideological assertion—that only a certain form of family is capable of meeting needs for care and producing individuals capable of moral behavior within a democratic society—is whether they can construct a counternarrative of family and private life with the potential to combat the narratives of "good mother," "good father," and "good citizen" to which conservatives appeal. The goal of articulating a new narrative means that each of the separate groups currently harmed needs to move away from trying to gain resources and power by proving that they can enact current norms. It also requires that these groups move beyond fixed understandings of identity and group, recognizing instead that the identity groups organizing today are historical constructions. Although these groups may sometimes need to appeal to a common identity, this identity itself only exists through exclusion, generally of those who are least able or willing to conform to the dominant constructions of society that in other ways oppress the group as a whole. Thus, gay/lesbian communities can define those who are not monogamous, or who do not have children, as outside of the mainstream gay community, but in doing this, the same norms that oppress all gay people are reinforced. This is a cycle that can only be broken by rejecting the central terms. One of these central or core terms is that the sexual family is a superior social organization for forming adult relationships and raising children. In concluding my argument, I want to focus on a question that brings very clearly to the surface the contradiction inherent in seeking social recognition and resources by reinforcing dominant constructions: How can adult gays and lesbians best support the opportunities and choices of those young people who would like to construct a sense of self-identity in opposition to the dominant heterosexual discourse? That is, What does considering how we can best provide care for gay youth tell us about family politics?

5

Who Are "Our" Children?

Asking the question "Who are our children?" can reveal a number of difficult issues that lesbian and gay communities must face in defining a politics of private life able to create the space necessary for enhanced agency and judgment. The "families" that lesbians and gays have created to supplement or replace the families into which we were born have often been rather odd families in that they tend to not be multigenerational. In particular, they are unlikely to include young people who are contesting sexuality and gender norms or elderly people who contest these norms. The consequences of each exclusion are negative, both because we are unable to provide support during what are often difficult times of life, and because we have few opportunities to learn from either the young or the old. In this chapter, I want to focus on the consequences of excluding young people from our communities. This dynamic places gays and lesbians in a unique position: We do not socialize those who will become part of our communities, if we understand the gay and lesbian communities to be centrally defined by sexual identity. In fact, this work is done by people and institutions often openly hostile to homosexual people and communities. At the same time, if we believe the data being collected by psychologists and lawyers, lesbians and gays are no more likely to raise gay children than are heterosexuals. Thus, we face another rather odd reality: Children in our families may not be part of what we define as a central community (and often an alternative family) in our adult lives.

These two "oddities" point to the necessity of rejecting the identification of gay and lesbian identity as equivalent to, or even similar to,
ethnic identities. In fact, if we consider intergenerational relations, the
necessity of queer politics framed within the radical democratic model
that I discussed in chapter 3 becomes more compelling. Central to such
a political agenda must be increased freedom for youth, freedom that
would help all children and adolescents to develop the skills and perspectives necessary to exercise agency, particularly sexual agency, and
judgment within a democratic society. If we begin to understand freedom for young people as more central to our political agendas, two
points become clear: (1) that we need to reconsider the economic relationships embedded in the privatized nuclear family and (2) that a
model of family that understands children as belonging to their parents
is inadequate for a society that seeks to enhance freedom and agency in
private life and in public life. As Kevin Jennings notes, "'If anybody's
going to fight for those kids, it has to be [gays and lesbians]. We've got
to act like gay kids are our children, because they really are'" (qtd. in
Moss 1997, 33). The model of private life and family that we need to set
forth must understand that enhanced freedom requires breaking down
moral boundaries. That is, we must challenge three ideas: that children
are best nurtured in the privacy of the family, that moral questions (such
as in what ways youth can and should be sexual) can be divorced from
politics, and that the most appropriate place from which to address
questions of youth and sexuality are from a disinterested (that is, adult
authority) voice.

In general, gays and lesbians stand in a unique location from which
to view family and from which to define a politics of family and private
life. This vantage point is one from which the privatized family, although sometimes appearing to be a positive retreat from a hostile
public world, often appears to be a place that is destructive to intergenerational relationships because the private world of the family denies us
connection to the next generations of youth who will resist the dominant construction of sexuality by defining themselves as gays, lesbians,
bisexuals, or queers. If we put the position of gay youth at the center of
the political project of gay and lesbian communities, we are able to reconsider political perspectives that enhance the importance of a private
world dominated by sexual families. Further, if we understand the difficulties that all adolescents face in constructing a sense of self, we are
better able to understand how reinforcing the power of parents over

children makes difficult the creation of a youth culture more hospitable to those who challenge norms of gender and sexuality.

Intergenerational Interdependence

In order to consider the role that children and youth play currently in gay and lesbian communities and might play in the future, it is useful to consider the role of children in the larger society. In agriculturally-based communities, having children was obviously a necessity: children were economic assets in that they provided labor critical to the survival of families; as adults, they provided for their parents in old age. As production has changed, so too has the role of children within society, and the roles of parents in relation to their children. The current construction of childhood contains remnants of changes that occurred as industrialization transformed social views of children from people able to engage in productive labor from an early age to people in need of education in order to become good citizens and good workers. Ideally, these dependents—despite their increasing cost to their parents—would be financially supported by their parents and would therefore be responsible to them. As the role of children changed with industrialization, so too did the number of children parented by "normal" families. Significant declines in fertility occurred as children became economic burdens rather than economic assets. By the 1860s, mothers had also become more likely than fathers to be deemed legally responsible by courts for their now costly children.

This construction of youth differed from constructions of the past and resulted in the formation of schools—or of a social institution focused specifically on socializing children and youth in the public realm—and a separate justice system. Although each of these two seemingly different systems provides some benefits to youth, they are also similar systems in that each socializes children into bourgeois values while curbing their antisocial tendencies, in the process producing "docile bodies" (Foucault 1995, 135–170). Producing properly masculine boys is a challenge that schools confront due to the overwhelming presence of women as teachers in the school system. This challenge is dealt with not only in the home, but also in institutions located in the public world, such as organized athletics and organizations such as the Boy Scouts. Despite the time that children spend outside of the family and the importance of this time for their socialization, parents retain the legal responsibility of guaranteeing that their children behave in pro-social ways. Thus, they also maintain the legal right to control their children's lives.

Although intergenerational interdependence was obvious in the past, it is now more hidden because social policy addresses many relatively age-specific needs that previously would have been met in the private realm of family. In significant ways, what these changes have done is to create a new level of interdependence that involves children and youth and the entire society in which they live. Thus, in old age we are now reliant not simply on our own children (though for many elderly Americans these children are the difference between comfort and poverty), but on all adults who pay taxes. Therefore, all members of society—not just parents—have an incentive to invest in the young, and for a society to not invest its resources in its youth is terribly short-sighted. Using the language of economists, Nancy Folbre observes that "children, like the environment, are a public good. The individual decisions that parents make about child rearing, and the level of resources that they can devote to this work, have economic consequences for everyone" (1994, 254). The increased ability of adults to survive economically without giving birth to or raising their own children is, of course, part of what allows for the development of gay identities, and for the importance of marriage and child rearing to decline for some people.[1]

Of course there are also other levels of interest in children, levels that develop as communities have become more heterogeneous, and as parents and state institutions have attempted either to infuse or strip away the ethnic and racial identities of children. This ethnic concern for the socialization of children is discussed by Charles Taylor (1985), who argues that ethnic minorities have a right to raise their children in such a way as to continue their cultural heritage, even as this heritage is subject to critique and transformation as it interacts with other cultures. This perspective is, however, one that is clearly contested within contemporary liberal democratic societies. Preserving multiple systems of values, some of which may be at odds with those of the dominant culture, may simply guarantee that we will never be able to avoid ethnic and racial conflict (Schlesinger 1992). This was certainly the perspective built into creating educational systems, systems particularly important for teaching the children of immigrants what it meant to be "American."

There are, then, multiple voices—often in conflict—speaking to how children should be socialized. Particularly within the political system, there is some recognition that these multiple voices exist and that they do not always have the same interest. Thus, a number of different actors have come to be seen as legitimate within the political system: parents, political and community leaders who are understood to represent parents, and the state bureaucracy. Three points are important for gay politics: (1) that those in the state bureaucracy have largely defined "American" values as including monogamous heterosexuality, (2) that youths themselves have virtually no voice, and (3) that those who are not parents—unless they happen to be part of the state bureaucracy— have almost no voice.[2] This lack of voice among nonparents exists despite our current financial contributions to children and families and the critical role that they will play in supporting us in old age, and thus the interest that we have in them as an "investment."

For gays and lesbians, then, the incentive to have children may be more complex than the representations that we saw in chapter 2 suggest. Having children provides greater security in old age, while also helping to legitimize one's voice in the politics of schooling and socializing the young. Importantly, because of fears surrounding lesbians and gays as recruiters of the young, having children is the only way for gays and lesbians to interact with youth without fear of being perceived as "dangerous," a construction that reinforces parental power while denying agency to both adults (including teachers) and youth. Gays and lesbians can respond to this construction either by arguing that we are not a threat to children since homosexuality is biological, or by questioning the continued definition of children as parental property, recognizing instead that our interdependence necessitates public debate about how children should be educated, and that democratic citizenship requires children and youth to be provided with the opportunities necessary to exercise agency and judgment, including sexual agency. If we choose the latter, we must be prepared to contest and confront arguments that our involvement is motivated solely by sexual interest.

The latter position is critical because unless we defend the right of children and youth to interact with those whom they choose, we are in danger of leaving youth who do not conform to normative sexual identity and/or normative gender identity to fend for themselves, existing in social institutions hostile to their existence until they are old enough to choose to act on their "natural" sexual desires or gender identities. The consequences of not creating conditions that allow for greater freedom are significant, not only because of high rates of teen suicide among those questioning sexual identity/gender identity,[3] but also because, as Patricia Warren discusses, many gay/lesbian youth who leave their families in order to act on their sexual desires face serious economic consequences. Describing youth with whom she is familiar as a result of her position as a commissioner of education, Warren writes:

> I have learned that students often pay a big price for being out: loss of financial support and financing for school. Some get thrown out and end up on the street. Others simply leave home, courageously holding down two or three little jobs while they continue their studies. And while for the present they shoulder a crushing economic load, the future doesn't look any brighter. With the skyrocketing cost of higher education—typically over $100,000 for an undergraduate degree—I am seeing promising students either opt for community college because it's all they can afford or recklessly encumbering themselves with big college loans. (1997, 5)

These are youth in whom we are not investing because they have chosen to act counter to familial and societal expectations.

Rethinking Youth and Agency

Although we have already discussed the negative impact on gay and lesbian politics of essentialist models of gay identity, it is important to understand how this interpretation of identity can affect interactions with youth and how youth construct their own sexual identities. In criticizing perspectives on gay identity that understand "gay" as having a fixed meaning, Gary Lehring observes: "We have created gay teen groups to assist questioning teens in the 'discovery' of their authentic sexuality. Adults, through therapy and self-exploration, reinterpret events in their life within the framework of this powerful new truth. . . . Choice has been removed from this debate" (1997, 191).

Despite the support that many youth receive from gay and lesbian agencies such as Horizons, a Chicago community organization, Herdt and Boxer's (1993) discussion of this agency also suggests some of the ways by which constructing sexual desire as a choice is removed from conversation. In fact, Herdt and Boxer suggest that constructing sexuality as a nonchoice is important for the ritualistic act of coming out. For example, they discuss the confusion that an adviser for the group feels when he realizes that a friend with whom he had "come out" now understands his sexual desires to be heterosexual. Despite his confusion over this change, and the implicit possibility that perhaps sexual identity is not fixed and predictable, the adviser does not see his story as appropriate for sharing with the youth group. Why, Herdt and Boxer ask, did he choose not to share this story with the group? One possibility, they note, is that advisers see using the group to help sort out their own feelings as inappropriate. But they also offer another possibility: "to intrude such a story—which suggests that someone can 'come out' as gay but later 'come out' as heterosexual, a sort of contemporary Tiresias—might undermine the tenuous confidence that the youth have in their own feelings" (1993, 119). In a society where so much undermines the confidence of these youth, the advisers feel a need to help the youth feel secure with their gayness. Yet this means that those youth who do not feel sure about whether or not they are gay, or who already identify as bisexual, may well be alienated from this "safe" space as well as from others places.

The reality of this alienation is apparent in Herdt and Boxer's discussion of a young man nicknamed "Straight Sam" by members of the youth group. This nickname was intended "in part to poke fun at him, and in part to mock his frequent assertion 'I'm straight'" (1993, 197). Yet Sam came to the group because he liked homosocial environments and because he was the target of antigay comments at his school. He was, however, a youth who obviously did not fit well with the construction of sexuality dominant in the youth group, and for whom a group trying to consolidate a secure and unquestioning understanding of identity had neither time nor patience. Youth who identify themselves as bisexual also do not fit with the accepted construction of sexual identity in the Horizons group, particularly that accepted and furthered by the advisers. This may be one reason that among the youth who come to Horizons few are bisexual, and that even those who identify as bisexual when they come initially come to identify themselves as having a lesbian or gay identity (Herdt and Boxer 1993, 132). For those who leave the group or for those who stay, choice and agency now have a much more restricted meaning than they might have if bisexual identity, or sexual identity as nonfixed, guided the perspective of the adults in the group.

Finally, it is important to note that the social construction of gay and lesbian identity as fixed, and as gays and lesbians as otherwise normal people, also has the potential consequence of dividing gay and lesbian youth from transsexual and transgendered youth. Herdt and Boxer note that one significant change in Chicago's gay culture and institutions is the decrease in drag shows and transvestites as "the gender roles of gay men and lesbians seem to be feeding into mainstream culture today" (1993, 234). This is also reflected in the opinions of the youth, some of whom felt that transsexuals should not be allowed in the Gay Pride parade. In this context, we might remember Eve Kofosky Sedgewick's (1993) assertion that unless we are able to create a culture that values effeminate boys, we will not be able to create a culture that positively values gay people. Nor will we be able to create a culture that values those whose visibility in transgressing gender and sexuality norms was central for making public gay identity possible (Kennedy and Davis 1993 , Feinberg 1993).

The belief that youth need to establish a clear and stable identity is not unique to gay/lesbian culture, yet critiquing this belief may have more obvious benefits in relation to youth questioning sexual identity than for many others. Creating institutions able to foster a more complex understanding of sexual identities depends upon fostering a society that is more able to see human identity as more complex than we do currently, and that is also able to see youth as people who, although confronted by multiple and often conflicting demands, can and must exercise agency. The formulation of sexuality and youth that I am advocating requires that the broader society replace our understanding of childhood and adolescence with a new understanding, one that recognizes the agency of youth not solely as a source of concern, but also as a source of strength and democratic initiative. If we understood youth in this way, we would be less inclined to see the building of significant relationships between young people and adults who are not family members as threatening. This seeming threat reinforces the power of parents by denying to children the possibility of alternative role models.[4]

As James Cote and Anton Allahar point out, because people need more and more credentials in order to get meaningful jobs that pay a livable wage, the time period in which young people are dependent has grown. In part, this has produced a large consumer group—in the United States, youths as consumers are worth about $2 billion a year (Cote and Allahar 1994, 119). It also leads human beings to spend a significant portion of their lives deeply embedded within systems of control, with few ways to play meaningful roles in society. Donna Gaines expresses well the frustration that many youth feel: "In reality, it was adult organization of young people's reality over the last several hundred years that *created* this miserable situation: one's youth as wasted years. Being wasted and getting wasted. Adults often wasted kids' time with meaningless activities, warehousing them in schools; kids in turn wasted their own time on drugs. Just to have something to do" (1991, 86). Cote and Allahar see the dissent caused by such control and meaninglessness as leading to crime and violence. Interestingly, adults have not yet responded by trying to rethink youth, or trying to build meaningful intergenerational relationships; instead, we have responded by passing laws that are increasingly punitive. Thus many adolescents (generally male) who break the law in violent ways are tried as adults, while adolescent females who are pregnant can be forced to either get a parent's permission to have an abortion or to live with their parents to receive welfare benefits. A socially constructed period of youth that, as Cote and Allahar point out, may have fit better with industrial societies[5] is coming into increasing contradiction with the lived reality of youth, yet social discourse still suggests that families can make adolescence work, with coercive support from the state.

Another increasingly clear contradiction is that which exists between the emphasis placed on parental rights and responsibility for their children's actions and the extraordinary influence that the public world plays in the lives of children and youth, an influence that will only grow because of technological innovation. Interestingly, this public influence will be difficult for adults to control because most youth have a greater proficiency for using computer and other communication technologies than their parents. A recent television advertisement indicates the ways by which technology allows youth to circumvent parental power: although the parents of a young dating couple do not permit them to see one another after an appointed hour, the parents are oblivious to the couple's computer communication. Technology may also provide a means for young gays and lesbians to engage in safe and affirming communication. Mark Poster recognizes the changes in family dynamics that occur as public life becomes more central for children and youth: "The diffusion of authority over the child to a multiplicity of rule-making social agents constitutes a situation in which the child confronts conflicting values, styles, and role models. This situation is very different from the situation of the child in the Oedipal family" (1989, 160). It is different largely because the Oedipal family provided for the internalization of a single person as the child formed a sense of self. Thus, s/he did not have to contend with multiplicity.

One response to the potential freedom offered to youth by technology is to attempt (largely unsuccessfully) to regulate it in order to restore the power of the father; an alternative response is to recognize that parental control is undesirable and impossible, and to foster in youth the ability to make judgments and exercise agency. Such skills would make them better, though perhaps less complacent, democratic citizens. Understanding these alternatives is particularly important at this moment in history because changing technologies and social conditions make it unlikely that change can be prevented for much longer. Seeing the impact of technology on the lives of young people, Poster writes:

> Middle-class families in Orange County are at a crossroads. Surrounded by an emerging new social formation, the mode of information, families have rejected the classical nuclear-family pattern. They are testing new family structures, some of which reject to a considerable degree earlier forms of domination in the family. One senses a tremendous burden on these micro-units of society and, accordingly, a deep contradiction in the emerging social formation. These Orange County families have great ambitions: they want to remove restrictions on women's life choices; they want to achieve emotional and sexual gratification; they want to develop in their children an ability for self-directed personal growth; they want to enjoy the sophisticated technologies available to them. These goals suggest a type of integration between the family and the community unique to the mode of information, one that places new demands on the social formation: families now want high-quality, plentiful day care, even in workplaces; richer community life; extensive sharing of information; and activities made possible by the new technologies. Yet the social formation resists the changes implied in these demands. The modern family thus constitutes itself as a segmented unit, adapting its goals to a recalcitrant environment and bearing what must be the stress of experimentation without social support. (1989, 168–169)

Although the "recalcitrant environment" can react to these changes by trying to impose control, a better strategy, particularly for a democratic society, would be to encourage the development of agency and judgment in youth, thus freeing them to explore multiple worlds. Such a reconceptualization of education and youth would have benefits for the many kids trying to better understand sexuality in their lives, but it would also have benefits that are far larger.

Opening up the public world is antithetical to family privacy in ways that may often be positive for gays and lesbians in many instances, but not in all situations. Gays and lesbians who are parents are in what might seem to be a contradictory situation. Their best means of protecting their own right to parent is to argue that they have a right to socialize their children as they see fit. At the same time, challenging parental rights may be necessary to protect gay and lesbian youth. This apparent contradiction fades, however, if we understand that all youth would benefit from a society that understands them as better able to exercise agency and that provides the support necessary for doing so.

Challenges of Nurturing Youth with Complex Identities

To authors such as Blankenhorn, the heterosexual nuclear family is necessary because it promotes the development of a particular kind of individual that many theorists see as necessary for social survival. This theoretical framework—which grew out of Freudian theory but which Lasch, Moynihan, and Blankenhorn, among others, have further developed—identifies secure and appropriate gender identity as fundamental to psychological and moral development, and therefore to the creation of an orderly society. Within the psychological development and moral development literatures, the impact of class, race/ethnicity, and sexuality on the lives of children and adolescents is rarely discussed. Because dynamics of identity other than gender are ignored, the complexity of identity and identity development is not discussed. Instead, it is asserted that proper family structure combined with "good enough" parenting can lead parents to produce children with a clear and coherent sense of identity and morality. The denial of the complexity of identity in this work is dangerous even for those who are white, middle class, and heterosexual because it denies the extent to which identity conflicts are inevitable in a rapidly-changing multicultural society. Such denial means that as a society, we do not consider how children and youth can best be helped to recognize and face the conflicts that they will experience as they try to develop a sense of identity in a world where race, ethnicity, class, and sexuality—in addition to gender—sometimes create conflicting demands, and where they will be called upon to make judgments that either reinforce privilege or challenge it. Instead, as the work of Horkheimer (1972 [1936]; see also Benjamin 1978) pointed out so well nearly forty years ago, privileged youth learn that by adapting to the standards and norms of their parents, including gender norms, they will receive some degree of privilege within society.

Psychologists often justify the focus on gender development in their work by pointing to the fact that children begin to differentiate and identify their gender at a very young age, about two years old. Since humans consolidate their gender identity so early, psychologists understand this identity as central to the understanding of self. While this may be an important insight, and while research on gender identity may well be important, this focus ignores the reality that children also learn racial identity, which psychologists study much less frequently, at a very young age. "Recent studies of preschoolers," Tracy Robinson and Janie Victoria Ward tell us, "demonstrate that by age three and four, children of different races are keenly aware that, in this society, white skin color is valued and preferred" (1991, 90). This knowledge of the importance of racial identity is not new, even if it has not been central to theories of development. In fact, this understanding led to the arguments underpinning desegregation. In his discussion of children's reactions to desegregation, Robert Coles discussed the significance of awareness of race for white children:

> The segregated social system comes to bear upon children, as well as adults, so that long before a white child goes to school he has learned that good and bad can find very real and convenient expression in black and white skin. Negro children are described as bad, ill-mannered, naughty, disobedient, dirty, careless, in sum, everything that the white child struggles so hard not to be. Moreover the child's sense of his own weakness, loneliness—or angry defiance—are also likely to be charged up to the Negro. (1967, 68)

The result is that the unitary self of middle-class white children can develop through splitting.[6] Obviously the same stereotypes and cultural images pose developmental challenges for children of color as well. These challenges, and how children confront them, are rarely the subject of social discourse.

In her discussion of elementary schools, Linda Grant highlights the ways that teachers reinforce a racialized sexism in their treatment of black girls. Black girls, her research suggests, rarely enter classrooms with teachers who assume that they will be academic achievers. Instead, they enter into classrooms with teachers inclined to see them as nonacademic helpers. "Black girls," Grant writes, "arrive at schools primed for service roles. The school environment reinforces this disposition" (1994, 51). It is also clear that peers learn and reinforce these expectations. Her observations indicate that white children, particularly boys, perceive intelligent black girls as a threat and respond by drawing upon already available racism to reassert a sense of superiority when their initial assumption of their superiority is threatened: "Five of the six [racist remarks] came in nearly identical circumstances. After a teacher had complemented a black girl for her work, a white boy of lesser achievement made a racist remark" (Grant 1994, 59).

Autobiographical writing, poetry, and literature provide discussions of the challenges—for both parents and children—of living in racist and classist society. For example, Audre Lorde's *Zami: A New Spelling of My Name* (1983) poignantly portrays the strategies employed by her parents in order to "shield" her from racism, strategies that often felt more persecutory than protective to Lorde as a child. *Zami* is indicative of the multiple, contradictory understandings of self that Lorde developed as a result of social forces and their interaction with family dynamics. Living in a multicultural society that asserts the primacy of one culture influences the family dynamics and conflicts within many families. Many children of color grow up simultaneously in at least two cultures and, therefore, are exposed constantly to two distinct understandings of gender, sexuality, and ethnic or religious values. The development of a self requires not that one of these cultures be accepted and internalized and the other rejected; it requires that the two be in dialogue with one another, with the encounter leading to questioning both and valuing both, even while forming a new understanding.

Interactions with the state pose significant challenges for both poor children of color and poor white children. One argument made by many who advocate replacing current systems of welfare with a guaranteed income is that the current system is demeaning, both in the fact that it *is* a public system and in the way that social services administers benefits. It is impossible to imagine that this demeaning factor does not have a devastating impact on the self-image of a child, no matter how hard her/his parent(s) may work to build a positive sense of self. Further, the ability to maintain a positive enough feeling about oneself to encourage the development of similar feelings in a child in spite of the regular onslaught of negative judgments by others seems almost impossible. Theresa Funiciello's critique of the welfare system in *Tyranny of Kindness* makes it clear that the system needs changing because it is an inhumane, shame-producing system—one that does not even provide adequate material resources. For example, she cites a policy requiring mothers of school-age children to go to the school to get written verification of their children's school attendance in order to be eligible for continued benefits. In evaluating this policy, Funiciello points out how the system can harm children: "The letters did not actually prove much of anything. They did cause untold humiliation of the welfare children, especially the older ones, because the other kids at school knew perfectly well what the periodic lineup of mothers meant. This increased truancy. The very next day the welfare kids were too ashamed to go back to school, as all had once again been reminded that they were on welfare" (1993, 56).

If social scientists focused less attention on the development of appropriate gender identity in white, middle-class youth, we might see how encounters such as that described by Funiciello affect youth negatively, as well as how youth have greater capabilities for negotiating identity and agency than we generally believe them to have. Identity, in this formulation, is derived from a complex interplay of contradictory, sometimes ambiguous messages coming at individuals from the private world of family and the public world. If we better understood this interplay, rather than blaming families for the failure to properly socialize their children, it would be necessary to understand the antisocial behavior of youth as a problem that requires not simply punishment, but social critique. For example, we might see gang-violence and other forms of "protest masculinity" not as the result of the impact on the psyches of young men of their parents' divorce or failure to marry, but as a collective practice that can only be changed by collective response. R. W. Connell describes the difference between his understanding of masculinity and Alfred Adler's more commonly accepted understanding of protest masculinity:

> Adler's concept [masculine protest] defined a pattern of motives arising from the childhood experience of powerlessness, and resulting in an exaggerated claim to the potency European culture attaches to masculinity. Among these young men too there is a response to powerlessness, a claim to the gendered position of power, a pressured exaggeration (bashing gays, wild riding) of masculine conventions. The difference is that this is a collective practice, not something inside the person. Very similar patterns appear in the collective practice of working-class, especially ethnic minority, street gangs in the United States. There seems to be no standard pattern developmental path into it, apart from the level of tension created by poverty and an ambiance of violence. (1995, 111)

Although Blankenhorn groups criminal behavior, violence against women, and the tendency to abandon one's own children as common characteristics of young men who have been raised without fathers, Connell points out that those who exercise protest masculinity in groups may well see and interact with women as equals, care for children, and perform other activities associated with femininity. The masculine identities of these young men are complex, contradictory, and changeable over time. But without political direction, the possibility of resolving the complexities of egalitarianism and misogyny in ways that are not antisocial is slight (1996, 172). It is important to note that resolving these contradictory attitudes and actions does not mean that the young men would come to a settled, positive understanding of the meaning of masculinity. In a society with multiple masculinities interacting with many other social identities, such closure is not possible. What is possible, however, is to bring these contradictions more to the surface and into dialogue, thus enabling the individual to act as an agent.

The identities of more privileged men are no less complex, although the dynamics may be less obvious. Connell's exploration of masculinity suggests that young men construct themselves in accord with hegemonic masculinity through resolving competing understandings of desire, acceptability, and opportunity. Without institutional structures through which to support developing more complex masculine identities, many young men will gain entrance to hegemonic masculinity by learning to repress and deny parts of themselves that they come to understand as incompatible with hegemonic masculinity, including homosexual desire. As Peggy Reeves Sanday (1990) has discussed, fraternities are a location where privileged young men take some parts of the self out of dialogue with the rest of the self in order to form a sense of self that is secure and superior at a vulnerable time in their lives. One of the parts of self taken out of dialogue in most fraternities is that which desires sexual contact with other men, though fraternity rituals may well have elements of repressed homosexual desire.

Gilligan's (1991) discussion of girls, and the loss of voice that develops in adolescence, indicates that this is a time period in which young people who wish to feel secure lose, or at least suppress, inner discourse. Institutional structures such as schools do little to maintain such discourse and often construct knowledge in ways which demand that students lose the ability to recognize complexity in order to succeed. In a world of ambiguity, multiplicity, and conflict, it is perhaps not surprising that adolescents and young adults who are not encouraged to enter into dialogue with their multiple and complex selves often choose self-destruction—whether through suicide, eating disorders, or dropping out of school—or attempt to destroy those socially constructed as a threat to the dominant order. Perhaps most seriously, there is little evidence that the primary social institutions with which children interact and into which children enter encourage the development of such dialogue. This should not surprise us since, in addition to acting with greater agency oneself, the awareness of contradictory discourses can lead to demands for social changes that enable individuals to have the freedom to enact their agency.

Schooling and Agency

There is significant evidence that young adults are capable of making complex and difficult decisions with intelligence. However, as with all of us, this is most likely to occur if they have others with whom to engage in reflection and discussion. Although sometimes parents might be ideal for this role, at other times they are too involved in their children's lives to be objective. This is why, Collins argues, othermothers are so important in black communities—communities where mother-child relationships have a particularly great intensity because mothers have to provide for and nurture children within oppressive systems (1990, 127–128). She quotes Renita Weems's writing about her relationship to both her mother and to othermothers: "In recounting how she dealt with intensity of her relationship to her mother, Weems describes the women teachers, neighbors, friends, and othermothers she turned to—women who, she observes, 'did not have the onus of providing for me, and so had the luxury of talking to me'" (1990, 128). Unfortunately, the social segregation of youth means that many young people do not have a person or people with whom they can engage in such conversation and reflection. They are, therefore, left to speak with peers who are often rivals, with each person trying to survive in a social system that encourages conformity and teaches few skills that encourage individual, critical thinking. Perhaps this is true nowhere more than in relation to sexual decision making.

By law, schools that wish to receive federal funds under legislation such as the 1996 Federal Welfare Reform Reconciliation Act (H.R. 3734) are constrained to provide sex education that focuses solely on abstinence. This bill defines abstinence education in ways that very clearly indicate its intent to provide a moral education designed to foster the continuance of the sexual family. As defined in the four of the bill's provisions, abstinence education "(D) teaches that a mutually faithful monogamous relationship in context of marriage is the expected standard of human sexual activity; (E) teaches that sexual activity outside of the context of marriage is likely to have harmful psychological and physical effects; (F) teaches that bearing children out-of-wedlock is likely to have harmful consequences for the child, the child's parents, and society;" and "(H) teaches the importance of attaining self-sufficiency before engaging in sexual activity" (1996, H.R. 3734, sec. 2301). It is not clear that these are the standards that would be chosen even by most parents. The assumption of those legislators who pass such limiting legislation is that if parents wish for their children to have any other kind of sex education, it will be provided by parents in the privacy of the home. In the public world of the school, it is impossible to provide any education but that which is in accord with commonly accepted community standards. The constraints that this assumption imposes in a society that either demonizes homosexuality or tries to hide it in the private sphere are obvious. It is also astounding that the same members of Congress who vote for federal legislation intended to deny funds to localities that define for themselves different community standards also vote for legislation that harms the poor in the name of devolution, or granting power to local communities. This combination of taking power away in the case of moral education, while increasing power when it can save money, is related to both the increasingly privatized state that Petchesky (1990) criticizes and to maintaining a society where the moral boundary between politics and ethics is upheld in such a way as to foster the continued dominance of an interpretation of Judeo-Christian values.

This becomes even more clear when we remember that a significant number of the children who receive this "community approved education" might either not define themselves as heterosexual or might live in families where at least one significant person in their life does not define her/himself as heterosexual. Public messages, in these cases, contradict the private knowledge that youth possess. By failing to provide space for discussing the concerns, hopes, and fears of these youth, schools reinforce feelings of shame that make the exercise of agency difficult. This failing is even more common if one adds in the number of youth who are themselves sexually active outside of marriage or who have a close family member or friend who is sexually active outside of the "community standards." Finally, it clearly establishes that youth themselves are not recognized as members of the community with the right to define community norms.

The difficulty of constructing a sense of oneself as an agent acting with the ability to sort through multiple subject positions becomes particularly clear when one focuses on what schools do teach. Schools are, of course, the primary institutional structure in the lives of most children. Research done on schooling in the United States indicates that schools foster not the complex, multiple view of the self that we have discussed as necessary for radical democratic agency, but rather a more simple understanding—one highly influenced by stereotyped images of race, class, and sex/gender and a limited understanding of psychology (Thorne 1993, Fine and Zane 1991). This may become more true as a child ages. As we consider how institutional structures reinforce the sense of self that is developing, it is important to remember that psychoanalysis may be wrong in seeing childhood as the critical moment in the development of a moral human being. There is much to suggest that although this is one important time period, it is equally important to consider the connections that adolescents and young adults build as they attempt to work through the contradictory understandings of the identities that they have internalized.

From the perspective of gays and lesbians, understanding the political dynamics of adolescence and young adulthood may be particularly critical. Beth Zemsky notes the lengthy process of coming out that is the reality for many lesbians: "Research has indicated that coming out is a lengthy developmental process, with an average of 16 years from first recognition to identity synthesis" (1991, 197). Adolescence is clearly a period when young gays and lesbians are at serious risk of not being able to reconcile the contradictions between messages that they are receiving and desires that they are experiencing, thus the high rate of suicide and suicide attempts among gay and lesbian youth. The loss of connection that many youth face during this period can be devastating, particularly because there are so few institutions willing to risk parental disapproval in order to provide support and nurturance. It would be a mistake, however, to see this dynamic as unique to gays and lesbians. For most adolescents, this is a period during which the contradictions between social messages of appropriateness—messages that are themselves often contradictory—and desires and needs come into conflict. Taylor, Gilligan, and Sullivan indicate that similar difficulties—in particular parent-child conflict around friends, dating, and sexuality, as well as conflict between the values of Hispanic culture and the values of American culture—are characteristic of first- and second-generation Latina American girls who attempt suicide (1995, 63).

Although adolescence is a critical time in the lives of children, schools can work to deny the complex identities that children at even earlier ages bring to them, working instead through stereotyped images. Barrie Thorne provides a complex discussion of how children and teachers in schools work together to build norms that reinforce not just gender/sex divisions but, along with these divisions, normative heterosexuality. Although teachers and other adults sometimes challenge dominant gender norms in their official instruction, they are likely to accept the gender divisions that children create, and with their own use of gender as a simple category for dividing the children, reinforce a competitive, difference-based relationship. From early in the process of schooling, the reinforcement of gender roles comes with the reinforcement not only of racial superiority, but also with the assertion of heterosexual superiority and homophobia. Overtly, this most often happens through exchanges between children. In discussing the use of "faggot" by schoolchildren, Barrie Thorne writes: "When asked about their elementary school experiences, male college students sometimes recall occasions when they were called 'sissy,' 'nerd,' 'wimp,' or 'fag.' The memories are painful, and the men I talked with remember trying to avoid or cope with the stinging insult" (1993, 117). As Ritch Savin-Williams (1995) reports, the pressures to behave in a gender typical fashion increase in adolescence. The most obvious way in which boys avoid the insult is by embracing more stereotypically heterosexual behaviors. For boys, this may mean gay-bashing or getting a girl pregnant; for girls who face similar though often severe pressures, it may mean demonstrating heterosexual behavior through visible pregnancy (Ruddick 1991, 110; Savin-Williams 1995, 176–177).

Thorne's observation that children actively engage in acting out and reproducing sex/gender roles is also important to note in relation to adolescents. For many girls who participated in the studies done by Taylor, Gilligan, and Sullivan (1995) and Gilligan, Rogers, and Tolman (1991) schools are negative places not because the girls do not like the academic work, but because schools are the location of rumors and conflict between peers, with much of the conflict revolving around heterosexual relationships and the performance of gender/sex norms. Michelle Fine and Nancie Zane's (1991) discussion of why girls drop out of school adds to this understanding, pointing out that for many girls the complexities of their lives and perspectives are not taken seriously. On one level, the division between the public life of the school and the private life of the person means that the conflicts many young women have between the responsibilities that they have outside of school—including caring for younger siblings as well as elderly relatives—goes unrecognized. Fine and Zane write: "Inside their lives, the needs of self and other are braided together. Inside their schools these needs are posited as incompatible. With families, boyfriends, girlfriends, and school all competing for top priority, these young women feel the emotional toll of being pulled in all directions. Perhaps this is why national and local data so consistently reveal that social class, family strain, and number of siblings predict so well female dropout rates" (1991, 86). The separation of public and private has consequences for these girls' lives.

Equally important, however, is that teachers fail to take the recognition of complexity and contradiction as a sign of engaged thought, instead seeing those unwilling to set forth simplistic answers based on curricular knowledge as inadequate because they do not provide the "correct" answers. These adolescents refuse to take a disinterested stance, preferring instead to explore the intersection of their lived experience and curricular knowledge. The complexities of the lives that most adolescents lead are excluded not simply from discussions in schools, but in general from public, intergenerational discourse. They remain instead central to the discussion of youth, with little opportunity to have the complexity of identity and thought recognized and valued. Fine and Zane (1991) see this as leading many poor and working-class girls to drop out of school.[7] Brown sees commonalties between these girls and middle-class girls: "The young women in this study, the young women at risk for eating disorders, the high school valedictorians, and the low-income adolescent girls who drop out of school may all have something in common. They are all described as particularly smart, sensitive, astute young women who, in their struggles, are some of the culture's sharpest critics. Yet each of these girls has confronted in her own way the painful and confusing discrepancy between her own experience and cultural conventions and stereotypes. Each has also solved a problem of exclusion in her own way; each tells a story of some form of exit" (1991, 68). The positive alternative to exit is voice (Hirschman

1970), but this would require the support necessary to engage in social critique and political action.

Fundamental change of schools is seen as necessary by Connell (1995) in his discussion of how hegemonic masculinity can be challenged; Ruddick (1991) in her discussion of teen pregnancy; Brown (1991) in her discussion of voice in middle-class girls; Fine and Zane (1991) in their discussion of why lower-class girls drop out of school; and Taylor, Gilligan, and Sullivan (1995) in their discussion of the loss of voice among working-class girls. For each, what is critical about schools is that they do not provide either children or adolescents with the opportunity to explore the complexities of their identities and desires. It is interesting that the writings of some gay and lesbian teachers suggest that gay/lesbian teachers who are out provide a space in which youth can explore identity, even if those youth are not gay (Respini 1994, Wilson 1994). Many, such as Blankenhorn, might argue that teachers being open about their own identities in ways that provide space for youth is inappropriate since parents should provide a moral education for their children. Yet this argument assumes that morality can be taught, rather than that morality is a more complex interplay of knowledge about oneself and the world—knowledge that leads to making decisions and exercising agency, rather than following precepts.

It is important, however, to understand the extent to which schools would need to be transformed in order for them to help students to develop complex understandings of identity and of democratic agency. If as Foucault, Cote and Allahar, Gaines, and many others have argued schools were created to manufacture complacent citizen/worker/ consumers, it will take a lot to make them integral to meaningful democratic discourse and productive adolescent lives. One way that schools regulate students is through regulating teachers. Madiha Didi Khayatt, a former high school teacher, describes how the social construction of "teacher" poses challenges for lesbian teachers: "Teachers in general are hired in conformity with an assumed standard. They are expected, to some extent, to reflect a conventionality that corresponds with the state's ideologically sanctioned model of behavior." She goes on to observe that given the history of women in the profession of teaching, "The notion of lesbian teachers inevitably and indubitably contradicts mainstream assumptions of the female teacher, a woman who was traditionally or stereotypically portrayed as either a 'mother-teacher' or a 'spinster' (a women who remained 'chaste' and allegedly frustrated, hoping for eventual fulfillment of her 'true' role of wife and mother)" (1992, 5). It is clear that schools try to maintain this image by silencing teachers. In one recent instance unique largely for the overtness of school officials, a Utah teacher who had recently ended her marriage and began living with a lesbian partner was asked to sign a statement stating that if she ever discussed sexual orientation with students, parents of students, or school staff, she would be fired.[8] The construction of teachers as either safe heterosexual mothers or chaste precludes teachers from interacting with students as real people who are themselves desiring sexual subjects, and who both face choices and conflicts as sexual beings and might be able to engage in informed discussions about such choices and conflicts with their students. Male teachers face a related, but different, problem: being seen as nurturing, without their support being sexualized. If, therefore, we want teachers to engage with students in different ways, we will have to make significant changes in how we think about schools and teachers, changes that will only come about with political activism that challenges the limits put on teachers.

Such activism, however, is made difficult by a view of children as the property of their parents, and therefore, of educational systems as subject to teaching values supported by parents, rather than values that might further democratic principles and society. For example, in discussing the potentially revolutionary aspects of new social movements, Allen Hunter presents what he sees as a commonly held ethical complication:

> It is one thing to deprive economic elites of their control over resources by anchoring property relations and economic transactions in egalitarian and economically sound practices. It is one thing to demand that homophobic religious fundamentalists act with a modicum of tolerance toward homosexuals in public. Both of these changes inhibit the freedom of some (economic elites and homphobes) to enhance the freedom of others (economic majorities and gays, lesbians, and heterosexuals committed to diversity and tolerance) by changing the structures of incentives for self-interested action. However, it is more invasive to require that people not only conform to new standards of behavior, but reject deeply held cultural values and welcome into schools, churches, and families a cultural politics designed to instill values they oppose. (1995, 338)

A successful social movement, he suggests, is one that is able to transform internalized values slowly, until this stark contrast in values is no longer problematic. It is not clear, however, in Hunter's essay what this means. I want to suggest that if we see children as more than blank slates to be written on by parents, this conflict—though politically real—need not be understood as invasive.

A number of replies to the problem stated by Hunter are obvious: gays, lesbians, and supportive heterosexuals may be in families headed by a member who stands opposed to gay freedom. Thus, the deeply held values within a family may be subject to disputes that are covered over by power, and that often put youth at risk. Savin-Williams writes: "Bisexual, gay male and lesbian youth may desire to avoid abuse and maintain the family secret but by coming out to their family they are often 'rejected, mistreated, or become the focus of the family's dysfunction.' If these abused youth run away they face a world that is all too ready to exploit them. They are thus at extreme risk for substance abuse, prostitution, and suicide" (1995, 176, quoting Gonsiorek 1988, 116). Joyce Hunter's study of five hundred youth receiving services from the Hetrick-Martin Institute in New York City confirms the prevalence of family violence in lives of gay youth: 40% of the youth reported experiencing violent physical attacks, and of these "46% reported that the assault was gay-related [with] 61% of the gay-related violence [occurring] in the family" (1992, 78). Until we begin to understand families not as units, but as collections of connected but separate individuals, each of whom may need support in different ways, we cannot as a society respond responsibly and with care to youth whose beliefs and actions may conflict with those of more powerful members of their families.

We can also address the issues embedded in Hunter's concern through the lens of an ethic of care. There are significant conflicts at work: In late twentieth-century post-industrial society, a vast variety of people provide care to children in multiple ways. Children who receive health insurance subsidized by employers are essentially being subsidized by anyone who supports the company that provides benefits. On the next level, publicly funded schools indicate that care is a public concern. Increasingly children receive even more day-to-day care outside of the home in after school programs and day care programs. If we take seriously the idea that those who provide the labor of care should have a voice in determining the needs of those for whom they care, it becomes impossible to define parents as those whose voice matters, while teachers are deemed irrelevant as participants in defining needs. Further, if we also take seriously the idea that those who receive care should have a voice in defining the care that they need, children themselves should gain increased power in relation to their own education as they age. The voice that they have in the school system should be more powerful and more meaningful than it is currently, because increased voice can help to influence schools in ways that make them better places for gay and lesbian youth: "In short, Massachusetts is addressing the real school experiences of gay and lesbian youth. 'The lesson we have learned is when students have a voice in this, it cuts through the homophobia. It makes teachers realize that these are just kids—like their own kids,' says David LaFontaine, chairman of the Governor's Commission on Gay and Lesbian Youth" (Bennett 1997). Taylor and Ward (1991) provide a model for the development of sex education programs in schools that embraces the logic that programs will be better and more effective if they include students, and if they are targeted at particular communities rather than constructed in relation to white, middle-class values. They argue that programs should be developed with the participation of adolescents, parents, local social service providers, and community leaders and teachers, thus allowing for a multiplicity of voices to engage in discussion and debate, and helping to eliminate stereotyped images of cultures and ethnicities. Such debate might also help to eliminate stereotyped images of women, lesbians, and gay men. Yet for such open discussion to occur, those with power need to create safe conditions for discussion. And, those who advocate alternative values need to be willing to actively voice their values, regardless of whether or not they are parents.

Even if we recognize as a society that since schools provide care many should have greater voice than is the case currently, schools will not quickly or easily become a haven for gay and lesbian youth or teachers. However, political mobilization around gay issues, gender issues, and multicultural issues would become a more legitimate ground of political debate because we would not start with the presumption that anything a child's parent(s) opposes should not happen. When the rights of parents foreclose political discussion, political discussion that is critical for our future as a democratic society is also foreclosed. Further, if gays and lesbians take seriously the lessons of the Children of the Rainbow Curriculum debate, it is clear that to take advantage of such a revised view of schools and community responsibility necessitates gays and lesbians building within their communities connections across racial lines in order to engage in critiques of schools with, rather than in opposition to, others who are oppressed. Lee et al. suggest that AIDS education and anti-violence movements are two areas where gay and lesbian organizing can connect to people's needs. Yet, the tendency of middle-class gay and lesbian groups to "drift away" from discussions about schools when Right-wing antigay initiatives are not a threat makes sustained alliance-building difficult (1996, 32–36).

In general, current perspectives on children focus on what social conditions will best lead to the development of a unified, clear sense of self in children. Since we live in a complex society with multiple understandings of "ethical" behavior, it is assumed that some combination of parental norms and the dominant social norms taught by schools will best enable children to develop this sense of self. "Outside" influences are seen as confusing. I have suggested that this is not a model that will work for youth who are questioning whether the sexual norms of their parents and of the dominant culture make sense. It is also a model that fails to work for any child or adolescent who is being socialized within or between two (or more) cultures. Finally, it is a model that fails to work if we wish to create the conditions where youth establish a positive sense of identity based on having developed and exercised their own agency, rather than on understanding themselves as superior to someone else.

The legal and assumed rights that parents currently have are in large part connected to the responsibilities that parents have in relation to children, responsibilities that are both financial and emotional. It may be, however, that the rights are greater than they should be given the resources, again both financial and emotional, that parents sometimes provide for their children. The fact that much care for children is being provided outside of the private realm of the family suggests that perhaps the larger communities that are providing care deserve greater input into decision making that affects children.[9] However, because there is no social consensus on the values that should guide such input, it remains easier to leave children in the hands of their parents.

At the same time, given that we want youth to be people able to make decisions that have a positive impact on themselves and the communities in which they live, we need to more carefully consider the rights and opportunities that they require in post-industrial, democratic society. In considering this broad question, we move beyond asking about what gay kids need, a question that only makes sense if we assume that identity is fixed, to ask how we can create conditions that better serve those youth who want to embrace gay/lesbian/bisexual/transgendered/queer identities and the young people who will be their peers. As we ask this broad question, we can bring together analyses that recognize increased sexual agency not as the consequence of an overly permissive society that lacks family values, but as a potential means of increasing freedom, and those that recognize the dominance of white, middle-class Christian values as central to maintaining class and racial/ethnic divisions. From here, if we are to address the complex issues embedded in these analyses, we are forced to articulate a new vision of the nurturance of children and youth. In concluding this chapter, I want to begin to articulate such a vision.

Community Connections and Developing Agency

Despite the obstacles that I have identified, many children are nurtured in ways that allow them to become agents capable of making decisions not by denying parts of themselves in order to create false unity, but by recognizing the conflicts and making decisions. What is clear is that in many such cases, the ability to interact not only with parents, but also with other adults, is critical. We can get some of the sense of the important role that other adults might play in the lives of working-class adolescents in the 1990s from Rubin's discussion of the tensions between adolescents and their parents. She notes that parents feel threatened because their children see the world very differently. In particular, young people do not make the same decisions about sexuality that their parents once did, nor do they feel shame or guilt as they move away from these values. As a result, parents try to control their children in a way that leads to conflict. Rubin suggests that parents' desire for control is connected to both their desire to not see their children suffer and to a psychological dimension: "For only if their children behave properly by their standards, only if they look and act in ways that reflect honor on the family, can the parents begin to relax about their status in the world, can they be assured that they will be distinguished from those below" (1994, 60). Thus, for parents it may be difficult to allow children to explore because of the heavy investment that they have made. Other adults, therefore, may be helpful to adolescents and young adults as they try to sort through their desires.

As briefly discussed earlier, Patricia Hill Collins suggests that such a role has been present in black communities. She writes that although communities expect blood mothers to care for children, "African and African-American communities have also recognized that vesting one person with full responsibility for mothering a child may not be wise or possible. As a result, othermothers—women who assist blood mothers by sharing mothering responsibilities—traditionally have been central to the institution of Black motherhood" (1990, 119). In her discussion of othermothering, Collins makes a number of points relevant for conceptualizing the role that nonblood-parent adults can play in the lives of children. First, she points out that having othermothering as an institutionalized part of child nurturance requires that children be seen as more than the possessions of their parents. Instead, children are conceptualized as valued and valuable community members who need broad networks of support and for whom adults should assume responsibility. Second, she argues that one important function of othermothers is "to help diffuse the emotional intensity of relationships between daughters and mothers" (1990, 128). This intensity, as we have seen, is particularly great because of the power of racism. Finally, Collins notes that othermothering serves important functions not just for children, but also for adults. On the one hand, othermothering allows women who have not given birth to achieve the status of mother. On the other hand, othermothering leads not simply to status within the community, but also to political engagement and activism. "Nurturing children in Black extended family networks," Collins notes, "stimulates a more generalized ethic of caring and personal accountability among African-American women who often feel accountable to all the Black community's children" (1990, 129).

Although there has been some debate about the extent to which such community ties and othermothering practices have been sustained as poverty has taken a larger toll on poor black communities in recent years, Barbara Omolade echoes the importance of networks of support for black single mothers. She suggests that to the extent that family networks have declined, they have been partially, and should be more extensively, replaced with activist organizations designed to encourage young women to provide support and assistance to one another. She cites the example of The Sisterhood, an organization created to help single mothers to name their own reality and support one another. One of the most successful programs the organization has supported,

Omolade reports, has been a big sister program for teen mothers (1994, 75). This program tries to help single mothers not through moral teaching, but through support, encouragement, and teaching practical skills. Programs such as these indicate that with support, teen mothers are capable of making intelligent choices for themselves and their children, yet such programs also recognize that adult support is necessary and desirable.

Other programs that help youth to build connections to adults other than parents have had some success, though such programs have not been extensively tried and it is not clear that relationships with no greater context than big brother or big sister programs are helpful for youth. Research indicates that such programs are worth pursuing and that they work best when there are real shared interests and experiences between the adult and the youth. When these relationships work, they provide as many benefits for the adults as for the youth. Unless we reconstruct social narratives so that we value the active involvement of adults who are not parents in children's lives, such relationships will remain small-scale experiments. As the youth interviewed by Due (1995) indicate, the cost of this continued lack of contact between youth and supportive adults may be particularly high for lesbian and gay youth. Although the ability to create our own families and nurture our own children might provide an incentive for gays and lesbians to become visible enough as parents so that gay and lesbian issues became more prominent in schools, the experiences of people of color suggest that it would take significant struggle for such transformation to take place. Rather than solely fighting this agenda, and reinforcing the idea that only parents have a legitimate voice, we might work to create conditions that enable more adults to play more significant roles in the lives of children and adolescents. By doing this, we also may be able to build a vision of adolescence that works better in post-industrial society.

Martha Minow (1997) reminds us that children's rights—along with civil rights, women's rights, and gay and lesbian rights—was part of the 1960s agenda to liberate people. In the 1990s, the least visible of these movements is children's rights. Minow suggests that the unique situation of children as visibly dependent on adults is one factor in the failure of this agenda to maintain visibility. Another critical factor is the political powerlessness of youth. Nevertheless, she argues that children need to be granted human rights,[10] rights that recognize the ways in which they are different from adults, while also recognizing that "as human beings children deserve the kind of dignity, respect, and freedom from arbitrary treatment signaled by rights" (1997, 119). Gays and lesbians need to understand the importance of furthering the human rights of children and participate in further defining how human rights language helps youth to have greater freedom and protection, as well as participate in creating the material conditions that could make these rights meaningful. Only in this way can we protect "our" children.

6

Creating the Conditions for Freedom in Private Life

How we perceive ourselves as agents is central to how we frame and justify our choices, both to ourselves and to others. Hegemonic narratives suggest that we are not successful adults unless we are able to marry, have children, and establish economically independent family lives. There are, as we have seen, gender variations in this story so that women expect to have primary responsibility for child care, while men expect to have primary responsibility for money making, but for either gender, the possibility of forming nonmonogamous sexual partnerships, defining one's life primarily around nonsexual friendships, mentoring an unrelated adolescent, or parenting as part of a group is denied by this hegemonic narrative. Generally, social discourse helps to create conditions whereby people view these alternative living arrangements with suspicion, often understanding them as a sign of immaturity and thus indicating that the gender and family understandings central to constructing and consolidating white, middle-class, heterosexual norms remain powerful. Nevertheless, many lesbians, gays, and heterosexual men and women do form families in different ways. The exercise of agency in these ways is critical for helping us to understand the ways by which identity, social roles, and social forces require us to exercise agency, as the following examples show:

- Minnie Bruce Pratt describes the difficulty, humor, and agency involved in sorting through roles at a "festive dinner," with her lover,
who might be her son's "drag stepdaddy," her son and "the woman
who is now his honey," and his friends. A key question emerges: Who
carves the turkey? In Pratt's words:

> How to negotiate the metaphors of blade, flesh, communion; mother,
> father, children; maleness, femaleness, domination, submission. Are my son
> and this woman our children? Are they the parents of the others? Am I ev-
> eryone's mother? And how can I be? Me who has just been making out
> with you by the stairs, not pure enough for a mother, too young in my flir-
> tatiousness, and with the wrong husband.
>
> When I return, everyone is seated but no one is at the head of the table.
> You are sitting to one side, next to an empty place and plate for me. But
> you have the blade in your hand and are slicing huge slabs of meat onto a
> platter. I begin to laugh. I say, "How did you end up with that?" And you
> say, "Don't even ask! I've never done this before in my life." But my son
> says, "It took a lot of courage to grasp that knife." (1995, 166–167)

- In describing raising her son and daughter, Audre Lorde highlights
the multiple ways by which oppression affects children and suggests
that lesbians can help children to face those challenges. She writes:

> Jonathon was three-and-one-half when Frances, my lover, and I met; he
> was seven when we all began to live together permanently. From the start,
> Frances' and my insistence that there be no secrets in our household about
> the fact that we were lesbians has been the source of problems and strength
> for both children. In the beginning, this insistence grew out of the knowl-
> edge, on both our parts, that whatever was hidden out of fear could be used
> either against the children or ourselves—one imperfect but useful argu-
> ment for honesty. The knowledge of fear can help make us free.
>
> *for the embattled*
> *there is no place*
> *that cannot be*
> *home*
> *nor is.*[1]
>
> For survival, Black children in america must be raised to be warriors.
> They must also be raised to recognize the enemies' many faces. Black chil-
> dren of lesbian couples have an advantage because they learn early, very
> early, that oppression comes in many forms, none of which have anything
> to do with their own worth. (1984, 75)[2]

- In a conversation about his partner Juan Lombard, Gil Mangaoang comments:

> I had always wanted a monogamous relationship. In the beginning, I had to grapple with the fact that Juan was not going to be monogamous whether I said I wanted it or not. I felt very jealous, and I questioned his commitment and responsibility to our relationship and to me. But we've managed to maintain our relationship with a lot of quality, and I don't feel the same threat I did before. I do feel the same jealousy, but I don't think it cheapens our relationship in any way. (Sherman 1992, 68)

He goes on to observe that communication has been critical, particularly communication about the different cultures and religious backgrounds from which he and Juan come.

Building and sustaining such relationships, in part because dominant discourses do not recognize them as legitimate, are acts that require agency. What often makes these relationships interesting models for social change and social discourse is not simply that they have been chosen, but that people chose them in opposition to social norms in ways that allow them to enhance care in their relationships. However, those who attempt to build these relationships continue to face severe constraints because the social and economic systems with which they interact as they build these relationships continue to presume that social rights and social benefits should be given to people not because as individuals we are inherently deserving members of society, but because as members of families we gain status, and therefore privileges and rights. Until the construction of social policy no longer rests on marital and family status, the ability to form alternative, caring living arrangements will remain risky, and most available to either those who are privileged or those who are so impoverished that extended community and kin ties are necessary for existence, even if they also require that people share in ways that technically break the law. In the latter case, however, the price of such ties will continue to be high.

Tronto argues that care need not be simply an ethical framework, but also can be a political concept with the power to help form strategies for organizing (1993, 175). It is obvious that social discourse which reveals the inadequacy of the care that many people in society receive can play a part in building and sustaining political movements of those who lack resources and care. It is less obvious that it can motivate those who do not feel themselves as lacking care. Yet, Tronto suggests that this may be possible: "Those with power rarely surrender it willingly; what I have suggested though is that care as a political value can help transform our public discussion in such a way that it exposes the ways in which the powerful have access to too many resources. At the same time, care provides the powerful with a vision of what they stand to gain in a well-ordered and well-cared for society" (1993, 177). For gays and lesbians with privilege—whether class, race, and/or gender privilege—it is tempting to try to gain access to private institutions in order to have our care needs met in the same ways that other privileged people do. Yet since the construction of gayness as "Other" is part of a normative system that rests on the relegation of care to the private world, and to the labor of women and people of color, there is much that even privileged lesbians and gays can gain from working to deconstruct this system. In part, this requires building an alternative discourse, yet it also requires the construction and sustenance of political organizations that work to make care a public concern.

The same Congress and President supported the recent passage of welfare reform legislation that forces recipients into the job market, limits lifetime benefits to five years, and bars legal immigrants from benefits, as supported the Defense of Marriage Bill. As I hope to have shown throughout the previous chapters, this is not coincidence. It is an attempt to maintain a class, race, sex/gender, and sexual hierarchy in a time when all are breaking down as a result of economic change and the combined power of social movements that were at their peak in the 1960s and 1970s. The critical question concerns not just how citizens can keep further reactionary policies from being enacted, but also how they can work to build alliances between the multiple and overlapping groups being harmed by the policies supported today by both Republicans and Democrats. As Judith Stacey (1996) argues, the ways by which gays and lesbians (such as those whom I cited in the beginning of the chapter) have chosen to construct their private lives can serve as models for the larger society. However, without an understanding of how race, class, and sometimes gender dynamics affect these choices *and* an understanding of how these choices have been limited by the family ideology, family law, and family policy of industrial capitalism and the liberal state, it is impossible to say much of anything about either the chances that others will work to create social conditions more conducive to choice and freedom in familial and nonfamilial relationships or the political goals that might guide gays and lesbians who want to extend relationship possibilities. In addition to challenging the dominant narrative of family and reconceptualizing ethics and decision-making processes so that they are compatible with a new vision, we must also work to create the material conditions that would allow people to make decisions without their decisions resting on or reinforcing the oppression of others.

Finding Time and Money for Private Life

There are two obvious approaches to considering how we might better guarantee the material basis of choice. The first, and most common, is to develop the welfare state so that it better provides for people. Given the role that the welfare state has played in exerting control and encouraging citizens to fit into their "proper roles," this alternative is less than attractive to many people. A second alternative is one that understands people as able to make choices for themselves if they have adequate resources. It is an alternative constructed around the possibility that current social problems—from the lack of adequate day care for children, to the alienation of youth, to the stress of many parent-workers, to the lack of connection that people feel to one another—have arisen because the family, state, and work systems of industrialization no longer effectively provide the care necessary in families and private life. Thus, it is important to consider how we can free people from the constraints of these institutions so that they have both necessary economic resources and time.

One proposal put forth that would enable greater numbers of people to attain financial security is to shorten the workweek. Joan Acker recognizes and critiques a proposal made by Social Democratic women in Sweden: "Social Democratic women have made a start [toward reorganizing work] with the demand for a six-hour working day at eight hours' pay. This might be a step toward eliminating the disadvantage of being a part-time worker. But, some have warned, the result might be that men simply have more time for relaxation and union work, while women's lives remain unchanged. In any case, with broad opposition from men, the six-hour-day proposal has made no progress" (1993, 46). Opposition is likely to be even greater in the United States where part-time work has remained more marginalized than in Sweden and most other European countries, countries in which part-time workers are guaranteed equal wages and are more likely to receive health insurance,[3] unemployment insurance, and paid annual vacations (Du Rivage and Jacobs 1993). Nevertheless, American unions such as the AFL-CIO have advocated a reduced workweek. In discussing progressive union demands, Susan Cowell recognizes that corporations are unlikely to see reduced working hours as compatible with international competitiveness; nevertheless, she argues that labor unions need to make this demand: "The corporate response to the need of women to work and care for children has been to track women into poorly paid and insecure part-time work. A progressive family policy needs to shorten working hours for all workers—and ensure that part-time work is secure, decently paid, and covered by benefits" (1993, 118).

In addition, Cowell argues that such a progressive agenda would encompass demands set forth by the Coalition of Labor Union Women (CLUW), including "the right to a job and economic security, the right to health care, the right to child and elder care, the right to family leave, the right to services for the elderly, the right to quality education, the right to equal opportunity, the right to equal pay for work of equal value, the right to shelter, and the right to live and work in a safe environment" (1993, 123). Despite CLUW's desire to broaden the understanding of family to include gay partnerships, single parents, extended families, and unmarried couples with and without families, these proposals are ones that privilege families, rather than provide both families and alternatives to the family with resources and social support. As Weeks reminds us, although families perform much caring work, the example of gay and lesbian reaction to the AIDS crisis is indicative of caring outside of families, that is, caring in moral communities. Thus, even these progressive policies, ones which move beyond those currently existing in any welfare state, may still be conceiving of the labor of care too narrowly.

The idea of reducing the workweek is also at the heart of Jeremy Rifkin's *The End of Work*. Central to Rifkin's argument is that the amount of labor necessary in the past is no longer necessary, thus leaving us with both serious problems, and new possibilities:

> In the coming decades, the shrinking role of the market and the public sector is going to affect the lives of working people in two significant ways. Those who remain employed will likely see a shortening of their workweek, leaving them with more leisure. Many on reduced work schedules are likely to be pressured to spend their leisure indulging in mass entertainment and stepped-up consumption. The increasing number of unemployed and underemployed

people, by contrast, will find themselves sinking inexorably into the permanent underclass. . . . Their cries for help will be largely ignored as governments tighten their purse strings and shift spending priorities from welfare and job-creation to beefed-up security and the building of more prisons. (1995, 238–239)

Rifkin continues by suggesting that reducing the workweek and increasing the role of the "third sector," or the voluntary sector, will be necessary if we are to respond to technological change in a humane manner.

Rifkin recognizes that feminists may not respond positively to this proposal because they are quite aware that, historically, volunteer work has been a way of using women's labor without valuing it. This is a recognition that he does not take as seriously as would be desirable, assuming both that it would possible to provide incentives for volunteer work and that with incentives men, as well as women, would respond. Further, he does not indicate whether such a system would help to challenge the class divisions that currently exist, although at times it sounds as if people would continue to do labor pretty similar to what they do now, but with some of it being voluntary. Finally, Rifkin never addresses how paid labor, third-sector labor, and private labor would come together. Thus, there are serious political questions that require political debate in order for this vision to be one that might address the questions of care that I have discussed. Yet the idea that we could, and should, use tax incentives and other public policies to encourage people to become actively involved in providing care in public life might be one that could frame political discussions and debates. It is a vision that sees the government as playing a significant, but also limited, role in community development.

Such a vision is one that is compatible with support for many organizations—such as AIDS organizations, women's health care centers, rape crisis centers, or community action groups—that have proven central for confronting multiple problems. In each case, organizations have come into existence because people concerned about the lack of support for a particular group of people have organized to provide the necessary care. For the most part, they have needed some support from the government, while also desiring to maintain independence and autonomy. A form of social benefits that worked less to professionalize and more to support the ability of individuals to work together voluntarily might both benefit organizations and enhance political participation within communities, since such volunteer work often results in people developing a greater understanding of social and political issues.

Building a gay and lesbian vision of family and a politics of family around care as a central concept—rather than around rights—would allow us to address the issues that I raise in the introduction in a more comprehensive and freedom-enhancing way. Once we understand human beings not simply as rights-bearing individuals (or in the case of children and youth, as potential rights-bearing individuals), but as democratic agents who are dependent upon the conditions negotiated in political debate with other democratic agents, we can begin to think differently about the stories that I discussed in the introduction. For example, rather than asking whether an individual's family status makes her/him eligible for health insurance, we can now ask whether providing health insurance and health care for that individual enhances his/her ability to be a responsible agent within society. Additionally, we can ask how the manner by which our society provides such resources affects our social understanding of care. In relation to another story, rather than asking who should have rights in relation to a child who has developed important relationships to both a biological parent or parents and a foster parent or parents, we might ask how both of these caring relationships can be sustained. Thus, the critical question becomes not who has rights, and therefore who should control the child, but rather how the care that is provided by multiple people can be recognized and preserved. This same concern would guide decision making about the complex relationships sometimes built between lesbians, gays, and children, whether in the context of nonmarital couple relationships or groups of adults who build relationships with one another by parenting together. If people were encouraged to build such extensive relationships, surrogacy, as well as adoption, might be less necessary mechanisms for adults who wish to share their lives with children or for children to receive the nurturance that they require. Finally, this perspective would help citizens, including gay and lesbian citizens, to recognize the intergenerational interdependence that exists and to work to support children, youth, and the elderly.

A perspective framed around care and enhancing democracy recognizes that without economic resources and political voice, the guarantee of rights, such as the right to marry and the right to construct a private life, have limited meaning. Yet this perspective can also contain an awareness that with socially provided resources come responsibilities,

responsibilities that are always subject to public and political definition and interpretation. Fostering political debate that calls into question the emphasis placed on families to provide a "haven in a heartless world" is critical to fostering a critique of current discourse and of the economic structures that maintain the family as the central institution of private life (Lasch 1977). Gays and lesbians, because we remain deeply dependent on external communities to raise children who will become part of our communities, are in a unique position to understand the importance of reframing political discussion and debate so that we can work to create greater freedom for youth and adults. Yet unless we are able and willing to question central institutional structures, rather than to seek equality by acting virtually normal enough to fit in with only minimal change, we will fail to fully bring the unique perspective that we have into political debate and discourse.

Notes

Introduction

1. This policy was actually closer to the laws passed by municipalities that generally include nonmarried heterosexual partners. Policies put into place by private businesses less often include nonmarried heterosexual couples.

2. As Ettelbrick notes, because these policies do not require *sexual* exclusivity, they are an advance over marriage law. However, because they allow for only one domestic partner to be registered, they do make it impossible to count more than one person and his/her children as central to one's life (1989).

3. Interestingly, even *Murphy Brown*, a television show that will perhaps always be remembered for Dan Quayle's attacks on Murphy's single-motherhood, ended the episode in which she gave birth with Murphy singing "You Make Me Feel Like a Natural Woman" to her newborn son.

4. Although the benefits that I receive as a result of my professional status give me more security than many people in society.

5. Kennedy and Davis's (1993) discussion of lesbian life in Buffalo makes it very clear that those whose lesbianism was most visible also made the greatest economic sacrifices. Thus, butch lesbians from earlier in the century are likely to have few resources in old age.

6. As I will discuss in more detail later, it is important to note the class bias that is also built into this ruling.

7. Lewin reports a similar case (1993, 189).

8. Due (1995) notes that San Francisco, considered a haven by gay kids as well as gay adults, provides no services explicitly directed at gay youth who are living on the streets.

9. Despite the fact that I agree with her analysis of the complex issues that need to be explored in relation to family, I find that Osborn's overall argument romanticizes gay and lesbian life and, as seen through the lens of modern social theory, presents a naive view of human development. For example, this quote concerning violence in families is followed by a discussion of the prevalence of violence in heterosexual relationships. The reality and seriousness of violence in lesbian and gay relationships is never mentioned.

10. Negative reaction to the Human Rights Campaign's endorsement of then Republican New York Senator Alphonse D'Amato in the most recent election suggests that many in gay and lesbian communities do want gay and lesbian organizations to further broadly democratic agendas.

Chapter 1

1. It is important to note that although HRC and NGLTF are both gay rights organizations, they do have somewhat different agendas. NGLTF is more inclined to recognize the importance of articulating a position on issues, such as welfare reform, that are not "gay issues."

2. This is an understanding of society that separates justice from ethics. Political theorist Michael Sandel summarizes this view of society in the following way: "Society, being composed of a plurality of persons, each with his own aims, interests, and conceptions of the good, is best arranged when it is governed by principles that do not *themselves* presuppose any conception of the good; what justifies these regulative principles above all is not that they maximize the social welfare, or otherwise promote the good, but that they conform to the conception of the *right*, a moral category given prior to the good and independent of it" (1982, 1). See also Tronto (1993).

2. In *Griswold v. Connecticut* (381 U.S. 479 (1965)) the Supreme Court ruled that married couples had the right to use contraceptive devices in the privacy of their own homes. This case was particularly important because this was the first time that the Court stated the privacy doctrine. This decision is reprinted in Rubenstein (1993).

3. In *Loving v. Virginia* (388 U.S. 1 (1967)), the privacy doctrine was invoked to overturn laws banning interracial marriage.

4. For example, this language is often used to frame the desire for school vouchers, a plan that is designed to allow children to attend private schools with at least some of the cost paid for publicly.

5. It is important to realize, however, that Locke did not believe that the necessary understanding could be found without proper nurturance. Thus, he not only wrote political theory, he also wrote what we would today consider a child-rearing manual, *Some Thoughts Concerning Education* (1964).

6. Although we may see liberalism as a political philosophy containing biases about the form of private life that is most compatible with liberal public life, there will necessarily be differences in the vision and institutionalization of these norms as a result of democratization, specific cultural factors (including race relations and gender relations), and changes in the economic system. Therefore, although historical writings about the family can reveal some continuity, it is most critical that we examine the United States, historically and today.

7. Patriarchy can be understood either as a system of male dominance or as the particular form of male dominance in which male authority is directly linked to paternity. I will use the term in the general sense of male dominance.

8. This is ambiguous, however. Women, and to a lesser extent children, have also been active in helping men to organize resistance. For example, the activism of

women in supporting striking workers is powerfully portrayed in Lorraine Gray's film *With Babies and Banners* (1978).

9. This is a point that I will discuss in great detail in later chapters.

10. The extent to which economic considerations continued to influence bourgeois relationships was noted by Engels, who suggested that most bourgeois marriages were little more than prostitution (1978 [1884], 82).

11. Once a contract is defined as a contract for prostitution, it is negated. For example, domestic partnership contracts that include sexual services are viewed as equivalent to prostitution, and therefore are illegal. This is part of a larger system of regulation that has been designed to channel all legitimate sexuality into marital relationships.

12. In this regard, George Chauncey makes an interesting and relevant point in his discussion of the development and maintenance of a thriving gay world prior to World War I: This world was made possible because cities offered cheap housing and domestic services, that is, work that otherwise would have required marriage (1994, 135). Men were able to live independently because they lived in a social system where they could purchase "women's" labor. At the same time, some middle-class women may have had some degree of freedom (and many did, in fact, choose not to marry), but this was possible because lower-class women replaced them in performing domestic services for some middle-class men. Neither a thriving gay world nor the less sexually overt but still very present world of independent women challenged the gendered division of labor consolidated during this time period.

13. Eskridge notes that Polikoff makes this observation in her critique of proponents of same-sex marriage. He does not, however, respond to the observation (1996, 61–62).

14. Frye writes in relation to a 1983 study of sex, which found that "only about one-third of lesbians in relationships of two years or longer 'had sex' once a week or more; 47% of lesbians in long-term relationships 'had sex' once a month or less, while among heterosexual married couples only 15% 'had sex' once a month or less. And they report that lesbians seem to be more limited in the range of their 'sexual' techniques than are other couples" (1990, 306).

15. It is important to note that those couples who see marriage as playing a role in consolidating relationships or building connections to others had themselves arranged and participated in marriage ceremonies. Given that such public celebrations are relatively common, it is important to understand that when I talk about marriage, I am talking about legally recognized marriage, not commitment ceremonies or religious ceremonies.

16. Wilton (1995, 186–187) discusses and refutes the argument that lesbians may be better off economically than heterosexual women. A more detailed analysis of this question is present in Dunne's (1997) discussion of a small sample of lesbians. She finds that although lesbians are more present in nontraditional jobs than heterosexual women, their incomes and opportunities are still not equal to men's. The Policy Institute of the National Gay and Lesbian Task Force and the Institute for Gay and Lesbian Strategic Studies recently published a report by M. V. Lee Badgett on the incomes of lesbian, gay, and bisexual Americans. Badgett notes that we would

expect the incomes of lesbian households to be lower due to the gender gap and cites that data support this expectation: "Klawitter and Flatt further analyzed the differences in household income controlling for the couple's geographical location, education, age, race, sex, and other relevant variables. Once these factors are taken into account, married couple households and male same-sex households have roughly equal household incomes, while female same-sex couples bring home 18–20% less income than a similar married couple's income" (1998, 15). Further, since 31% of lesbian households include children (compared to 37% of heterosexual women's households), lesbians are often supporting children on these lower incomes (Bladgett 1998, 17).

17. It should be noted, however, that marriage rights do not necessarily provide parental rights. In a number of countries where gays and lesbians have marriage rights, the law is specifically written to exclude adoption rights. It is likely that a U.S. law permitting same-sex marriage would also not guarantee co-partners any rights in relation to children.

18. I want to note the important difference in reproduction between the situation for gay men and the situation for lesbians that Eskridge avoids in his phrasing. It is certainly possible in the case of lesbians to have an anonymous sperm donor who neither has nor desires legal rights in relation to the child. It is not currently possible for gay men to reproduce without a third-party (such as a surrogate) who is quite differently situated. This difference in reproductive capacity makes the development of a new norm of parenting more important for gay men who wish to reproduce than for fertile lesbians. The difference between the interests and power of men and women must be recognized, because these differences can create serious challenges to building a unified lesbian and gay—or perhaps, queer—analysis of family.

19. I will discuss this issue in greater detail in chapter 4.

20. This dual argument in itself raises an interesting question. Can it simultaneously be the case that marriage rights would aid gays economically while not costing corporations much and possibly saving the state money? It may be that both would happen because the extension of rights would have different impacts on different gay people. For a poor couple, marrying might mean the loss of welfare benefits; for a middle-class couple, it might mean the extension of health benefits. For a middle-class dual-earner couple, marriage might actually have economic costs because of the structure of the tax system.

21. A classic analysis of this dynamic may be found in Frances Fox Piven and Richard Cloward's *Poor People's Movements* (1977).

Chapter 2

1. Blankenhorn writes: "There are exceptions of course, but here is the rule: Boys raised by traditionally masculine fathers do not commit crimes. Fatherless boys commit crimes" (1995, 30). Similarly, "for boys, the most socially acute manifestation of paternal disinvestment is juvenile violence. For girls, it is juvenile and out-of-wedlock childbearing" (1995, 45).

2. I do not mean to imply that such policies are always bad. Certainly in cases where a child's parents want to live together but cannot afford to do so because living together leads to lower levels of benefits, there is irrationality built into policy that ought to be changed. But the program reported in the *New York Times* does not simply address these irrationalities; it uses public policy to provide greater benefits for children who have fathers present in the housing project than for those who do not. Given this, it would not be surprising if the program reinforced the normative concepts that it is supposed to reflect: children who are economically better off because of the program might do better than those children who are in families receiving less adequate benefits simply because the structure of those families is demonized by policymakers.

3. This is a construction that ignores another possibility—women who have actively chosen to leave their husbands or partners.

4. I assume that Hillary Clinton is referring to Moynihan's *The Negro Family: The Case for National Action* (1965), a work that has been highly criticized for failing to recognize that black women, who are oppressed within the race and gender structure of the United States, are not "matriarchs" (Davis 1981). Further, Carol Stack's classic work *All Our Kin* (1974) provides evidence with which one can argue that black men are not present in the lives of black boys only if s/he understands the only possible means of support as taking place in the nuclear family. If the vision of family is expanded to include extended families and non-kin nurturers, Stack argues, it is apparent that many black men are involved in the lives of black boys and male youth.

5. Adoptive fathers would also count as adequate to Blankenhorn. He identifies stepfathers as highly problematic, however, in particular because they are more likely to sexually abuse children.

6. Whereas Pateman reads these myths as an indication of the presence of patriarchy at the founding of liberalism, Blankenhorn seems to read them as prescient social analysis and as a prediction of the disarray into which a society without fathers as authority figures will fall. As I will suggest, the parallel between his ideas and those of Hobbes and Locke may simply be a function of their common liberalism.

7. This position could be used to provide a theoretical justification of an American cultural fear that gay men who interact with children will molest them.

8. It is, of course, often not the case that gay parents abandon their children. In fact, many fight hard for custody rights, though courts may well be hesitant to grant custody rights to these parents. See, for example, Pratt (1990).

9. Or, for particular people within a culture.

10. Lehring goes on to point out that this rejection of gay liberation is based on understanding sexuality as natural and fixed.

11. The threat to middle-class masculinity was made greater by the increasing role of women in socializing boys in both the home and the school.

12. For further discussion of the historical developments that helped to give rise to and shape modern homosexual identities, see D'Emilio and Freedman (1988) and D'Emilio (1983).

13. Dunne points to keeping finances separate, dividing bills proportionately with income, and living at a level comfortable for the partner who has the lower earnings (1997, 196).

14. See Fung (1991) for a discussion of how gay male culture reinforces sexual stereotypes of Asian men.

15. At least minimal *visible* external support. The social cost of providing home loans, tax deductions, health care, education, etc., is hidden in social discourse. As a result, the only children who appear to receive state support are those who receive benefits through social welfare policies.

16. By "lesbian mothering" I mean mothering by women who consciously identify as lesbian and have chosen to give birth either in a lesbian relationship or as single mothers. The literature on lesbian mothers focuses increasingly on the experiences of these women, as opposed to earlier research that focused on women who had children as part of a heterosexual relationship, or relationships, before they came out.

17. Though, as I will argue in chapter 4, it is also important to construct and use a language of agency carefully, particularly in a society where many lack the resources to make real choices.

18. Success rates for in vitro fertilization are about 9 percent. The cost for attempting in vitro fertilization is between $4,000 and $7,000 per cycle. Many women continue attempting to "succeed" until they either can no longer afford the procedures or get divorced.

19. In relation to Weeks's work, Seidman writes: "While Weeks argues that we grasp the meaning of sex acts by situating them in their context and relating them to the intentions of the agent, only the issue of choice versus constraint guides his moral assessment. The pragmatic concern with the consequences of the act plays no role in his moral standpoint. But why should we concern ourselves only with whether agents choose or were constrained to act as they did while ignoring the moral implications of the effects of their acts?" (1992, 207 n. 7).

Chapter 3

1. It is important to note that ethnicity itself does not have to be, nor should it be, understood as fixed and stable, a point that I will return to at the end of this chapter. See Phelan (1994) for a discussion of what lesbian and gay politics can learn from work, including that of lesbians of color (such as Gloria Anzaldua 1987), that moves away from such essentialist understandings of ethnicity.

2. This is, of course, the argument that has been used to reject affirmative action. It is also an argument that has been used in antigay ballot initiatives.

3. From "My Brother" in *Jonestown and Other Madness* by Pat Parker. Reprinted with permission from Firebrand Books, Ithaca, New York. Copyright © 1985 by Pat Parker.

4. There are other interpretations of the effect of drag performances, interpretations that understand drag less as progressive deconstruction and more as a means of reasserting gender roles by illustrating the humor of men playing women. See, for example, Frye (1983).

5. See Berlant and Freeman (1993) for a positive interpretation of the intent of this action.

6. Lugones also lists "practicing trickstery and foolery" as one of the curdling processes (1994, 478).

7. Crimp and Ralston report the following events that occurred after ACT UP demonstrations in New York, San Francisco, and London: "The following day Wellcome PLC shares fell substantially on the London stock exchange. Four days later Burroughs Wellcome announced a twenty percent reduction in the price of AZT" (1990, 118).

8. Kadi further suggests that "queerness" may be an important link between working-class people (people like her who are "on the margins of the class hierarchy without any hope of being 'normal,' that is, middle class," [1997, 31] who may feel pride in class identity) and those who identify as sexually queer. The difficulty, however, is that those who feel not class identity and pride, but rather shame because of their class status, may have difficulty accepting sexually queer people who openly display their sexuality: "My parents can't embrace their queerness; they're doing everything possible to escape it. So it makes sense that they let loose with homophobic condemnation when I come out and embrace one particular form of queerness" (1997, 34).

9. As I understand them, Laclau and Mouffe argue not that transformed discourse in itself has the power to challenge social structures, but rather that without transformed discourse, those who might benefit from social and political change will not be able to organize to effect this change. This is the case, they assert, because there are no pre-constituted radical agents:

> From the point of view of the determining of the fundamental antagonisms, the basic obstacle, as we have seen, has been *classism:* that is to say, the idea that the working class represents the privilege agent in which the fundamental impulse of social change resides—without perceiving that the very orientation of the working class depends upon a political balance of forces and the radicalization of a plurality of democratic struggles which are decided in good part *outside* the class itself. (Laclau and Mouffe 1985, 177)

Although the struggles may not take place within the working class, this does not mean that class analysis should, or can, be absent.

10. In making this argument, I am drawing on the analysis of Zillah Eisenstein (1981) in *The Radical Future of Liberal Feminism.*

11. This decision is reprinted in Rubenstein (1993).

Chapter 4

1. In fact, the number of hate crimes in general continues to increase: "According to the Justice Department, 8,759 bias crimes were reported in 1996, up from 7,947 in 1995. Sexual orientation was a factor in 12% of those cases. Race was a factor in 63% of all reported crimes, followed by religion at 14% and ethnic origin at 11%" ("Hate Crimes" 1997, 16).

2. Friedan's proposed response to this problem was not to get the father more

involved in the household, but rather, to get the educated, white, middle-class mother more involved in the public world. The implications of this strategy for poor women and women of color was not discussed by Friedan.

3. See Lehring (1997) for an excellent critique of Elshtain.

4. If we do this we also lose the opportunity to ask, as Sandra Pollack (1987, 322) believes we should, whether the children of gays and lesbians might actually have advantages over other children. For example, Charlotte Patterson reports one study that found that children raised by lesbian mothers felt more reactions to stress, but had a greater sense of well-being. She suggests that this could be because these children "were better able to acknowledge both positive and negative aspects of their emotional experience" (1995, 238).

5. Gay conservatives might respond that divorce is too easy in all cases, and that gay married couples, like heterosexual couples, could be encouraged to stay together by ending policies like no-fault divorce. To support such policy change, however, is to create conditions where agency is denied to individuals in the name of an ideal family form.

6. I am talking about constructions of black and white families exclusively in this section because the black/white binarism has been so central to discourses of "normalcy" in the United States. All people of color, however, are judged in accord with white, middle-class norms. It is also worth noting that for Native Americans, the economic support of children was for a long time controlled by the state through removing children from their families and cultures and sending them to boarding schools to be "properly" socialized.

7. It is interesting in this context that Hawaii, the state most likely to legalize gay marriage, also has the least punitive welfare reform programs in place (see Swarns 1997 for a discussion of welfare reform and Hawaii).

8. A literary example of this kind of relationship is present in E. Lynn Harris's (1996) novel *And This Too Shall Pass*, in which a main character, a gay man, is a central figure in the life of his nephew, who is being raised by a "single mother."

9. Sullivan's reply to Harkes is that even in the doubtful case that these men's problems result from not being married to a woman, rather than that they are caused by not being married, this does not mean that gay men would not be better off in stable, loving relationships.

10. Some policies have also been advocated by particular groups of women, even if it is possible to argue that the policies enacted had a negative impact on women as a group. For example, protective legislation divided women.

11. West earlier connects this angst to "the eclipse of hope and collapse of meaning" that is linked to "the structural dynamics of corporate market institutions that affect all Americans. Under these circumstances black existential angst derives from the lived experience of ontological wounds and emotional scars inflicted by white supremacist beliefs and images permeating U.S. society and culture" (1993, 17).

12. Burr argues that cloning offers "nothing new in the way of reproductive freedom," but he also notes that "if having a homosexual kid is important to you, cloning gives you your best odds" (1997, 9). Bull (1997) reports on the different perspectives on cloning among gay and lesbian activists.

13. See Lewin (1993, 50). It is important to recognize that because of race-matching, white gays and lesbians have a hard time adopting U.S. children of color. Bartholet's discussion of race matching in adoption suggests how difficult it is currently for white prospective parents to adopt children of color: "An initial order of business for most adoption agencies is the separation of children and prospective parents into racial classifications and subclassifications. Children in need of homes are typically separated into black and white pools. The children in the black pool are then separated by skin tone—light, medium, dark—and sometimes by nationality, ethnicity, or other cultural characteristics. The prospective parent pool is similarly divided and classified. An attempt is then made to match children in the various 'black' pools with their parent counterparts. The goal is to assign the light-skinned black child to the light-skinned parents, the Haitian child to the Haitian parents, and so on. White children are matched with white prospective parents" (1994, 70). It is interesting that those children most likely to be available to gay and lesbian potential parents are mixed-race children who do not neatly fit into the categories.

14. Stacey (1996) states that adoption remains a primary means by which lesbians acquire children.

15. Petchesky (1990) argues that one way of developing a pro-abortion argument that avoids the problems of a rights-based approach is to ask when pregnant women and fetuses begin to build a relationship. From this perspective, allowing abortion before "quickening" (or the time when the woman begins to feel the fetus move) makes considerable sense.

16. As Nelson (1996) notes, because birth control was less widely available and used, this is a question that would have been nonsensical until recently. Despite (or because of) the reality that people had children without actively choosing to do so, there was not widespread questioning of whether parents (particularly those who were white and middle class) loved their "accidental" children.

17. There are, of course, more questions that could be asked as well, including ones that focus on the increasingly mandatory nature of prenatal screening, promoted in the name of increasing the parents' ability to make choices. For discussions of this issue, see Rose (1987) and Richard (1995).

18. It is important to understand that even this level of assistance is not available for most pregnant women. As a result, they are more likely to be incarcerated until their children are born than provided with services. As Schroedel and Peretz point out, this is an irrational way to assure the health of a fetus since miscarriage rates are significantly higher in prisons. Additionally, many do not provide adequate prenatal care to inmates (1995, 98).

19. In arguing that an ethic of care should be central to treatment programs, I do not mean that society should not hold individuals responsible for the potential negative outcomes of their actions, including the possibility of giving birth to a drug-addicted child. In this sense, Louise Erdrich's (1989) impassioned defense of incarcerating alcohol-addicted women so that children are not born with fetal alcohol syndrome like her adopted son is understandable, yet it fails to consider both the real consequences of incarceration into a prison culture that is by no means drug or alcohol free, and the possibility that programs can combine treatment and poli-

tics in ways that help addicted women who are pregnant to join with community organizations to foster change. This approach, Young (1995) argues, is more caring and likely to be more successful because it recognizes that personal empowerment rests upon community empowerment.

Chapter 5

1. Given that women are less likely to have high paying jobs, they are also less likely to receive adequate benefits in old age. Therefore, the social necessity of marriage has declined less for most women than for most men.

2. And even those who are part of the state are most likely to have an effective voice if they do not publicly challenge dominant norms.

3. See Gibson (1989). A more recent study suggests that the risk of suicide is particularly great for young men. *The Advocate* reports on a study done in Minnesota that found "bisexual and gay males ages 13 to 18 are seven times more likely to attempt suicide than heterosexual males." Among female teens, 20.5 percent of lesbian teens reported thoughts of suicide compared to 14.5 percent of heterosexual females ("Youth at Risk" 1997).

4. We might understand the social construction of gay men as predators as embedded in the construction of men as dangerous outside of the context of family. Those men who are properly socialized will care about their own children; those who care about the children of others must have other, more nefarious motives. This formulation of proper, nonthreatening masculinity plays a critical role in positioning women as natural and safe caretakers of children, even while it denies to nonfathers the ability to provide care for children and youth.

5. Though even here it may have fit because the control that was exerted was functional, not because it enhanced freedom.

6. For boys, the self will also develop through splitting in relation to gender. The work of Weis and Maccleod indicates that this dynamic is not restricted to middle-class youth.

7. As Fine and Zane note, when pregnant girls drop out, it is seen by school officials and teachers as most acceptable if the girl is planning to marry. Writing in response to a counselor's positive evaluation of Elisa, who was pregnant and planning to marry at 15, Fine and Zane note, "No one told Elisa that teen pregnancy compounded by marriage is more likely to result in divorce, domestic violence, a second child, and a disrupted education" (1991, 88–89). Again, the valorization of marriage and fathering is present. Ruddick extends this analysis by pointing out that "adolescent mothers urgently need elders who forgo blame, help them to feel and be more competent, and organize with them to secure the services support they deserve" (1991, 113). When young mothers are in communities that provide such support, teen parenting can be a positive experience for both mother and child.

8. See "Utah Officials Illegally Ban Free Speech of Veteran High School Teacher" (1997). The ACLU has filed suit on behalf of the teacher. In this context, it should be noted that a primary obstacle to the passage of the Employment Non-Discrimination Act, a piece of legislation that would protect gays and lesbians from employment discrimination, is the belief among some members of Congress that

schools should be able to discriminate. This belief is justified on the grounds that parents should have the right to determine the morals taught to their children. It should be noted, however, that only slightly more parents object to their child being taught by an openly gay teacher than feel comfortable with their child having an openly gay teacher (Biewen 1997).

9. This position would also have an impact on debates about whether parents should be held legally liable for the acts of their children.

10. Minow suggests that her use of "human rights" is intended to convey something different than what children would get from other rights frameworks (1997, 119). I see her use of human rights as similar to Martha Nussbaum's (1992) understanding that societies should work to allow human beings to develop their capabilities (see also Nussbaum and Sen 1993). Tronto recognizes Nussbaum's work as closely connected to her own arguments about the potential of an ethic of care (1993, 140).

Chapter 6

1. Lorde includes her poem from *The Black Unicorn* (1978).

2. Reprinted with permission from "Man Child: A Black Lesbian Feminist's Response" in *Sister Outside: Essays and Speeches* by Audre Lorde, © 1984. Published by The Crossing Press, P.O. Box 1048, Freedom, CA 95019.

3. Generally as part of universal systems.

References

Abramowitz, Mimi. 1988. *Regulating the Lives of Women: Social Welfare Policy from Colonial Times to the Present.* Boston: South End Press.

Acker, Joan. 1993. "Women, Families, and Public Policy in Sweden" in *Women, the Family, and Policy.* Edited by Esther Ngan-ling Chow and Catherine White Berheide. Albany, N.Y.: SUNY Press.

"Advocate Marketspace." 1998. *The Advocate* 753:69.

Altman, Dennis. 1987. *AIDS in the Mind of America.* Garden City, N.Y.: Anchor Books.

Amott, Teresa. 1990. "Black Women and AFDC: Entitlement Out of Necessity" in *Women, the State, and Welfare.* Edited by Linda Gordon. Madison: University of Wisconsin Press.

Amott, Teresa. 1993. *Caught in the Crisis: Women and the U.S. Economy Today.* New York: Monthly Review Press.

Anzaldua, Gloria. 1987. *Borderlands/La Frontera: The New Mestiza.* San Francisco: Spinsters Aunt Lute.

Aronowitz, Stanley. 1992. *The Politics of Identity: Class, Culture, and Social Movements.* New York: Routledge.

Barrett, Michele. 1980. *Women's Oppression Today: Problems in Marxist Feminist Analysis.* London: Verso.

Bartholet, Elizabeth. 1994. "Where Do Black Children Belong? The Politics of Race Matching in Adoption" in *Child, Parent, and State: Law and Policy Reader.* Edited by S. Randall Humm, Beate Anna Ort, Martin Mazen Anbari, Wendy S. Lader, and William Scott Biel. Philadelphia: Temple University Press.

Bawer, Bruce. 1993. *A Place at the Table: The Gay Individual in American Society.* New York: Poseidon Press.

Benjamin, Jessica. 1978. "Authority and the Family Revisited." *New German Critique* 13:35–57.

Benkov, Laura. 1994. *Reinventing the Family.* New York: Crown Publishers.

Bennett, Lisa. 1997. "Break the Silence." *Teaching Tolerance* 6:24–29.

Berlant, Lauren, and Elizabeth Freeman. 1993. "Queer Nationality" in *Fear of a*

Queer Planet: Queer Politics and Social Theory. Edited by Michael Warner. Minneapolis: University of Minnesota Press.

Berube, Allan. 1997. "Intellectual Desire" in *Queerly Classed: Gay Men and Lesbians Write about Class*. Edited by Susan Raffo. Boston: South End Press.

Biewen, John. 1997. *All Things Considered*. National Public Radio. 21 October.

Birch, Elizabeth. 1997. Human Rights Campaign Fund Marriage Booklet. http://www.hcrusa.org/issues/marriage/guide.html.

Bladgett, M. V. Lee. 1998. *Income Inflation: The Myth of Affluence Among Gay, Lesbian, and Bisexual Americans*. Joint publication of the Policy Institute of the National Gay and Lesbian Task Force and the Institute for Gay and Lesbian Strategic Studies. Available at www.ngltf.org.

Blankenhorn, David. 1995. *Fatherless America: Confronting Our Most Urgent Social Problem*. New York: Basic Books.

Blasingame, Brenda Marie. 1992. "The Roots of Biphobia: Racism and Internalized Heterosexism" in *Closer to Home: Bisexuality and Feminism*. Edited by Elizabeth Reba Weise. Seattle: Seal Press.

Blasius, Mark. 1994. *Gay and Lesbian Politics: Sexuality and the Emergence of a New Ethic*. Philadelphia: Temple University Press.

Bloch, Ruth. 1987. "The Gendered Meaning of Virtue in Revolutionary America." *Signs* 13 (1): 37–58.

Boris, Eileen, and Peter Bardaglio. 1983. "The Transformation of Patriarchy" in *Families, Politics, and Public Policy*. Edited by Irene Diamond. New York: Longman Press.

Bower, Lisa C. 1995. "The Trope of the Dark Continent in the Fetal Harm Debates: 'Africanism' and the Right to Choice" in *Expecting Trouble: Surrogacy, Fetal Abuse, and New Reproductive Technologies*. Edited by Patricia Boling. Boulder: Westview Press.

Bronner, Stephen Eric. 1991. *Moments of Decision*. New York: Routledge.

Brown, Carol. 1981. "Mothers, Fathers, and Children: From Private to Public Patriarchy" in *Women and Revolution*. Edited by Linda Sargent. Boston: South End Press.

Brown, Laura S. 1995. "Lesbian Identities: Concepts and Issues" in *Lesbian, Gay, and Bisexual Identities Over the Lifespan*. Edited by Anthony R. D'Augelli and Charlotte J. Patterson. New York: Oxford University Press.

Brown, Lyn Mikel. 1991. "A Problem of Vision: The Development Voice and Relational Knowledge in Girls Ages Seven to Sixteen." *Women's Studies Quarterly* 19 (1/2): 77–99.

Brown, Wendy. 1995. *States of Injury: Power and Freedom in Late Modernity*. Princeton: Princeton University Press.

Bull, Chris. 1993. "A Mother's Nightmare." *The Advocate* 640: 24–27.

Bull, Chris. 1997. "Send in the Clones." *The Advocate* 731: 37–38.

Burke, Phyllis. 1993. *Family Values*. New York: Random House.

Burr, Chandler. 1997. "Cloning for Survival." *The Advocate* 731: 9.

Butler, Judith. 1990. *Gender Trouble: Feminism and the Subversion of Identity*. New York: Routledge.

Cagan, Lisa. 1990. "Community Organizing and the Religious Right: Lessons from Oregon's Measure Nine Campaign," interview with Suzanne Pharr. *Radical America* 24:67–75. (Published 1993.)

Carter, Julian. 1997. "Normality, Whiteness, and Authorship: Evolutionary Sexology and the Primitive Pervert" in *Sciences and Homosexualities*. Edited by Vernon A. Rosario. New York: Routledge.

Cerullo, Margaret, and Marla Erlien. 1986. "Beyond the 'Normal Family': A Cultural Critique of Women's Poverty" in *For Crying Out Loud: Women and Poverty in the United States*. Edited by Rochelle Lefkowitz and Ann Withorn. New York: The Pilgrim Press.

Chang, Grace. 1994. "Undocumented Latinas: Welfare Burdens or Beasts of Burden." *Socialist Review* 23:151–185.

Chauncey, George. 1994. *Gay New York: Gender, Urban Culture, and the Making of the Gay Male World, 1890–1940*. New York: Basic Books.

Chee, Alex S. 1991. "A Queer Nationalism." *Out/Look* 11:15–19.

Clinton, Hillary Rodham. 1996. *It Takes a Village*. New York: Simon and Schuster.

Cochran, Susan D., and Vickie M. Mays. 1995. "Sociocultural Facets of the Black Gay Male Experience" in *Men's Lives*. 3d ed. Edited by Michael S. Kimmel and Michael Messner. Boston: Allyn and Bacon.

Cohen, Cathy J. 1996. "Contested Membership: Black Gay Identities and the Politics of AIDS" in *Queer Theory/Sociology*. Edited by Steven Seidman. Cambridge, Mass.: Blackwell Publishers.

Coles, Robert. 1967. *Children of Crisis: A Study of Courage and Fear*. Boston: Little Brown.

Collier, Jane, Michelle Z. Rosaldo, and Sylvia Yanagisako. 1982. "Is There a Family? New Anthropological Views" in *Rethinking the Family*. Edited by Barrie Thorne and Marilyn Yalom. New York: Longman Press.

Collier, Richard. 1995. *Masculinity, Law, and the Family*. London and New York: Routledge Press.

Collins, Patricia Hill. 1990. *Black Feminist Thought: Knowledge, Consciousness, and the Politics of Empowerment*. Boston: Unwin Hyman.

Collins, Patricia Hill. 1992. "Black Women and Motherhood" in *Rethinking the Family: Some Feminist Questions*. Rev. ed. Edited by Barrie Thorne and Marilyn Yalom. Boston: Northeastern University Press.

Condon, Lee. 1997. "Executive Order: Enough Hate Already." *The Advocate* 744: 29–30.

Conerly, Gregory. 1996. "The Politics of Black Lesbian, Gay, and Bisexual Identities" in *Queer Studies: A Lesbian, Gay, Bisexual, and Transgender Anthology*. Edited by Brett Beemyn and Mickey Eliason. New York: New York University Press.

Connell, R. W. 1995. *Masculinities: Knowledge, Power, and Social Change*. Berkeley: University of California Press.

Connell, R. W. 1996. "Gender Theory, Masculinity Research, Gender Politics." *Ethnos* 61:157–176.

Connolly, William E. 1991. *Identity/Subjectivity: Democratic Negotiations of Political Paradox*. Ithaca: Cornell University Press.

Cooper, Davina. 1995. *Power in Struggle: Feminism, Sexuality, and the State*. Buckingham: Open University Press.

Cornell, Drucilla. 1992. "Gender, Sex, and Equivalent Rights" in *Feminists Theorize the Political.* Edited by Judith Butler and Joan W. Scott. New York: Routledge.

Cote, James E., and Anton L. Allahar. 1994. *Generation on Hold: Coming of Age in the Late Twentieth Century.* Toronto: Stoddart Publishing.

Cowell, Susan. 1993. "Family Policy: A Union Approach" in *Women and Unions.* Edited by Dorothy Sue Cobble. Ithaca: Cornell University Press.

Crimp, Douglas, with A. Rolston. 1990. *AIDS Demographics.* Seattle: Bay Press.

Davis, Angela. 1981. *Women, Race, and Class.* New York: Vintage Books.

D'Emilio, John. 1983. *Sexual Politics, Sexual Communities: The Making of a Homosexual Minority in the United States, 1940–1970.* Chicago: University of Chicago Press.

D'Emilio, John, and Estelle Freedman. 1988. *Intimate Matters: A History of Sexuality in America.* New York: Harper and Row.

Du Rivage, Virginia, and David C. Jacobs. 1993. "Social Policy and Part-Time Work: Lessons from Western Europe" in *Women and Unions.* Edited by Dorothy Sue Cobble. Ithaca: Cornell University Press.

Due, Linnea. 1995. *Joining the Tribe: Growing Up Gay and Lesbian in the '90s.* New York: Anchor Books.

Dunne, Gillian. 1997. *Lesbian Lifestyles: Women's Work and the Politics of Sexuality.* Toronto: University of Toronto Press.

Dupuis, Martin. 1995. "The Impact of Culture, Society, and History on the Legal Process: An Analysis of Legal Same-Sex Marriage in the United States and Denmark." *International Journal of Law and the Family* 9:86–118.

Ehrenreich, Barbara, and Deirdre English. 1978. *For Her Own Good: 150 Years of Expert Advice to Women.* New York: Anchor Books.

Eisenstein, Hester. 1991. *Gender Shock: Practicing Feminism on Two Continents.* Boston: Beacon Press.

Eisenstein, Zillah. 1981. *The Radical Future of Liberal Feminism.* New York: Longman.

Eisenstein, Zillah. 1994. *The Color of Gender: Reimaging Democracy.* Berkeley: University of California Press.

Elshtain, Jean Bethke. 1981. *Public Man, Private Woman: Women in Social and Political Thought.* Princeton: Princeton University Press.

Engels, Friedrich. 1978 [1884]. *Origins of the Family, Private Property and the State.* Peking: Foreign Language Press.

Epstein, Barbara. 1990. "Reappraising Social Movement Theory." *Socialist Review* 20 (1):36–63.

Erdrich, Louise. 1989. "Foreword." *The Broken Cord.* By Michael Dorris. New York: Harper and Row.

Eskridge, William N., Jr. 1996. *The Case for Same-Sex Marriage.* New York: The Free Press.

Ettelbrick, Paula L. 1989. "Since When is Marriage a Path to Liberation?" *Outlook* Fall:9, 14–16.

Evans, David T. 1993. *Sexual Citizenship: The Material Construction of Sexualities.* London: Routledge.

"Fatherless America (Book Review)." 1995. *The Futurist* 29:61–62.

Feinberg, Leslie. 1993. *Stone Butch Blues*. Ithaca: Firebrand Books.

"Feminist-Reversing Fatherless." 1995. *The Futurist*. 29:60–61.

Ferguson, Kathy E. 1993. *The Man Question: Visions of Subjectivity in Feminist Theory*. Berkeley: University of California Press.

Fine, Michelle, and Nancie Zane. 1991. "Bein' Wrapped Too Tight: When Low Income Women Drop Out of School." *Women's Studies Quarterly*, 19 (1/22): 77–99.

Fine, Michelle et al. 1997. "(In)Secure Times: Constructing White Working Class Masculinities in the Late Twentieth Century." *Gender and Society* (11)1:52–68.

Fineman, Martha Albertson. 1995. *The Neutered Mother, the Sexual Family, and Other Twentieth Century Tragedies*. New York: Routledge.

Folbre, Nancy. 1994. *Who Pays for the Kids? Gender and the Structures of Constraint*. London: Routledge.

Ford, Sara. 1994. "I'd Rather the Honesty" in *One Teacher in Ten: Gay and Lesbian Educators Tell Their Stories*. Edited by Kevin Jennings. Boston: Alyson Publications.

Foss, Karen A. 1994. "The Logic of Folly in the Political Campaigns of Harvey Milk" in *Queer Words, Queer Images: Communication and the Construction of Homosexuality*. Edited by R. Jeffrey Ringer. New York: New York University Press.

Foucault, Michel. 1995. *Discipline and Punish*. 2d ed. Translated by Alan Sheridan. New York: Vintage Books.

Franzen, Trisha. 1996. *Spinsters and Lesbians: Independent Womanhood in the United States*. New York: New York University Press.

Fraser, Nancy. 1989. *Unruly Practices: Power, Discourse, and Gender in Contemporary Social Theory*. Minneapolis: University of Minnesota Press.

Fraser, Nancy. 1995. "False Antitheses" in *Feminist Contention: A Philosophical Exchange*. Seyla Benhabib, Judith Butler, Drucilla Cornell, and Nancy Fraser, contributors, with an introduction by Linda Nicholson. New York: Routledge.

Friedan, Betty. 1963. *The Feminine Mystique*. New York: Norton.

Frye, Marilyn. 1983. *The Politics of Reality: Essays in Feminist Theory*. Freedom, Calif.: The Crossing Press.

Frye, Marilyn. 1990. "Lesbian 'Sex'" in *Lesbian Philosophies and Cultures*. Edited by Jeffner Allen. Albany, N.Y.: SUNY Press.

Fung, Richard. 1991. "Looking for My Penis: The Eroticized Asian in Gay Video Porn" in *How Do I Look?: Queer Film and Video*. Edited by Bad Object-Choices. Seattle: Bay Press.

Funiciello, Theresa. 1993. *Tyranny of Kindness: Dismantling the Welfare System to End Poverty in America*. New York: Atlantic Monthly Press.

Gaines, Donna. 1991. *Teenage Wasteland: Suburbia's Dead End Kids*. New York: Pantheon Books.

Gamson, Joshua. 1996. "Must Identity Movements Self-Destruct?: A Queer Dilemma" in *Queer Theory/Sociology*. Edited by Steven Seidman. Cambridge, Mass.: Blackwell Publishers.

Gibson, P. 1989. "Gay and Lesbian Youth Suicide" in *Report to the Secretary's Task Force on Youth Suicide, Volume 3: Prevention and Intervention in Youth Suicide*. Washington, D.C.: U.S. Department of Health and Human Services.

Gilligan, Carol. 1982. *In a Different Voice*. Cambridge: Harvard University Press.

Gilligan, Carol. 1991. "Women's Psychological Development: Implications for Psychotherapy" in *Women, Girls, and Psychotherapy*. Edited by Carol Gilligan, Annie C. Rogers, and Deborah Tolman. New York: Harrington Park Press.

Gilligan, Carol, Annie C. Rogers, and Deborah Tolman, eds. 1991. *Women, Girls, and Psychotherapy*. New York: Harrington Park Press.

Gillis, John R. 1988. "From Ritual to Romance: Toward an Alternative History of Love" in *Emotion and Social Change: Toward a New Psychology*. Edited by Carol Z. Stearns and Peter N. Stearns. New York: Holmes and Meier.

Gitlin, Todd. 1993. "The Rise of 'Identity Politics.'" *Dissent* Spring:172–177.

Glendon, Mary Anne. 1987. *Abortion and Divorce in Western Law*. Cambridge: Harvard University Press.

Gonsiorek, J. C. 1988. "Mental Health Issues of Gay and Lesbian Adolescents." *Journal of Adolescent Health Care* 9:114–122.

Gover, Tzivia. 1996a. "Fighting For Our Children." *The Advocate* 721:22–30.

Gover, Tzivia. 1996b. "The Other Mothers." *The Advocate* 721:31.

Gover, Tzivia. 1997. "Hate that Goes Boom in the Night." *The Advocate* 730:41–42.

Grant, Linda. 1994. "Helpers, Enforcers, and Go-Betweens: Black Females in Elementary School Classrooms" in *Women of Color in U.S. Society*. Edited by Maxine Baca Zinn and Bonnie Thornton Dill. Philadelphia: Temple University Press.

Gray, Stan. 1987. "Sharing the Shop Floor" in *Beyond Patriarchy*. Edited by Michael Kaufman. Oxford: Oxford University Press.

Greenberg, David F., and Marcia H. Bystryn. 1996. "Capitalism, Bureaucracy, and Male Homosexuality" in *Queer Theory/Sociology*. Edited by Steven Seidman. Cambridge, Mass.: Blackwell Publishers.

Hall, Stuart, and David Held. 1990. "Citizens and Citizenship" in *New Times: The Changing Face of Politics in the 1990s*. Edited by Stuart Hall and Martin Jaques. London: Verso Press.

Hansen, Gary L. 1996. "Review: Fatherless America: Confronting Our Most Urgent Social Problem." *Family Relations* 45:120–121.

Harris, E. Lynn. 1996. *And This Too Shall Pass*. New York: Anchor Books.

"Hate Crimes: A Step Toward Protection." 1997. *The Advocate* 749:16.

Hawkeswood, William G. 1996. *One of the Children: Gay Black Men in Harlem*. Berkeley: University of California Press.

Hemmings, Clare. 1995. "Locating Bisexual Identities: Discourses of Bisexuality and Contemporary Feminist Theory" in *Mapping Desire: Geographies of Sexualities*. Edited by David Bell and Gill Valentine. London and New York: Routledge.

Hemphill, Essex. 1992. *Ceremonies: Prose and Poetry*. New York: Plume.

Hennessy, Rosemary. 1993. *Materialist Feminism and the Politics of Discourse*. New York: Routledge.

Herdt, Gilbert, and Andrew Boxer. 1993. *Children of Horizons: How Gay and Lesbian Teens are Leading a New Way Out of the Closet*. Boston: Beacon Press.

Hirschman, Albert O. 1970. *Exit, Voice, and Loyalty*. Cambridge: Harvard University Press.

hooks, bell. 1984. *Feminist Theory: From Margin to Center*. Boston: South End Press.

hooks, bell. 1989. *Talking Back*. Boston: South End Press.

Horkheimer, Max. 1972 [1936]. *Critical Theory*. Translated by J. Cummings. New York: Herder and Herder.

Humphries, Jane. 1982. "The Working Class Family: A Marxist Perspective" in *The Family in Political Thought*. Edited by Jean Elshtain. Amherst: University of Massachusetts Press.

Hunter, Allen. 1995. "Rethinking Revolution in Light of the New Social Movements" in *Cultural Politics and Social Movements*. Edited by Marcy Darnovsky, Barbara Epstein, and Robert Flacks. Philadelphia: Temple University Press.

Hunter, Joyce. 1992. "Violence against Lesbian and Gay Male Youth" in *Hate Crimes: Confronting Violence against Lesbians and Gay Men*. Edited by Gregory Herek and Kevin Berrill. Newbury Park: Sage.

Jay, Karla, and Allan Young, eds. 1972. *Out of the Closets: Voices from Gay Liberation*. New York: Douglas Book Corp.

Jernigan, David. 1988. "Why Gay Leadership is Hard to Find." *OUT/LOOK* 2: 33–49.

Jeter, Jon. 1997. "Making Family a Man's World." *The Washington Post*. July 8, B1.

Johnson, Dirk. 1996. "No-Fault Divorce is Under Attack." *New York Times*. February 12, A10.

Kadi, Joanna. 1997. "Homophobic Workers or Elitist Queers?" in *Queerly Classed: Gay Men and Lesbians Write about Class*. Edited by Susan Raffo. Boston: South End Press.

Kauffman, L. A. 1990. "The Anti-Politics of Identity." *Radical America* 20 (1): 67–80.

Khayatt, Madiha Didi. 1992. *Lesbian Teachers: An Invisible Presence*. Albany: State University of New York Press.

Kennedy, Elizabeth Lapovsky, and Madeline D. Davis. 1993. *Boots of Leather, Slippers of Gold: The History of a Lesbian Community*. New York and London: Routledge.

Klepfisz, Irena. 1987. "Women without Children/Women without Families/Women Alone" in *Politics of the Heart: A Lesbian Parenting Anthology*. Edited by Sandra Pollack and Jeanne Vaughn. Ithaca: Firebrand Books.

Kornblum, Janet. 1997. "Gay and Gray." *The Advocate* 737: 46–48.

Laclau, Ernesto, and Chantal Mouffe. 1985. *Hegemony and Socialist Strategy: Toward a Radical Democratic Politics*. London: Verso Press.

Lasch, Christopher. 1977. *Haven in a Heartless World: The Family Besieged*. New York: Basic Books.

Lasch, Christopher. 1984a. "Family and Authority" in *Capitalism and Infancy: Essays on Psychoanalysis and Politics*. Edited by Barry Richards. Atlantic Highlands, N.J.: Humanities Press.

Lasch, Christopher. 1984b. *The Minimal Self*. New York: Norton.

Lee, N'Tanya, Don Murphy, and Juliet Ucelli. 1990. "Whose Kids? Our Kids!: Race, Sexuality, and the Right in New York City's Curriculum Battles." *Radical America* 25: 9–21. (Published 1993.)

Lee, N'Tanya, Don Murphy, Lisa North and Juliet Ucelli. 1996. "Bridging Race, Class, and Sexuality for School Reform" in *Beyond Identity Politics: Emerging Social Movements in Communities of Color*. Boston: South End Press.

Lehr, Valerie. 1993. "The Difficulty of Leaving 'Home': Gay and Lesbian Organizing to Confront AIDS" in *Mobilizing the Community: Local Politics in the Era of the Global City*. Edited by Robert Fisher and Joseph Kling. Urban Affairs Annual Review 41. New York: Sage.

Lehring, Gary. 1997. "Essentialism and the Political Articulation of Identity" in *Playing With Fire: Queer Politics, Queer Theories*. New York: Routledge.

Lewin, Ellen. 1993. *Lesbian Mothers: Accounts of Gender in American Culture*. Ithaca: Cornell University Press.

Lewin, Tamar. 1998. "U.S. Colleges Begin to Ask, Where Have the Men Gone?" *New York Times*, December 6. p. 1.

Lind, Michael. 1998. "The Beige and the Black." *New York Times Magazine*. August 6, 38–39.

Locke, John. 1963 [1698]. *Two Treatises on Government*. Rev. ed. New York: Mentor Books.

Locke, John. 1964 [1693]. *Some Thoughts Concerning Education*. Abridged and edited by F. W. Garforth. Woodbury, N.Y.: Barron's Educational Series.

Loeb, Paul Rogat. 1994. *Generation at the Crossroads: Apathy and Action on the American Campus*. New Brunswick, N.J.: Rutgers University Press.

Lorde, Audre. 1978. *The Black Unicorn*. New York: Norton.

Lorde, Audre. 1983. *Zami: A New Spelling of My Name*. Trumansburg, N.Y.: Crossing Press.

Lorde, Audre. 1984. *Sister Outsider: Essays and Speeches*. Trumansburg, N.Y.: Crossing Press.

Lugones, Maria. 1994. "Purity, Impurity, and Separation." *Signs: Journal of Women in Culture and Society* 19:458–479.

Lugones, Maria, with Pat Alake Rosezelle. 1995. "Sisterhood and Friendship as Feminist Models" in *Feminism and Community*. Edited by Penny A. Weiss and Marilyn Friedman. Philadelphia: Temple University Press.

MacLeod, Jay. 1987. *Ain't No Makin' It: Leveled Aspirations in a Low-Income Neighborhood*. Boulder: Westview Press.

Macpherson, C. B. 1962. *The Political Theory of Possessive Individualism*. Oxford: Oxford University Press.

Mann, Patricia. 1994. *Micro-Politics: Agency in a Post Feminist Era*. Minneapolis: University of Minnesota Press.

Melucci, Alberto. 1989. *Nomads of the Present*. Philadelphia: Temple University Press.

Meyers, Diana Tietjens. 1994. *Subjection and Subjectivity: Psychoanalytic Feminism and Moral Philosophy*. New York: Routledge.

Minow, Martha. 1997. "Whatever Happened to Children's Rights?" in *Reassessing the Sixties: Debating the Cultural and Political Legacy*. Edited by Stephen Macedo. New York: Norton.

Morgan, Kathryn Pauly. 1989. "Of *Woman* Born? How Old-Fashioned!—New Reproductive Technologies and Women's Oppression" in *The Future of Human Reproduction*. Edited by Christine Overall. Toronto: The Women's Press.

Moss, J. Jennings. 1997. "Classroom Warfare: Public Schools Have Become the Battleground of Choice for Antigay Conservatives." *The Advocate* 728:32–33.

"Mother's Boys—Fatherless America." 1995. *The Economist* 335:79.

Mouffe, Chantal. 1991. "Democratic Citizenship and the Political Community" in *Community at Loose Ends*. Edited by the Miami Theory Collective. Minneapolis: University of Minnesota Press.

Mouffe, Chantal. 1992. "Feminism, Citizenship, and Radical Democratic Politics" in *Feminists Theorize the Political*. Edited by Judith Butler and Joan W. Scott. New York: Routledge.

Moynihan, Daniel Patrick. 1965. *The Negro Family: The Case for National Action*. Washington, D.C.: Government Printing Service. Prepared for the Office of Policy Planning and Research of the Department of Labor.

Narayan, Uma. 1995. "The 'Gift' of a Child: Commercial Surrogacy, Gift Surrogacy, and Motherhood" in *Expecting Trouble: Surrogacy, Fetal Abuse, and New Reproductive Technologies*. Edited by Patricia Boling. Boulder: Westview Press.

Neisser, Philip, and Sanford Schram. 1994. "Industrial Welfare Policy Meets Post Industrial Society." Presented at the Annual Meetings of the American Political Science Association. New York.

Nelson, Fiona. 1996. *Lesbian Motherhood: An Exploration of Canadian Lesbian Families*. Toronto: University of Toronto Press.

Nussbaum, Martha C. 1992. "Human Functioning and Social Justice: In Defense of Aristotelian Essentialism." *Political Theory* 20:202–246.

Nussbaum, Martha C., and Amartya Sen, eds. 1993. *The Quality of Life*. Oxford: Clarendon Press.

O'Donnell, William J., and David A. Jones. 1982. *The Law of Marriage and Marital Alternatives*. Lexington, Mass.: Lexington Books.

Okin, Susan Moller. 1989. *Justice, Gender, and the Family*. New York: Basic Books.

Omolade, Barbara. 1994. *The Rising Song of African American Women*. New York: Routledge.

Osborn, Torie. 1996. *Coming Home to America*. New York: St. Martin's Press.

Parker, Pat. 1985. *Jonestown and Other Madness*. Ithaca: Firebrand Books.

Pateman, Carole. 1988. *The Sexual Contract*. Stanford: Stanford University Press.

Patterson, Charlotte J. 1995. "Lesbian Mothers, Gay Fathers, and Their Children" in *Lesbian, Gay, and Bisexual Identities Over the Lifespan*. Edited by Anthony R. D'Augelli and Charlotte J. Patterson. New York: Oxford University Press.

Pearce, Diane. 1990. "Welfare is *not* for Women" in *Women, the State, and Welfare*. Edited by Linda Gordon. Madison: University of Wisconsin Press.

Petchesky, Rosalind. 1990. *Abortion and Women's Choice: The State, Sexuality, and Reproductive Freedom*. Rev. ed. Boston: Northeastern University Press.

Phelan, Shane. 1989. *Identity Politics: Lesbian Feminism and the Limits of Community*. Philadelphia: Temple University Press.

Phelan, Shane. 1994. *Getting Specific: Postmodern Lesbian Politics*. Minneapolis: University of Minnesota Press.

Piven, Frances Fox, and Richard Cloward. 1977. *Poor People's Movements: Why They Succeed, How They Fail.* New York: Pantheon Books.

Polikoff, Nancy. 1987. "Lesbians Choosing Children: The Personal is Political" in *Politics of the Heart: A Lesbian Parenting Anthology.* Edited by Sandra Pollack and Jeanne Vaughn. Ithaca: Firebrand Books.

Pollack, Sandra. 1987. "Lesbian Mothers: A Lesbian Feminist Perspective on Research" in *Politics of the Heart: A Lesbian Parenting Anthology.* Edited by Sandra Pollack and Jeanne Vaughn. Ithaca: Firebrand Books.

Poster, Mark. 1978. *Critical Theory of the Family.* New York: Seabury Press.

Poster, Mark. 1989. *Critical Theory and Poststructuralism.* Ithaca: Cornell University Press.

Pratt, Minnie Bruce. 1990. *Crime Against Nature.* Ithaca: Firebrand Books.

Pratt, Minnie Bruce. 1995. *S/HE.* Ithaca: Firebrand Books.

Rabinowitz, Jonathan. 1996. "A Hartford Program to Put Fathers to Work." *New York Times,* June 16, p. 1.

Raymond, Janice G. 1993. *Women as Wombs.* San Francisco: Harper Books.

Reagon, Bernice Johnson. 1983. "Coalition Politics: Turning the Century" in *Home Girls: A Black Feminist Anthology.* Edited by Barbara Smith. New York: Kitchen Table: Women of Color Press.

Renzetti, Claire. 1992. *Violent Betrayal: Partner Abuse in Lesbian Relationships.* New York: Sage Press.

Respini, Blake. 1994. "Shelly, Hallie, Jack, and Me" in *One Teacher in 10: Gay and Lesbian Educators Tell their Stories.* Edited by Kevin Jennings. Boston: Alyson Publications.

Rich, Adrienne. 1976. *Of Woman Born: Motherhood as Experience and Institution.* New York: Norton.

Rich, Adrienne. 1980. "Compulsory Heterosexuality and Lesbian Existence." *Signs: Journal of Women in Culture and Society* 5:631–680.

Richard, Patricia Bayer. 1995. "The Tailor-Made Child: Implications for Women and the State" in *Expecting Trouble: Surrogacy, Fetal Abuse, and New Reproductive Technologies.* Edited by Patricia Boling. Boulder: Westview Press.

Rifkin, Jeremy. 1995. *The End of Work: The Decline of the Global Labor Force and the Dawn of the Post-Market Era.* New York: Putnam.

Ripley, Rebecca. 1992. "The Language of Desire: Sexuality, Identity, and Language" in *Closer to Home: Bisexuality and Feminism.* Edited by Elizabeth Reba Weise. Seattle: Seal Press.

Robinson, Tracy, and Julia Victoria Ward. 1991. "'A Belief in Self Far Greater Than Anyone's Disbelief': Cultivating Resistance Among African-American Female Adolescents" in *Women, Girls, and Psychotherapy.* Edited by Carol Gilligan, Annie C. Rogers, and Deborah Tolman. New York: Harrington Park Press.

Robson, Ruthann. 1994. "Resisting the Family: Repositioning Lesbians in Legal Theory." *Signs* (19) 4:975–996.

Rose, Hilary. 1987. "Victorian Values in the Test-Tube: The Politics of Reproductive Science and Technology" in *Reproductive Technologies: Gender, Motherhood, and Science.* Edited by Michelle Stanworth. Oxford: Polity Press.

Rose, Nancy E. 1993. "Gender, Race, and the Welfare State: Government Work Programs from the 1930s to the Present." *Feminist Studies* 19:319–342.

Rotundo, E. Anthony. 1987. "Patriarchs and Participants: A Historical Perspective on Fatherhood in America" in *Beyond Patriarchy*. Edited by Michael Kaufman. Oxford: Oxford University Press.

Rubenstein, William, ed. 1993. *Lesbians, Gay Men, and the Law*. New York: New York University Press.

Rubin, Lillian. 1994. *Families on the Faultline*. New York: Harper Collins.

Ruddick, Sara. 1991. "Educating for Procreative Choice: The 'Case' of Adolescent Women." *Women's Studies Quarterly*. 19 (1/2):102–120.

Rust, Paula. 1996. "Sexual Identity and Bisexual Identities: The Struggle for Self-Description in a Changing Sexual Landscape" in *Queer Studies: A Lesbian, Gay, Bisexual, and Transgender Anthology*. Edited by Brett Beemyn and Mickey Eliason. New York: New York University Press.

Saalfield, Catherine, and Scot Nakagawa. 1997. "Lucky: A Conversation in Many Parts" in *Queerly Classed: Gay Men and Lesbians Write About Class*. Edited by Susan Roffe. Boston: South End Press.

Samuels, Andrew. 1995. "The Good-Enough Father of Whatever Sex." *Feminism and Psychology* 5 (4):511–530.

Sanday, Peggy Reeves. 1990. *Fraternity Gang Rape*. New York: New York University Press.

Sandel, Michael. 1982. *Liberalism and the Limits of Justice*. Cambridge: Cambridge University Press.

Sapiro, Virginia. 1990. "The Gender Basis of the American Social Policy" in *Women, the State, and Welfare*. Edited by Linda Gordon. Madison: University of Wisconsin Press.

Savin-Williams, Ritch. 1995. "Lesbian, Gay Male, and Bisexual Adolescents" in *Lesbian, Gay, and Bisexual Identities Over the Lifespan*. Edited by Anthony R. D'Augelli and Charlotte J. Patterson. New York: Oxford University Press.

Schlesinger, Arthur M., Jr. 1992. *The Disuniting of America: Reflections of a Multicultural Society*. New York: W. W. Norton and Company.

Schroedel, Jean Reith, and Paul Peretz. 1995. "A Gender Analysis of Policy Formation: The Case of Fetal Abuse" in *Expecting Trouble: Surrogacy, Fetal Abuse, and New Reproductive Technologies*. Edited by Patricia Boling. Boulder: Westview Press.

Sedgewick, Eve Kofosky. 1993. "How to Bring Your Kids Up Gay" in *Fear of a Queer Planet: Queer Politics and Social Theory*. Edited by Michael Warner. Minneapolis: University of Minnesota Press.

Segal, Lynne. 1990. *Slow Motion: Changing Masculinities, Changing Men*. New Brunswick, N.J.: Rutgers University Press.

Seidman, Steven. 1992. *Embattled Eros: Sexual Politics and Ethics in Contemporary America*. New York: Routledge.

Seidman, Steven. 1996. "Introduction" in *Queer Theory/Sociology*. Edited by Steven Seidman. Cambridge, Mass.: Blackwell Publishers.

Shanley, Mary Lyndon. 1995. "'Surrogate Mothering' and Women's Freedom: A

Critique of Contracts for Human Reproduction" in *Expecting Trouble: Surrogacy, Fetal Abuse, and New Reproductive Technologies*. Edited by Patricia Boling. Boulder: Westview Press.

Sherman, Suzanne, ed. 1992. *Lesbian and Gay Marriage: Private Commitments, Public Ceremonies*. Philadelphia: Temple University Press.

Shilts, Randy. 1987. *And the Band Played On*. New York: Penguin Books.

Sklar, Kathryn Kish. 1993. "The Historical Foundation of Women's Power in the Creation of the American Welfare State, 1830–1930" in *Mothers of a New World: Maternalist Politics and the Origins of Welfare States*. Edited by Seth Koven and Sonya Michel. New York: Routledge.

Smith-Rosenberg, Carroll. 1989. "Discourses of Sexuality and Subjectivity: The New Woman: 1870–1936" in *Hidden from History: Reclaiming the Lesbian and Gay Past*. Edited by Martin Bauml Duberman, Martha Vicinus, and George Chauncey, Jr. New York: New American Library.

Solinger, Rickie. 1992. *Wake Up Little Susie: Single Pregnancy and Race before Roe v. Wade*. New York: Routledge.

Stacey, Judith. 1996. *In the Name of the Family: Rethinking Family Values in the Postmodern Age*. Boston: Beacon Press.

Stack, Carol. 1974. *All Our Kin: Strategies for Survival in a Black Community*. New York: Harper Colophon Books.

Stein, Arlene, and Ken Plummer. 1996. "'I Can't Even Think Straight': 'Queer' Theory and the Missing Sexual Revolution in Sociology" in *Queer Theory/Sociology*. Edited by Steven Seidman. Cambridge, Mass.: Blackwell Publishers.

Stoddard, Thomas B. 1989. "Why Gay People Should Seek the Right to Marry." *Outlook* Fall: 9–13.

Sullivan, Andrew. 1996. *Virtually Normal: An Argument about Homosexuality*. New York: Vintage Books.

Swarns, Rachel L. 1997. "Hawaii Bucks Trend on Welfare Reform." *New York Times*, September 28, sec. 4, p. 3.

Tarcov, Nathan. 1986. *Locke's Education for Liberty*. Chicago: University of Chicago Press.

Taylor, Charles. 1985. *Human Agency and Language*. Cambridge: Cambridge University Press.

Taylor, Jill McLean, Carol Gilligan, and Amy M. Sullivan. 1995. *Between Voice and Silence: Women and Girls, Race and Relationship*. Cambridge: Harvard University Press.

Taylor, Jill McLean, and Janie Victoria Ward. 1991. "Culture, Sexuality, and School: Perspectives from Focus Groups in Six Different Cultural Communities." *Women's Studies Quarterly* 19: 121–137.

Thorne, Barrie. 1993. *Gender Play: Boys and Girls in School*. New Brunswick: Rutgers University Press.

Touraine. Alain. 1988. *Return of the Actor*. Translated by Myrna Godzich. Minneapolis: University of Minnesota Press.

Trnka, Susanna. 1992. "A Pretty Good Bisexual Kiss There . . ." in *Closer to Home: Bisexuality and Feminism*. Edited by Elizabeth Reba Weise. Seattle: Seal Press.

Tronto, Joan C. 1989. "Women and Caring: What Can Feminists Learn about Morality from Caring?" in *Gender/Body/Knowledge: Feminist Reconstructions of Being and Knowing*. Edited by Allison M. Jagger and Susan R. Bordo. New Brunswick: Rutgers University Press.

Tronto, Joan. 1993. *Moral Boundaries*. New York: Routledge.

Udis-Kessler, Amanda. 1996. "Identity Politics: Historical Sources of the Bisexual Movement" in *Queer Studies: A Lesbian, Gay, Bisexual, and Transgender Anthology*. Edited by Brett Beemyn and Mickey Eliason. New York: New York University Press.

"Utah Officials Illegally Ban Free Speech of Veteran High School Teacher." 1997. American Civil Liberties Union Report. www.aclu.org/news/n10/2197a.html.

Vaid, Urvashi. 1996. *Virtual Equality: The Mainstreaming of Gay and Lesbian Liberation*. New York: Anchor Books.

Warren, Patricia Nell. 1997. "Down and Out." *The Advocate* 739/740:5.

Weeks, Jeffrey. 1991. *Against Nature: Essays on History, Sexuality and Identity*. London: Rivers Oram Press.

Weeks, Jeffrey. 1995. *Invented Moralities: Sexual Values in an Age of Uncertainty*. New York: Columbia University Press.

Weis, Lois. 1990. *Working Class without Work*. New York: Routledge.

West, Cornel. 1993. *Race Matters*. Boston: Beacon Press.

Weston, Kath. 1991. *Families We Choose*. New York: Columbia University Press.

Weston, Kath. 1996. "Requiem for a Street Fighter" in *Out in the Field: Reflections of Lesbian and Gay Anthropologists*. Edited by Ellen Lewin and William L. Leap. Urbana and Chicago: University of Illinois Press.

Wilkerson, Isabel. 1995. "Middle Class Blacks Try to Grip a Ladder while Lending a Hand" in *Race, Class, and Gender in the United States: An Integrated Anthology*, 3d ed. Edited by Paula S. Rothenberg. New York: St. Martin's Press.

Williams, Linda. 1989. "No Relief until the End: The Physical and Emotional Costs of In Vitro Fertilization" in *The Future of Human Reproduction*. Edited by Christine Overall. Toronto: The Women's Press.

Willis, Paul. 1981. *Learning to Labor: How Working Class Kids Get Working Class Jobs*. New York: Columbia University Press.

Wilson, Elizabeth. 1993. "Is Transgression Transgressive?" in *Activating Theory: Lesbian, Gay, Bisexual Politics*. Edited by Joseph Bristow and Angelina R. Wilson. London: Lawrence and Wishart.

Wilson, Rodney. 1994. "Telling Our Stories, Winning Our Freedom" in *One Teacher in 10: Gay and Lesbian Educators Tell Their Stories*. Edited by Kevin Jennings. Boston: Alyson Publications.

Wilton, Tamsin. 1995. *Lesbian Studies: Setting an Agenda*. London: Routledge.

With Babies and Banners. 1978. Videotape. Directed by Lorraine Gray. New Day Films.

Wittman, Carl. 1972. "A Gay Manifesto" in *Out of the Closets: Voices from Gay Liberation*. Edited by Karla Jay and Allan Young. New York: Douglas Book Corp.

Young, Iris Marion. 1990. *Justice and the Politics of Difference*. Princeton: Princeton University Press.

Young, Iris Marion. 1995. "Punishment, Treatment, and Empowerment: Three Approaches to Policy for Pregnant Addicts" in *Expecting Trouble: Surrogacy, Fetal*

Abuse, and New Reproductive Technologies. Edited by Patricia Boling. Boulder: Westview Press.

"Youth at Risk." 1997. *The Advocate* 744:15.

Zaretsky, Eli. 1982. "The Place of the Family in the Origins of the Welfare State" in *Rethinking the Family.* Edited by Barrie Thorne and Marilyn Yalom. New York: Longman Press.

Zemsky, Beth. 1991. "Coming Out against All Odds" in *Women, Girls, and Psychotherapy.* Edited by Carol Gilligan, Annie C. Rogers, and Deborah Tolman. New York: Harrington Park Press.

Index

abortion politics, 38, 185n19; and violence, 106

abortion, 136; and social conditions, 131

Abramowitz, Mimi, 111

Acker, Joan, 172

Adolescents. *See* youth

adoption, 33, 126–29, 175, 180n17; children of color, 127–28; by gay men and lesbians, 128, 185n13; mixed-race children, 185n13 race matching, 185n13; white babies, 112, 130. *See also* second-parent adoption

adoptive fathers, 181n5

affirmative action, 118, 123–24, 182n2

AFL-CIO, 173

African American communities: adoption and, 127–28; child nurturance in, 113, 165; deindustrialization and, 122; male influence on boys, 181n4; value of children in, 125, 165; *See also* black gay men, othermothers.

African Americans: family ideology and, 111–14; Religious Right and, 104–05; homosexuality and, 65, 111; sexual stereotypes and, 64, 112, 114, 125–26. *See also* black children; black existential angst; black lesbian and gay identities

Agency, 45, 67, 95, 99–103, 109, 134, 136,139–40, 143, 145, 152, 154–56, 168, 182n17; democratic, 169–77; schools and, 159–64; youth, 146–49, 163–67

AIDS Coalition to Unleash Power (ACT UP), 91–93, 183n7

AIDS service organizations, 174

AIDS, 32, 136–37, 173; communities of color, 91; education, 163; gay men, 55, 69–72, 115; IV drug users, 91; women, 91

All Our Kin, 181n4

Allahar, Anton, 146–47, 159

alliance building, 42, 91, 97–98, 103–05, 106, 108, 110, 113, 126–28, 133, 163

Altman, Dennis, 55

American Civil Liberties Union, 186n8

Amott, Teresa, 27, 112, 121

And the Band Played On, 115

anger, 85, 89, 92, 106

anti-equal rights rhetoric, 107, 124, 163

anti-gay violence, 98, 106–07, 124, 152, 157; changing economy and, 118–25; conservative politics and, 119; masculinity and, 116

antigay ballot initiatives, 2, 124, 182n2

Anzaldua, Gloria, 182n1

Arkes, Hadley, 115

Aronowitz, Stanley, 119, 122

Arthur, Kate, 89

artificial insemination. *See* donor insemination

Asian Americans: sexual stereotypes, 182n14

backlash against social change, 125

Badgett, M.V. Lee, 179n16

Baird, Zoe 26

Bardaglio, Peter, 119

Barrett, Michelle, 19, 21, 185n13

Bartholet, Elizabeth, 127

"Bash Back," 89, 183n5

Bawer, Bruce, 56, 111

Benjamin, Jessica, 149

Benkov, Laura, 66–67

Bennett, Lisa, 162

203